THE ANCIENT ECONOMY

THE ANCIENT ECONOMY

Evidence and Models

Edited by

J. G. MANNING AND IAN MORRIS

STANFORD UNIVERSITY PRESS

Stanford, California

Stanford University Press
Stanford, California
© 2005 by the Board of Trustees of the Leland Stanford
Junior University.
All rights reserved.

Printed in the United States of America on acid-free, archival-quality paper

Library of Congress Cataloging-in-Publication Data

The ancient economy : evidence and models /
edited by J. G. Manning and Ian Morris.
   p. cm.—(Social science history)
Includes bibliographical references and index.
ISBN 0-8047-4805-5 (cloth : alk. paper)
ISBN 0-8047-5755-0 (pbk : alk. paper)
   1. Economic history—To 500. I. Manning, Joseph
Gilbert. II. Morris, Ian, date- III. Series.
HC31.A524 2005
330.93—dc22   2004025985

Original Printing 2005

Typeset by G & S Typesetters in 10.5 on 13 Bembo AR

In memory of Michael H. Jameson (1924–2004).
For all his contributions to ancient economic history
and to Stanford.

CONTENTS

FIGURES

CONTRIBUTORS

Takeshi Amemiya Edward Ames Edmonds Professor of Economics, Stanford University

Roger S. Bagnall Professor of Classics and History, Columbia University

Peter R. Bedford Associate Professor of History (Ancient Near East), Edith Cowan University

John K. Davies Leverhume Professor of Ancient History, University of Liverpool

Mark Granovetter John Butler Ford Professor in the School of Humanities and Sciences, Professor of Sociology, Stanford University

Avner Greif Professor of Economics, The Bowman Family Endowed Professor in Humanities and Sciences and Senior Fellow, Stanford International Studies, Stanford University

R. Bruce Hitchner Professor of Classics, Chair, Tufts University

Mario Liverani Professor of Ancient Near Eastern History, University of Rome "La Sapienza"

J. G. Manning Associate Professor of Classics, Stanford University

Ian Morris Jean and Rebecca Willard Professor of Classics and Professor of History, Stanford University

Richard Saller Provost, Edward L. Ryerson Distinguished Service Professor of History and Classics, University of Chicago

THE ANCIENT ECONOMY

Chapter 1

Introduction

IAN MORRIS AND J. G. MANNING

Ancient historians conventionally draw a line through maps of the Mediterranean basin. On one side of it are the Greek and Roman worlds; on the other, Egypt and the Near East. Aeschylus and Herodotus already made a similar distinction twenty-five hundred years ago, but since the late eighteenth century AD the delineation has provided the basic structure for studying the ancient Mediterranean world. After 250 years of scholarly consensus about the reality and importance of this Greco-Roman/Egyptian–Near Eastern boundary, a major shift of opinions began in the late 1980s. Some specialists announced that there was just one East Mediterranean culture in antiquity, stretching from Mesopotamia to the Adriatic. Others asserted that while this had been true in the Bronze and Early Iron Ages, the East Mediterranean *koine* had fragmented in the fifth century BC. Others still acknowledged the merits of the traditional view that classical Greco-Roman and Egyptian–Near Eastern cultures were fairly distinct but believed the former had strong Afroasiatic roots in the latter. Finally, some insisted that there was no point trying to make distinctions within the Mediterranean at all, since the entire basin had been tied together in a kaleidoscopic pattern of constantly shifting interactions. Throughout the 1990s the old dividing line was arguably the most prominent academic battlefield in ancient Mediterranean studies.

The fiercest clashes have been among students of ancient literature, art, and myth. But challenging the traditional divided-Mediterranean model also has profound implications for economic historians. If—as many philologists and art historians now claim—Greco-Roman culture was an offshoot of Egyptian and Near Eastern culture, why were the economic systems of these two broad regions of the Mediterranean as different as historians have traditionally believed? The debates over Mediterranean culture require economic historians to ask new questions; and the answers to these economic questions will necessarily feed back into the debates among cultural historians. In this volume, economic historians of various regions try to lay the foundation for a systematic comparative economic history of the ancient Mediterranean. They highlight key problems in the evidence, models, and intellectual traditions of the economic history of different regions of the Mediterranean in different periods of time. The book is merely a first step: Our main goal is to clear away some of the conceptual fog and empirical ignorance that currently bedevil comparative economic analysis.

This introductory chapter is a position paper. We define the central problem and explain the state of the debate as we understand it. We also make some recommendations for research in the next decade. It has become fashionable in the last few years to complain that ancient economic history has run its course, and that there is no hope of real progress.[1] We disagree completely. Serious economic analysis of the ancient Mediterranean world has barely begun. A century of important work has created a large (but problematic) database, honed powerful (but somewhat narrow) methods, and identified fundamental (but unresolved) problems. Ancient historians should be proud of these achievements. But the field remains radically undertheorized and methodologically impoverished. Theory, method, and data are inseparable. Archaeologists and historians have made great advances in classifying and analyzing the primary sources but have not thought enough about how to build models or how to relate models to the empirical facts.

We see four particular limitations in the way research is currently organized:

1. In the late eighteenth and late nineteenth centuries, ancient historians debated the purpose of their field—its function in the world and how it should be organized so as to perform that function. The divided-Mediterranean model is a legacy of these debates. Whether this division helps or hinders our understanding depends on the particular historian's notion of the purpose of ancient economic history.

2. No matter the region of study—Egypt, western Asia, Greece, or Rome—almost all ancient historians work within a broad, shared tradition. Ancient history is empiricist, positivist, inductive, and particularistic, driven mainly by philological agendas created in the nineteenth century. For most practitioners, economic history provides background information that will help scholars interpret more important cultural activities. There is little sense that ancient economic history contributes to any larger questions. The fields reward technical expertise in reading texts or recovering artifacts but put little emphasis on model building, methodology, or comparison. The result is economic history without economics.

3. Beneath the level of this shared tradition, there are deep divisions between Classics, Egyptology, and Near Eastern studies. Scholars in each field tend to be located in separate university or museum departments, and the emphasis that all these fields put on very specific linguistic skills discourages shared graduate programs. The separate scholarly communities use terms in different ways, and while work across these boundaries is more common than it was a generation ago, it remains the exception. The separation of disciplines by language reinforces perceived differences in socioeconomic structure, greatly inhibiting systematic comparison of economic systems.

4. Different kinds of evidence survive from different parts of the Mediterranean. For example, Egypt is rich in documentary papyri recording family and individual economic transactions. Greece has little or no evidence of this kind but has a sophisticated literary tradition that addresses the morality of economic behavior. Given the positivism of these fields, "economic history" has come to have very different meanings to scholars specializing in different parts of the Mediterranean. Egyptologists and papyrologists lean toward detailed accounts of specifics; Hellenists, toward sweeping overviews of ideologies. There are few generalizations that can be made across disciplinary boundaries because of the contrasts in the kinds of evidence available. Progress depends on careful consideration of how we build models, how our conceptual frameworks relate to the data, and how we can develop methods that will allow us to test models across regions.

We see six ways to resolve these problems:

1. *Conduct more discussion of the metanarratives that structure arguments*: By "metanarratives" we mean the grand stories within which some questions assume importance, while others are rendered irrelevant.

Charles Tilly (1984: 1) once suggested that historical sociologists "bear the nineteenth century like an incubus." Ancient historians are afflicted by similar spirits, but some of them are even older, haunting us from the eighteenth century. Only by self-conscious discussion of metanarratives can we decide if we still want to ask the same questions as Weber or Marx (let alone Winckelmann or Niebuhr). If we exorcize their ghosts, we need to know what we want to put in their place.

2. *A deliberate turn toward social science history*: We define what we mean by this in more detail below, but for the moment we sum it up as a commitment to assuming the basic rationality of economic actors and systems, formulating explicit explanatory models, and exposing these models to the risk of falsification. Social science historians have developed powerful tools for the analysis of economic systems and for rigorous comparisons across space and time. It is both arrogant and ignorant for ancient historians to assume that they can do good economic history without these tools.

3. *A broader approach to economic history*: Historians must focus on both the *performance* and *structure* of ancient economies. This will require new models, new methods, and new kinds of evidence.

4. *More thoughtful integration of archaeology into ancient economic history*: In many contexts archaeology provides the only data that can be quantified on a large scale, and there can be no real economic history without quantification. The archaeological record is subject to formation processes every bit as complex as those behind the written record, so this is not simply a matter of using an objective material record to correct a subjective textual one. But on the other hand, some classes of archaeological data can potentially be recovered from all regions of the ancient Mediterranean, vastly improving our ability to write comparative history.

5. *More emphasis on ancient demography and technology*: Economic history depends on understanding demographic trends and the production possibilities set by technology.

6. *More detailed comparisons of economic institutions through time and space*: There has been little work on whether superficially different institutions in different parts of the Mediterranean were functional equivalents, or whether similar-looking institutions in fact functioned differently. It is telling that the only extended comparative study of premodern financial systems—including ancient Mesopotamia,

Periclean Athens, and Augustan Rome—is by an economist, not an ancient historian (Goldsmith 1987).

This volume is a step toward these goals. It began in 1997 with discussions at the dinner seminars of Stanford's Social Science History Institute, which led to the institute hosting a conference on evidence and models in ancient economic history in the spring of 1998. The conference featured four pairs of specialists on the regions of the Near East, Greece, Egypt, and the Roman Empire; responses came from social science historians based in Stanford's Economics, Sociology, and Political Science Departments. Participants hoped to cross two sets of barriers: those dividing ancient history from the social sciences, and those dividing specialists within Mediterranean studies.

There was a flurry of conferences on the ancient economy in the late 1990s, but the Stanford gathering was rather unusual. John Davies, who took part in several of these meetings, concluded that "in general, two main messages stemmed from the Stanford conference. The first was a continuous undercurrent of determined deconstruction of the Finley divided-Mediterranean model as static, simplistic, useless, and retrograde. The second comprised a set of signals that the pre-Alexander economies of the Ancient Near East were vastly more complex and diverse than conventional wisdom dreamed of" (Davies 2001: 13).

Rather than rushing the papers into print, we have taken several years to discuss them and reflect upon their potential impact. Important new studies have appeared since 1998, allowing us to refine our goals more clearly. This is not a systematic review of ancient Mediterranean economies or a fully developed model (desirable as both of these would be). It is simply an attempt to open up discussion. There have been plenty of conferences of classical historians featuring a token Near Eastern specialist (for example, Parkins and Smith 1998), or of Near Easterners with a token classicist (Bongenaar 2000), but few attempts to bring the fields together as equal participants. We want to move toward agreement on questions, methods, terminology, and problems. No two contributors have exactly the same ideas about how the field should move, nor do they each address the whole range of issues listed above. Some chapters concentrate on describing the dominant models in a particular field; others, on new kinds of evidence or forms of argument. But all are united by a commitment to building a generalizing and comparative ancient economic history, connected to debates in the social sciences as well as—but not instead of—those in the humanities.

The Nature of the Problem

Europeans and their colonists on other continents have studied parts of the ancient Mediterranean world intensively for centuries, largely because many of them saw the Bible and Greco-Roman literature as the two main foundations of their cultural identity. Theology and Latin dominated medieval education. In the nineteenth century theology retreated and Greek joined Latin; and in the twentieth century Greek and Latin both lost ground to sciences and modern languages. But even in the early twenty-first century Classics and biblical studies remain huge scholarly enterprises, with annual meetings attracting thousands of professionals. At the editors' own university, the introductory undergraduate courses in Egyptian and Greek history draw more students than those in any other field except U.S. history.

The formalization of scientific universities in the nineteenth century preserved the emphasis on ancient Mediterranean studies in two main clusters. The first was analysis of Greco-Roman society, called Classics in the English-speaking world, and *Altertumswissenschaft*—the science of antiquity—by German speakers. This was normally defined chronologically as beginning with Homer's poetry around 700 BC and continuing at least until the Emperor Constantine's conversion to Christianity, roughly a thousand years later. The discovery of the Aegean Bronze Age in the 1870s raised new questions; some archaeologists felt that it was part of Classics, while others thought that it was not properly Greek. The chronological boundaries also shifted with geography, as Greek and Roman political power waxed and waned. Down to about 335 BC the classical lands were restricted to the shores of the Aegean Sea, central Italy, and the Greek colonies scattered around the Mediterranean. After 335, Alexander's conquests carried Hellenism to Afghanistan and India, but this larger Hellenistic world (an English term coined after the German *Hellenismus*, itself a creation of the nineteenth century) was widely seen as not being fully classical. In the second century BC Rome began taking over the western Mediterranean. Some scholars included England and Romania in the classical realm, since those regions fell to Roman legions; while others limited the "real" classical world to the shores of the Mediterranean.

The second scholarly cluster was the study of societies linked to the Bible. Some academics extended this region as far east as Iran, while others stopped it in Mesopotamia. Egypt was generally seen as part of this world, although it was often studied in a separate department. The biblical stories of the Hebrews' wanderings meant that—unlike the situation in Classics—there was complete agreement that the Bronze Age was part of Near Eastern studies. Chronological disputes were pushed back into the Neolithic; sometimes this was ceded to archaeologists in Anthropology or Archaeology Departments, and sometimes not. Most specialists drew a line with Alexander's conquests, abandoning the Hellenistic kingdoms and Roman Near East to the classicists, even if classicists were not always very keen to embrace them.

The West Mediterranean was little analyzed, except insofar as it was affected by Greek colonization and incorporated into the Roman Empire. Most often, specialists on the literature, material culture, thought, and history of the ancient Mediterranean were concentrated in free-standing departments of Classics or Near Eastern studies rather than being distributed across Departments of History, Literature, Philosophy, Art, or Linguistics, as was the case with specialists in most other world civilizations. Classics and the Near East, were, in a sense, the original Area Studies programs.[2]

In common with many humanists and social scientists of the later nineteenth and earlier twentieth century, scholars of the ancient Mediterranean sought to explain the European invention of modernity; that is, how Europe had diverged from, and become superior to, the rest of the world. Most of the grand theorists of modernity had classical educations, and Karl Marx and Max Weber made particularly extensive use of the ancient Mediterranean in their general frameworks. On the whole, the experts—in Near Eastern studies as well as in Classics—concluded that race, climate, or sociology meant that Egyptians and Asians, in the great river valleys, got a precocious start in civilization but ran up against limits they could not exceed. The Greeks then took over the torch, passing it on to the Romans and ultimately to Western Europe. In one of the most influential books ever written, Johann Joachim Winckelmann proposed that Egyptian art

> is to be compared to a tree which, though well cultivated, has been checked and arrested in its growth by a worm, or other casualties; for it remained unchanged, precisely the same, yet without attaining its perfection, until the period when Greek kings held sway over them . . . the same thing may have happened to [art] as to the mythology; for the fables of the Egyptians were seemingly born anew beneath the skies of Greece, and took an entirely different form, and other names. (Winckelmann 1880 [1764]: 132–33, 135)

Similar sentiments were repeated thousands of times between the 1760s and 1960s.

The institutional forms created in the nineteenth century provided effective structures for pursuing this argument. But as the twentieth century wore on, the larger scholarly community lost faith in the basic assumptions behind it. World Wars I and II, decolonization, and the Vietnam War eroded humanists' confidence that there was any such thing as "European superiority" to explain. Rejecting eighteenth-century agendas—"the project of the Enlightenment," as they have come to be called—humanists and humanistically oriented social scientists have focused instead on the discourses that legitimate inequality (for example, Said 1978; Hardt and Negri 2000). Social scientists still interested in historical explanations of European and North American power developed new models in the past fifty years, from dependency theory to evolutionism, but few of these left much room for eighteenth-century theories of a racial/cultural inheritance going back to the Greeks.[3]

Despite their declining relevance to the rest of the humanities and social sciences, eighteenth- and nineteenth-century structures of thought and institutional arrangements have survived largely intact in ancient Mediterranean studies. This has had two main effects. First, scholars of the ancient Mediterranean have been partially shielded from potentially corrosive new ideas. Debates among classicists and biblical scholars have certainly changed noticeably since the 1980s, but taken as a whole, these fields remain more conservative than, say, comparative literature or cultural anthropology. Second, while many scholars of the ancient Mediterranean have managed to maintain research agendas not so different from those that were common in the 1950s, they have done so at the cost of increasing marginality to larger debates in the humanities and social sciences. In this volume, the contributors concentrate on one particular aspect: Whether the 250-year-old division of Mediterranean studies into two branches, ultimately driven by Greco-Latin philology and biblical exegesis, is a barrier to understanding ancient economics.

What's the Question? Metanarratives

In the last quarter-century, scholarship on the ancient Mediterranean has gone through its most profound transformation in more than two centuries. The outcome remains unclear, but the metanarratives of European identity that have guided the field since the eighteenth century are shifting under our feet. Even defenders of the idea of a distinct Western civilization are casting their defenses in forms very different from those common fifty years ago (Gress 1998; Lind 2000).

Jean-François Lyotard famously spoke of a growing "incredulity toward metanarratives" in the 1980s. He insisted that "to the obsolescence of the metanarrative apparatus of legitimation corresponds, most notably, the crisis of metaphysical philosophy and of the university institution which in the past relied on it." Metanarrative, he claimed, "is being dispersed in clouds of narrative language elements" (Lyotard 1984: xxiv). In the 1990s Lyotard's assertions entered mainstream historical thought, and it was not unusual to encounter claims that we must replace Eurocentric metanarratives with an "interminable pattern without meaning" (Ermarth 1992: 212). But the belief that historians can escape metanarratives altogether is simplistic (Berkhofer 1995). As is often pointed out, critiques of metanarrative usually turn out merely to be arguments in favor of other metanarratives; the postmodern rejection of metanarrative is itself "a (quite totalizing) piece of historical narrative" (Reddy 1992: 137).

In the late eighteenth century and again in the late nineteenth, ancient historians went through anguished debates about the overarching questions that shaped their inquiries, but contemporary scholars of the ancient Mediterranean too often act as if there is nothing to discuss. In the early twentieth century, a once-radical idea—Europe's superiority to the rest of the world—became a truism, so securely established that it no longer needed to be explained. With the overarching metanarrative secure, the experts could focus on what Thomas Kuhn (1970 [1962]) called normal science, generating a mass of detailed scholarly analysis. Most experts on the ancient Mediterranean defined their topics in narrow geographical and chronological terms. If a body of primary and secondary literature expands without any corresponding relaxation of the assumption that a serious scholar must read everything written on the subject, increasingly narrow research topics tend to follow. Large-scale comparative work might have blurred the simple contrast between Greco-Roman and Near Eastern–Egyptian-biblical research topics, but professional ancient historians undertook few studies of this kind, while those evolutionary theorists who addressed larger questions generally operated at such a high level of abstraction that most ancient historians felt that they could safely ignore them.

In the next section we summarize the most influential versions of the divided-Mediterranean model. We then address some of the main alternatives, looking at Fernand Braudel's vision of a single Mediterranean, the East Mediterranean models advocated by Martin Bernal and others, and Peregrine Horden and Nicholas Purcell's recent revival of pan-Mediterraneanism. We close by considering a different metanarrative, which seems to us to open up more fruitful questions. This calls for a new form of global history, committed neither to justifying European domination nor to explaining it away. This approach starts from the fact of

European and American global dominance but argues that it has only shallow historical roots. The comparative historians who developed this model in the late 1990s suggest that prior to the eighteenth, or perhaps even the nineteenth, century, the similarities between Eurasian civilizations vastly outweighed the differences. The central problem is not to find out what was special about premodern Europe but to build general models of the forces that inhibit economic growth and to explain the circumstances that relax these constraints. From this perspective, the Greco-Roman/Egyptian–Near Eastern divide is just not very important. Some ancient Mediterranean societies achieved limited economic growth, which are very significant in global perspective (Goldstone 2002; Saller, Chapter 11 of this volume). But drawing lines across the map will not help us do good economic history.

TWO MEDITERRANEANS: MARX, WEBER,
POLANYI, AND FINLEY

Malleability has been of the greatest strength of the divided-Mediterranean model developed in eighteenth-century Europe. Despite their political differences, Marxists, Weberians, and theorists of a long-lasting "Western civilization" have all found the East-West division perfectly compatible with their reconstructions. The *Communist Manifesto* opens by drawing a direct line between the struggles of the Roman patricians and plebeians and those of contemporary bourgeois and proletarians (Marx and Engels 1848). Marx and Engels distinguished between Asiatic and Classical Modes of Production, seeing the Middle East, India, and China as characterized by cyclical history, in contrast with the European evolutionary mainstream. Uniquely in Europe, contradictions within primitive communism generated a Greco-Roman Classical (or Slave) Mode of Production. Weakened by the struggle between citizens and slaves, this fused with a Germanic Mode to create the Feudal Mode. A series of bourgeois revolutions, beginning in seventeenth-century England, transformed this into the capitalist order and would ultimately lead to communism (Marx 1964 [1857/58]: 69–74).

Engels (1972 [1884]) presented this interpretation of ancient history to a wide audience. In communist countries this became the orthodoxy, although elsewhere its impact was more limited. Some Near Eastern scholars, especially in interwar Germany, found Marxist frameworks useful (see Liverani, Chapter 2), and there have been notable Marxist accounts of Roman history in Italy (Giardina and Schiavone 1981; Carandini 1985; Giardina 1986). But in the English-speaking world, even Geoffrey de Ste. Croix's monumental *The Class Struggle in the Ancient Greek World* (1981), the first sustained attempt to systematize Marxist Greco-Roman history, has been admired more than emulated.

But the divided-Mediterranean model could also be deployed for very different ends. In 1917 Woodrow Wilson's administration asked leading colleges across the United States to design classes that would justify the war effort. The most successful identified a distinct history of Western civilization that could have Near Eastern and Egyptian roots, but really began with classical Athens. When transplanted from elite universities like Chicago and Columbia to hundreds of small colleges, classes in the history of Western civilization provided a useful way to make sense of America's assimilation of citizens from very different parts of Europe (Gress 1998: 31–37). The Cold War gave new relevance to liberal histories of Western civilization. The University of Chicago redesigned its interwar program in the late 1940s (McNeill 1949), promoting a "Greek-centered model [that] define[d] the West as an ahistorical set of great ideas migrating, unsullied by history and passion, from Plato to NATO" (Gress 1998: 411). But while the Soviet Union exported Marxism all over Eastern Europe after 1945, scholars in the pluralistic NATO alliance felt perfectly free to ignore the Western civilization model, which had little to contribute to West European national identities. Even within the United States, it did more to structure teaching and textbooks than detailed professional research; but through these avenues it had a massive impact on how several generations of Americans perceived the ancient Mediterranean.[4]

Weber drew a third set of conclusions from ancient Mediterranean history but also grounded it firmly in an East-West distinction. Like Marx and the Western civilization theorists, he asked why Europeans had created modernity. But instead of seeking continuities from Greco-Roman society to industrial Western Europe, he contrasted an ideal type model of early modern Europe, on the verge of the capitalist take-off, with ideal types of other advanced civilizations that did not experience such a take-off. Weber identified the crucial variable, present in Europe and absent elsewhere, as a "spirit of capitalism," which involved using rationally organized, formally free labor in a regular orientation toward the achievement of profit through nominally peaceful economic exchange.[5] Weber argued that prior to the rise of Calvinism in sixteenth-century Western Europe, market relations were everywhere subordinated to other status concerns, which prevented the emergence of this spirit of capitalism. He wrote about Rome in detail, and also about Greece, the Near East, and Egypt (Weber 1958 [1921]; 1976b [1909]). He argued that ancient status structures rarely came close to breaking down, even under the stress of debt crises (Weber 1968: 303–4, 931).

For Weber the most important contrast was between modern Western rationality on the one hand and all previous forms of society on the other. These others had depended chiefly on traditional authority. But he also saw big differences between Greco-Roman citizenship and Near Eastern theocracy. One of the most important distinctions was the link between hydraulic agriculture and centralized power in the great river valleys of Egypt and Mesopotamia. The need to control irrigation networks, the argument ran, led directly to despotic forms of rule. Near Eastern state development led to rural poverty and the concentration of wealth in the hands of political elites, in contrast to decentralized, democratic patterns in Greece and Italy (see Wittfogel 1957; Springborg 1992).

Weber had few direct followers among Mediterranean specialists, but Karl Polanyi's reformulation of his ideas as "substantivism" fared better. The prominent Near Eastern historian Leo Oppenheim and Greek historian Moses Finley were both members of Polanyi's seminar at Columbia University in the 1950s. With a few exceptions (for example, Janssen 1975, 1981; Kemp 1989: 232–60), Egyptologists found little use for substantivism, but Oppenheim (1957, 1977) and Finley (1981 [1953–78]; 1985a [1973]) established it as a leading approach in Near Eastern and classical economic history.

Substantivism never became *the* leading approach to ancient Mediterranean history, which has remained a weakly defined liberal humanism (see pp. 26–27 below). But despite the great differences between these schools of thought, each took a Greco-Roman / Egyptian–Near Eastern division for granted. None of them made the division itself a major topic of research, perhaps due to the combined weight of two centuries of scholarship and the fact that postwar Europe itself had been riven in two.

The most developed version of the divided-Mediterranean thesis in economic history was Moses Finley's 1973 book, *The Ancient Economy*. Finley often criticized Polanyi (Finley 1970) but also built on Polanyi's typology of nonmarket economic systems. Polanyi had argued that the ancient Near East had been dominated by palatial redistribution, while the classical Greeks favored reciprocity, moving toward market exchange in the fourth century BC (Polanyi et al. 1957). For Finley, "the Graeco-Roman world was essentially and precisely one of private ownership, whether of a few acres or of the enormous domains of Roman senators and emperors, a world of private trade, private manufacture" (Finley 1985a [1973]: 29). By contrast, he suggested,

> The Near Eastern economies were dominated by large palace- or temple-complexes, who owned the greater part of the arable, virtually

monopolized anything that can be called "industrial production" as well as foreign trade (which includes inter-city trade, not merely trade with foreign parts), and organized the economic, military, political and religious life of the society through a single complicated, bureaucratic, record-keeping operation for which the word "rationing," taken very broadly, is as good a one-word description as I can think of. (Finley 1985a: 28)

As a result, Finley explained, "Were I to define 'ancient' to embrace both worlds, there is not a single topic I could discuss without resorting to disconnected sections, employing different concepts and models" (Finley 1985a: 28). Finley understood probably better than any other ancient historian the methodological challenges of broad, ideal-typical contrasts (Finley 1985b: 47–66). He spelled out his perception of the Greco-Roman/Near Eastern distinction:

I do not wish to over-simplify. There were private holdings of land in the Near East, privately worked; there were "independent" craftsmen and pedlars in the towns. Our evidence does not permit quantification, but I do not believe it is possible to elevate these people to the prevailing pattern of economy . . . [The classical and Near Eastern] worlds had their secondary, atypical, marginal people, such as the nomads who were a chronic threat to the settled river-valley communities in Mesopotamia and Egypt, perhaps the Phoenician cities on the coast of Syria, certainly the Spartans in Greece. Furthermore, Phrygians, Medes and Persians were not Babylonians or Egyptians, while the government of the Roman Empire became as autocratic and bureaucratic, in some ways, as the Ptolemies, and before them the Pharaohs, of Egypt. But not in all ways. We must concentrate on the dominant types, the characteristic modes of behaviour. (Finley 1985a: 28–29)

Finley conceded that "the Graeco-Roman world is of course an abstraction, and an elusive one when we try to anchor it in time and space" but suggested that "in very round numbers we shall be dealing with the period between 1000 BC and AD 500" (1985a: 29). Spatially, he identified it with the Roman Empire at its peak, with a focus around the Mediterranean Sea (1985a: 29–33).

Finley developed his model of the Greco-Roman economy across the remaining two hundred pages of *The Ancient Economy*. He saw an overwhelmingly agricultural world, characterized by small surpluses. Bulk commodities were usually traded only over short distances; only low-weight, high-value luxury goods could have been moved profitably across long distances. Transport, transaction, and information costs were high. There were low levels of monetization and a general preference for avoiding the risks of market exchange. Society was structured around male citizenship, in some cases leading to a polarization between free citizens and chattel slaves. Economic activity was subordinated to status considerations and, above all, ideas of citizenship. Citizens generally avoided activities that might seem to involve exploitation of their fellow citizens, including money lending, retail, and trade. This world was relatively static from the age of Homer to the third-century AD crisis of the Roman Empire.

Finley did not say whether he thought that the Egyptian–Near Eastern economies had the same kind of agricultural base, cellular arrangement, and lack of market integration as the Greco-Roman. He probably would have seen many similarities, but they were not important for his larger questions. For these, what mattered was the *social structure* of the economies under study. For Finley, like Weber, the most interesting question was why the Greco-Roman economy, for all its size and complexity, did not experience a capitalist transformation (I. Morris 1999: xx–xxiii). Like the nineteenth-century primitivists, Finley downplayed the scale of the Greco-Roman economy, but to reduce his argument to a case for primitivism—as so many ancient historians do—is to miss his point. As Richard Saller notes in Chapter 11, Finley recognized the size of the Greco-Roman economy just as well as Michael Rostovtzeff, the leading twentieth-century "modernist" historian. His real interest was its status structure: like Weber, he argued that citizenship acted as a brake on the development of factor markets, technology, and trade, preventing economic class from becoming the dominant social relationship (for example, Finley 1985a: 51, 60, 61). Approaching the ancient evidence with these questions in mind, Finley concluded that the prominence of free or chattel-slave labor in the Greco-Roman world as compared to complex gradations of status in the Egyptian–Near Eastern world, in conjunction with the prominence of great redistributive institutions of temple and palace in the latter and their virtual absence in the former, made it pointless to lump Greek, Romans, Egyptians, and Babylonians together. He may have thought that a separate study of Egyptian or Near Eastern economies (like Oppenheim's) might underline his and Weber's point that status structures prevented market take-offs in antiquity; but he saw nothing to gain from conflating two distinct sociological systems.

ONE MEDITERRANEAN: BRAUDEL

While it is an exaggeration to call Finley's model "a new orthodoxy" (K. Hopkins 1983: xi) or to claim that "the ghost of M. I. Finley is everywhere" (Paterson 1998: 157), Finley has had close followers in both Greek (P. Millett 1991; Möller 2000) and Roman history (Jongman 1988; Whittaker 1995). Unlike most English-language ancient historians, he won a wide readership in Italy and France (Vidal-Naquet 1965; Andreau and Étienne 1984; Andreau and Hartog 1987–89; Andreau 1995). By the 1990s most discussions of Greco-Roman economic history with pretensions to go beyond description began from his model (Andreau et al. 1994; Cornell and Lomas 1995; Descat 1995; Parkins 1997a; Parkins and Smith 1998; Lo Cascio 2000; Bresson 2000; Archibald et al. 2001; Mattingly and Salmon 2001; Cartledge et al. 2001; Temin 2001; Scheidel and von Reden 2002).

In part this attention is understandable, since Ste. Croix's version of Marxism has been the only coherent alternative economic model to the neo-Weberian tradition. But in another way it is very surprising. The most important argument for the unity of the Mediterranean, Fernand Braudel's *La Méditerranée et le monde méditerranéen à l'époque de Philippe II*, appeared in 1949, while Finley was sitting in Polanyi's seminar and finishing his doctorate. Braudel set out to challenge the obsessive focus on national histories in early modern Europe. He argued that "the Turkish Mediterranean lived and breathed with the same rhythms as the Christian, that the whole sea shared a common destiny, a heavy one indeed, with identical problems and general trends if not identical consequences" (Braudel 1972a: 14).

Braudel was unusual in blurring the boundaries between the Christian and Muslim Mediterraneans. In common with some of the other innovative French thinkers of his time, Braudel spent many years outside the Parisian establishment (Burke 1990: 32–33). Like Claude Lévi-Strauss, he taught in Brazil (at São Paulo, 1935–37); and like Pierre Bourdieu, he lived for several years in Algeria (1923–32). Immanuel Wallerstein (1976) celebrated the *Annales* school as a center of resistance to scholarly hegemonies, and we might see Braudel's project in that light, although there is little in his own work to support such a reading. J. H. Hexter (1972), on the other hand, suggested that the most interesting question was not so much why Braudel chose to write what he did (after all, there are always eccentrics), but, rather, why a twelve-hundred-page dissertation, arguing a very unorthodox thesis, became a classic. Hexter's answer was characteristically caustic: Braudel, whom Lucien Febvre had adopted into the *Annales* school as "un enfant de la maison" when they met on the long voyage back to France from Brazil in 1937, was positioned as no American scholar ever could be. When *La Méditerranée* came out, Braudel also succeeded to a chair at the Collège de France and codirectorship (with Febvre) of the Sixth Section of the École Pratique des Hautes Études. In 1951–52 he launched three series of publications to follow up the themes of his book, and by 1956–57 he became the dominant figure in the *Annales* editorial board (Burke 1990: 43–44). The Sixth Section was home to hundreds of historians, most of them moving in the directions advocated by the editors of the *Annales*. Hexter asked himself, "Where in the United States would one find an advanced History faculty of such dimensions, not to speak of such shared inclination? Indeed, where in the United States would one find a university ready to concern itself with the care and feeding of such a gaggle of advanced historical scholars?" He concluded that "to achieve in the United States what Febvre and Braudel achieved in France was beyond the capacities of [Oscar] Handlin, beyond the capacity of any historian in the United States. It would, I believe, have been beyond the capacities of Febvre and Braudel" (Hexter 1972).

It is perhaps not so surprising, then, that *La Méditerranée* had little impact on ancient historians' conceptions of their field. Through the 1950s and 1960s its main impact was within France, where the institutions of the *Annales* and the Sixth Section mattered most. And even within France, ancient historians' responses were initially muted. The book had its problematic aspects: As the most important Anglophone review of the French edition insisted (Bailyn 1951), it lacked a clear focus, in sharp contrast to Febvre's and Bloch's visions of *Annales* history. Braudel claimed that the real subject of his book was not the Mediterranean at all, but his tripartite model of levels of temporality (Braudel 1972a: 21–22). Further, Braudel never defined the Mediterranean. Despite insisting on the need for clarity (17–18), at times he included all of France, Portugal, the Balkans, and Anatolia (394–96). Braudel hinted at the relevance of his work for early periods but said little about them, and his lengthy manuscript *Mémoires de la Méditerranée* only appeared in 1998 (Braudel 2001 [1998]). The inventive school of Greek scholars working in Paris in the 1950s and 1960s was more influenced by Lévi-Strauss than by Braudel, although this trend began to change in the 1970s (Andreau and Etienne 1986). In the 1990s, French ancient historians and archaeologists were pioneers in taking the entire Mediterranean as their basic unit of analysis (Bresson and Rouillard 1993; Gras 1995; Ruby 1999).

Quite possibly Finley thought deeply about Braudel's challenge and rejected it. He worked with Jean-Pierre Vernant and Pierre Vidal-Naquet in Paris in the 1960s and could hardly have been unaware of Braudel's pan-Mediterraneanism. But if Finley did engage with Braudel, there is no sign of it in his writings: Braudel does not appear in the indices of his books.

The appearance of *La Méditerranée* in English in 1972 had a dramatic impact on Anglophone historians.[6] Brent Shaw says that he "can still see the sudden arrival of the paperback edition of Braudel's 'Mediterranean' in 1975 in the bookstores of Cambridge, and the ripples of excitement as the whole coterie of young research students in ancient history hurried to acquire their own copies" (Shaw 2001: 419–20). Yet even as late as the 1980s there are few signs that Braudel's pan-Mediterraneanism, which directly challenged the basic classical–Near Eastern division of intellectual labor among ancient specialists, seriously worried the leading ancient historians in any country. The peculiarities of Braudel's institutional position no doubt partly account for Finley's ability to ignore Braudel's central thesis and the failure of reviewers to call Finley to task on it. But it is striking that Braudel's reconceptualization of the Mediterranean had as much or more impact on historians of India and China than on those of the ancient Mediterranean (for example, Chaudhuri 1985, 1990; Wong 2001; Aymard 2001). We suggest that the unusual rigidity of institutional structures in both the classical and biblical branches of ancient Mediterranean scholarship protected these experts from having to confront an incompatible thesis in an adjacent field, even when it had become the most celebrated historical work of the twentieth century.

ONE EAST MEDITERRANEAN: WEST, BURKERT, AND BERNAL

At all times since the eighteenth century, a few scholars have questioned the East-West division. A generation ago the Oxford philologist Martin West concluded (though without defining his terms) that the similarities between Hesiod's poem the *Theogony* from the seventh century BC and Hittite religious texts from the Bronze Age meant that "Greece is part of Asia; Greek literature is a Near Eastern literature" (West 1966: 30–31). The Swiss philologist Walter Burkert later put flesh on these bones, arguing that ideas flowed freely from western Asia to Greece in the eighth and seventh centuries BC, creating a common culture in the East Mediterranean (Burkert 1992 [1984]).

West's arguments for a single Greco–Near Eastern culture were largely ignored in the 1960s and 1970s, while Burkert's small book saw a greater impact among classicists. However, these discussions were overshadowed by the uproar created by the first volume of Martin Bernal's *Black Athena* (1987). Bernal, a Sinologist, turned to the ancient Mediterranean in response to the

Vietnam War (Bernal 1987: xii–xiii). He saw striking parallels between East Asia and the East Mediterranean. He alleged that while ancient Greek authors had known that their civilization had Egyptian and Semitic roots, nineteenth-century classicists had deliberately obscured the origins to create a racist distinction between pure Europeans—tracing their descent to Greece—and inferior Asiatics, who lacked this pedigree. The book reached a wide audience, particularly in the United States, where it provided grist for the mill of scholars who had already rejected the eighteenth-century European meta-narrative. *Black Athena* stimulated public debates and raised awareness of what was at stake in ancient Mediterranean history (see Lefkowitz 1996; Lefkowitz and Rogers 1996; Hanson and Heath 1998; Berlinerblau 2001; Bernal 2001; duBois 2001). But neither Bernal nor his critics showed much interest in developing clear theoretical and methodological criteria, let alone in producing competent intellectual history (Marchand and Grafton 1997). Rather than stimulating a serious debate over the Greco-Roman / Egyptian–Near Eastern division, the *Black Athena* debate degenerated into ideological posturing.

In parallel to the public controversy, professional scholars raised more nuanced versions of some of the same questions (Kopcke and Tokumaru 1992; S. P. Morris 1992; M. Miller 1997). In conference panels, public debates, and special issues of journals they mapped out new areas for debate. By the late 1990s some of the many questions in the field asked which areas of the Near East played the biggest part in transmitting ideas to Greece (Egypt? Anatolia? the Levant?), when the major transmission took place (in the Bronze Age, in the seventh century BC, or continuously?), and whether the key issue is Greek borrowing or the development of a common culture.

However, the 1990s arguments over Greek–Near Eastern interactions were seriously undertheorized, presenting no coherent account of the workings of the hypothesized East Mediterranean culture; the interactions between literature, art, social structure, and economics; or even defining their terms and specifying standards for falsification (I. Morris 2000: 102–5). For Burkert (1992: 7), "the sheer fact of [Greek] borrowing" from the Near East is the end of analysis; and for West, the only methodological discussion required in a 650-page survey of west Asian influences on Greek poetry is that "culture, like all forms of gas, tends to spread out from where it is densest into adjacent areas where it is less dense" (1997: 1).

So far, art historians and philologists have dominated English-language scholarly debates, although continental scholars have made forays into comparative social history (Raaflaub and Müller-Luckner 1993). There seems to be strong agreement among younger specialists that Greek culture can only be understood in an East Mediterranean context, but economic historians have not followed up the challenge that this poses.

MANY MEDITERRANEANS IN ONE:
HORDEN AND PURCELL

These 1990s arguments concerned a relatively limited question, of cultural relationships among Greece, Egypt, and Western Asia. Peregrine Horden and Nicholas Purcell's book *The Corrupting Sea: A Study in Mediterranean History* (2000) is much more ambitious. It began life as an Oxford seminar stimulated by Braudel's work: "*The Mediterranean* induced a simple question. Could such a work have been written taking as its eponymous ruler an imperial potentate from Antiquity or the Middle Ages?" It evolved into "a distinction of subject matter between, on the one hand, history *in* the region, contingently Mediterranean or best conceived under some other heading, and, on the other hand, history *of* it—history either of the whole Mediterranean or of an aspect of it to which the whole is an indispensable framework" (Horden and Purcell 2000: 1, 2). Horden and Purcell concluded that they needed to write a history *of* the Mediterranean, embracing the entire period from later prehistory to the nineteenth century, because

> the distinctiveness of Mediterranean history results (we propose) from
> the paradoxical coexistence of a milieu of relatively easy seaborne
> communications with a quite unusually fragmented topography of
> microregions in the sea's coastlands and islands. . . . Against interpreta-
> tions that emphasize radical change and violent discontinuity in the
> Mediterranean past, our approach sustains the hope that valuable
> comparisons can be drawn, and certain continuities inferred, across
> extremes of time. (Horden and Purcell 2000: 5)

Consequently,

> As we have argued throughout, the region is only loosely unified,
> distinguishable from its neighbors to degrees that vary with time,
> geographical direction and topic. Its boundaries are not of the sort
> to be drawn easily on a map. Its continuities are best thought of as
> continuities of form or pattern, within which all is mutability.
> (Horden and Purcell 2000: 523)

"History *of*" is the antithesis of the divided-Mediterranean models going back to Winckelmann. Where Finley saw fixity, boundaries, institutions, and cities, Horden and Purcell identify fluidity, connectivity, individual action, and a rural-urban continuum. Where Finley and others marked out a

Greco-Roman economy, they see a vastly larger unity. Finley's Mediterranean had high transport, information, and transaction costs; Horden and Purcell's involves people moving around in "patterns of interaction too various and detailed to be called routes" (2000: 172). They assume low transport costs, making travel from one end of the Mediterranean to the other perfectly feasible across their entire time span; but they emphasize most strongly what they call *cabotage*, small-scale, individual movements of petty traders and travelers, uncontrolled by the state or any other entity. In Horden and Purcell's premodern Mediterranean, dispersed hinterlands and intervisible microregions are tied together "under the heading of the aggregates of 'short distances' that correspond to the definite places" (2000: 143). They see tremendous mobility and a constantly shifting diaspora: "We cannot unpick the weave of this tangled mass of ethnic origins" (2000: 400). Their premodern Mediterranean was decentralized. The institutional nodes of power that historians conventionally focus on—cities, states, empires— are no help. They argue at length (2000: 91–122) against setting up urban/rural distinctions, and more briefly (2000: 86–87, 375–77) against focusing on states. Empires and imperialism do not even appear in the index. The logic of what they call "inescapable redistribution" (2000: 342–44) sidelined these clumsy institutions, which responded to the "matrix" of diverse microecologies linked by the sea less effectively than did the uncoordinated actions of *caboteurs* and migrants. Consequently, they reject out of hand "the strategy of *classifying economies chronologically*. The search for common denominators using the comparative approach across wide spans of space and time seems to us more promising than asserting schizophrenic splits of historical experience created around 'turning points' on the teleoscopic scale" (2000: 147; emphasis in original). They are at pains to insist that we should not ignore fixed empires and trade routes altogether (2000: 151, 152, 172), but the most extended empirical discussion in the book is nevertheless an argument that there was far less of a decline in interregional connectivity in early medieval times than historians have supposed (2000: 153–72).

The ideas and language of *The Corrupting Sea* are strikingly like those developed by theorists of globalization (I. Morris 2003).[7] Since the late 1980s—the same period in which critiques of models of the divided Mediterranean have multiplied—technological changes have connected people as never before, revolutionizing finance and slashing the costs of moving goods, people, capital, and ideas around the world. Everything seems to be in flux. Globalization theorists regularly suggest that the cultural trend widely termed "postmodernism" is an aesthetic and philosophical response to the new economy (Harvey 1989).

One of the most common techniques for illuminating globalization has been to contrast the world that has emerged since the 1980s with that of the Cold War era. The Cold War international landscape was dominated by division; the new order, by integration. The Cold War was symbolized by the Wall; the new order, by the Web. The Cold War, by fixed rules and confrontation; the new order, by fluidity and shapelessness. Hierarchical states and firms, the inflexible institutions that dominated life in the Northern Hemisphere during the Cold War, have changed profoundly. In a classic essay, Ronald Coase (1937) argued that business firms exist because, under certain circumstances, top-down command structures function more efficiently in the market than Smithian freebooting entrepreneurs. Other analysts (particularly North 1990) extended this model to the state. Through much of the twentieth century, the level of technology and the forms of competition made the concentration of capital and labor in massive, rigid, Fordist enterprises the most efficient way to create wealth (whether in capitalist or socialist economies). Similar forces favored strong states with welfare programs and mighty armies, controlling national currencies and policing their economic as well as political frontiers. But the new technology and interconnectedness that emerged in the last quarter of the twentieth century mean that this situation no longer prevails. Most businesses need to outsource activities and decentralize decision-making to survive. So too states, which are having to adapt their power to meet new threats, while cities are evolving into something completely new (Harvey 1989; Soja 2000). To harness the power of the new economy, states relentlessly deregulate, lower tariffs, and submit their power to the discipline of global markets. Astonishing levels of mobility of labor and capital spelled disaster for those who refused, from IBM to the Soviet Union. The New World Order, like Horden and Purcell's world of *caboteurs*, has few real routes to dominate.

Globalization has changed how academics think. To say this is not to dismiss Horden and Purcell's book as "mere ideology"; the world is a different place now than it was in the 1950s. It is hard to disagree with Eric Carr's observation: "I am not sure that I should envy any historian who could honestly claim to have lived through the earth-shaking events of the past fifty years without some radical modifications of his outlook" (Carr 1961: 40). All formulations of the shape of history necessarily take many things for granted. In Finley's case, these were things that made a great deal of sense in the Cold War world. Horden and Purcell take different things for granted, and these are things that make a great deal of sense in the globalizing world. Finley's was an ancient Mediterranean of divisions, rigid structures, and powerful institutions; Horden and Purcell's is one of mobility, connectivity, and decentering.

The Corrupting Sea is a major work, forcing ancient historians to confront Braudel's challenge and its limitations. It raises some of the same issues as the present volume and speaks of grounding cultural analysis in ecology and economics, with a promise to examine demography in a further book. But Horden and Purcell pursue these issues in a very different way from us. Where we emphasize the need to define concepts clearly and to operationalize them, to build models, and to expose conjectures to the risk of refutation, they consistently avoid these activities. In one of the most original parts of their book, spelling out the shortcomings of attempts to define cities in the Mediterranean, they comment that "since this chapter is 'against *villes*', the gist of our argument at this point might be described as 'against typologies'" (2000: 101). This might serve as a motto not just for their fourth chapter, but for their whole method. The vastness and complexity of the "history of" the Mediterranean seems to them to rule out any attempt to pin down definitions, concepts, methods, or periods. Their method has something in common with what Joan Wallach Scott (1991) has called "history without foundations," a deconstructive approach eschewing definitions and categories in favor of constant mutability and reinvention.

NO MEDITERRANEANS: WRIGLEY, JONES, AND GOLDSTONE

While globalization was shifting the ground under our feet and multicultural and postcolonial critiques of the eighteenth-century metanarrative were gaining visibility, a group of economic historians was raising another set of questions with serious implications for the ancient Mediterranean. They suggest that the English Industrial Revolution, the historical rupture at the center of the metanarratives discussed above, was a more complex, gradual, and contingent phenomenon than is normally assumed; and that once we understand this, a whole new set of questions needs to be asked.

In a highly influential book, E. A. Wrigley (1988) broke the English Industrial Revolution down into two separate processes, covering a long timespan. The first, he argued, was an example of Smithian growth, beginning around 1550. Improvements in the organization of agriculture, transport, and the use of animal power significantly raised output per capita, while social institutions and belief systems loosened to allow labor to leave the agricultural sector, rather than consuming the gains in underemployment. In most of Europe real wages improved sharply after the Black Death, only to fall back to pre-1347 levels by 1600. Robert Allen (1999, 2001) has shown that this did not happen in England and the Low Countries, where real wages stayed around fifteenth-century levels until the early nineteenth century. In England, population grew seven-fold between about 1500 and 1750, while farm output increased only by a factor of roughly 2.25, meaning that the bulk of the achievement of maintaining living standards in a period of population growth must be put down to Wrigley's Smithian growth.

By 1750 English families were typically better off than those on the continent. But, Wrigley argues, what prevented diminishing returns setting in and returning the economy to a stationary state, as the classical economists (Smith, Ricardo, Mill) all predicted, was the beginning of a second process: technological advances that dramatically reduced the costs of exploiting energy trapped in fossil fuels. Diminishing returns did apply here, but initially the amounts of energy were so vast that there were constant or even increasing returns to scale, and by 1870 real wages were rising impressively. Wrigley calls societies like those of seventeenth-century England advanced organic economies, dependent on organic energy (muscle power plus vegetable foods, fuel, clothing, and shelter). Such societies can experience per capita economic growth through expanding markets or improving communications and organization but can only be transformed into a new kind of system, a mineral-based energy economy, if they succeed in tapping readily available fossil fuels.

At just the same time, Eric Jones (2000 [1988]) argued that pre-eighteenth-century economic history was more cyclical than historians had realized. Many societies, he suggested, had experienced *extensive* growth (overall increases in output), but they rarely succeeded in turning these into *intensive* growth, producing sustained rises in per capita output and standards of living. He saw the explanation in rent-seeking behavior by rulers. In a few cases, like Sung China and early modern Western Europe, this constraint was relaxed. "Perhaps," Jones concludes, "growth can occur only within an 'optimality band' where factor and commodity markets are freed and the government is neither too grasping nor too weak" (Jones 2000: 187).

A combination of Wrigley's and Jones's theses produces a very different metanarrative from Weber's. Many societies have achieved extensive growth and even raised output to the level of advanced organic societies. Measured across the very long-run, there has been a slow accumulation of physical and human capital and a gradual upward trend in per capita output. In any given society, periods of expansion normally broke down as rulers' pursuit of short-term gain blocked and then reversed the forces of growth. Contrary to the assumptions of nineteenth-century theorists, there were few significant long-term differences in social, cultural, and demographic trends in Europe and Asia (Wong 1998; Lee and Wang 1999; Pomeranz 2000). As late as the seventeenth century, the similarities between Europe, Ottoman Turkey, and

China were more striking than the contrasts (Goldstone 1991, 1998). Extensive growth verged on becoming intensive growth in several parts of the world, and, some historians argue, contingent factors—fortuitous political reforms in England in 1688, the distribution of mineral resources, and Europe's easier access to the physical resources of the Americas—pushed Europe over the edge first (Goldstone 2000; Frank [1998] argues a somewhat similar case, but with less subtlety). Europe's breakthrough spelled disaster for the civilizations of Asia, which experienced economic collapse in the nineteenth and earlier twentieth centuries.

These arguments substitute a new metanarrative for Eurocentrism. Gale Stokes sums up this thesis as "see[ing] the last thousand years as an era dominated primarily by the cultures of Asia, especially China, with a relatively brief and likely to be transient burst of European power in the last quarter of the millennium" (2001: 509). Sinocentrism is as speculative as Weber's Eurocentrism and involves just as many untestable counterfactuals: There is simply no way to know, for example, if China—assuming for a moment the Glorious Revolution in England had failed—would have become a mineral-based energy economy in the nineteenth century and created an empire in Africa, Europe, and America. Other counterfactuals, like asking what would have happened if America had been further from Europe or coal harder to find in England, fail to meet the basic criterion of plausibility (Tetlock and Belkin 1996).

But, that said, recent macrohistory has shaken the foundations of the nineteenth-century assumptions that much ancient Mediterranean history still rests on. If there is no European economic or cultural uniqueness with deep roots going back into antiquity, or even some special early modern European quality that we can show to have been absent in Rome (as well as India and China), Weber's metanarrative and those derived from it by Polanyi and Finley lose much of their force. If economic performance did improve substantially across Greco-Roman antiquity (see Morris, Hitchner, and Saller in this volume), we should link the gains with other cases of what Jack Goldstone (2002) calls "efflorescences" in world history, asking—with North, Wrigley, and Jones—what generated these episodes of growth and what interrupted them. We will need a much more complicated history of demography, institutions, and ideologies (North 1981: 3–68).

Shifting our focus in this way opens up new questions. It does *not* mean returning to the 1890s "primitivist-modernist" debate; Weber and Finley showed long ago that this cannot account for the realities of the ancient world. But instead of carrying on asking whether Europe was already different from the rest of the world in the first millennium BC, we now need to ask how well different societies unleashed the forces of growth, and how standards of living fluctuated. Once we raise these questions, different issues from the old Greece/Rome versus Egypt/Near East opposition come into focus. Relatively advanced organic economies developed in Western Asia and Egypt in the third millennium BC then spread both east and west. New questions proliferate. How advanced were these ancient organic economies? How did their performance and structure compare with those of, say, Sung China and Tudor-Stuart England? What caused ancient economic growth, and what retarded and eventually undermined it? Do Wrigley's categories work well on this macroscale? How far did advanced organic economies spread? Why did expansion stop when and where it did? Alternatively, we might see a quite different boundary as important, between the advanced organic economies of the last few millennia BC and the later Roman Empire, where a partial shift away from muscle power and toward water power began (Wilson 2000, 2002). This was still a far cry from the mineral-based energy economy of eighteenth-century England, but as Greif points out in Chapter 12, it is an important break with the organic economies.

CONCLUSION

We have suggested that most ancient economic history rests on pernicious postulates inherited from the eighteenth century. These reveal themselves not only in the ways historians work but also in the ways that they divide up the Mediterranean. Some ancient historians look more to postulates derived from nineteenth-century thinkers such as Marx and Weber, and in the 1980s and 1990s new ideas entered the field, some inspired by critiques of Eurocentrism, others by new ideas accompanying globalization. The developments of the last twenty years are rarely consistent with the eighteenth- and nineteenth-century frameworks. But so far ancient historians have formulated their challenges poorly and have failed to develop methods adequate to pursuing them. In the next section, we argue that a more explicitly social-science history will provide the rigor needed for a proper comparative study of ancient Mediterranean economies.

Social-Science History

As a first step toward defining social-science history, it might be useful to break down approaches to ancient history into two broad ideal types of "humanistic" and "social scientific" practice.[8] Making a sweeping generalization, we suggest that what makes a scholar humanistic is that he or she tries to *understand* the world, whereas the foundation of being a social scientist is in trying to *explain* it. The humanities are about drawing out the meanings and complexity of life. God is in the details, and good scholarship explicates the richness of culture. The social sciences, on the other hand, aim to cut through the messy details of reality to find underlying structures and principles. We might say that in the humanist's eyes, reducing the world to a handful of principles reveals little because it leaves out precisely those particulars that we most need to understand. In the social scientist's eyes, humanists focus on dependent variables, sticking to the surface of problems rather than digging down to real explanations. We subdivide these broad categories into "liberal" and "new" humanities on the one hand, and "economic" and "sociological" social sciences on the other.

LIBERAL HUMANISM

By liberal humanism we mean the mainstream of humanistic thought that took shape in the nineteenth century. Liberal humanists rarely define what they do, but in one of the most explicit statements, Ronald Crane (a University of Chicago literature professor) described the subject matter of the humanities as

> all those things which . . . are . . . not amenable to adequate explanation in terms of general laws of natural processes, physical or biological, or in terms of collective social conditions or forces. They are the things which we cannot predict, in any scientific way, that men individually or in groups will do, but which, when they are done, we recognize as signs, not of any natural or social necessities but of possibilities inherent in man's peculiar nature. They are, in short, what we commonly speak of as human achievements. (Crane 1967: 8)

Contrasting this vision of the humanities with his idea of science, he concluded that

> the sciences are most successful when they seek to move from the diversity and particularity of their observations toward as high a degree of unity, uniformity, simplicity, and necessity as their materials permit. The humanities, on the other hand, are most alive when they reverse this process, and look for devices of explanation and appreciation that will enable them to preserve as much as possible of the variety, the uniqueness, the unexpectedness, the complexity, the originality, that distinguish what men are capable of doing at their best from what they must do, or tend generally to do, as biological organisms or members of a community. (Crane 1967: 12)

Liberal humanists are even more reticent about the point of their inquiries, but individual internal enrichment seems to be one of the major issues. Appreciating the best that has been said and thought improves the humanist as a person, raising up society as a whole by creating better citizens. To a degree, liberal humanism defines itself against materialism and mass consumption, diverting the trained mind toward loftier issues.

The methods of liberal humanism are normally highly empirical, involving close reading of texts or art objects selected as outstanding, rather than representative, examples. Philology, connoisseurship, and sensitivity to nuance are the most important skills. On the whole, liberal humanists work inductively.

Ancient historians overwhelmingly come from this background. One consequence has been a focus on high culture at the expense of banausic matters like economics. In Greek history, Augustus Boeckh's *Stadtaushaltung der Athener* (1817) has still not been superseded. The highly literary nature of most surviving Greek and Latin texts makes economic history a difficult exercise, which no doubt accounts for some of the classicists' lack of enthusiasm. But while there has been nothing to stop archaeologists from focusing on sites of economic significance, only in the 1980s did this begin to be normal (I. Morris 1999b); and in the 1990s, archaeologists transformed our knowledge of Roman economics and technology (Mattingly 1995; Leveau 1996; Lewis 1997; Greene 2000; Mattingly and Salmon 2001; Wilson 2000, 2002; Hitchner, Chapter 10). By contrast with Greece and Rome, Mesopotamia and Egypt have been the sites of excavations of hundreds of thousands of economic tablets and papyri. The comprehensive traditions of *Altertumswissenschaft* prevent historians from ignoring these bodies of data, but scholars have studied a far smaller proportion of them compared to literary texts (Frier 1989; Bagnall 1995: 90–108; van de Mieroop 1999: 106) and in Ptolemaic Egypt have, until recently, consistently favored Greek texts over demotic Egyptian, which preserve private economic transactions and reveal the ancient institutional structure of Egypt. Liberal humanism puts economics on the back burner.

THE NEW HUMANITIES

Liberal humanism was always anathema to Marxists. Terry Eagleton, one of the leading Marxist literary critics, calls it "the impotent conscience of bourgeois society, gentle, sensitive, and ineffectual" (1983: 199). Orthodox Marxism treated culture as important because it was the home of ideology, the false consciousness that blinded people to the true nature of the Mode of Production that expropriated their surplus labor. But Marxist critiques of

culture often struck Western liberal humanists as naive and crude. From the
1950s to the 1970s, particularly in Paris, Marxist intellectuals responded by
accommodating Marx's economic determinism to such philosophical currents as existentialism, psychoanalysis, structuralism, poststructuralism, and
feminism. Rather than seeing culture as an epiphenomenon, legitimating the
economic infrastructure and institutional structure, some Marxist humanists
argued that these structures were culturally constituted. Michel Foucault developed an influential model of discursive structures, or regimes of truth, in
which all thought coheres into a dominant, diffuse, and controlling discourse from which escape was impossible. Deconstructionists went further
still, dismissing the liberal goal of identifying the meaning of great art and
texts as misguided, because meaning is indeterminate, indefinitely deferred
by chains of signifiers that only lead to other signifiers.

Unlike liberal humanists, new humanists pay great attention to economics but generally argue that economic categories are culturally constructed
as merely one dimension of the creation of a new set of subjectivities, narratives, and gender relations (Woodmansee and Osteen 1999).

New humanistic approaches have affected most fields of ancient Mediterranean studies, but poststructuralist literary critiques of economic categories have gone furthest among Hellenists. A sharp debate has developed
over the role of early Greek coinage in aristocratic self-fashioning. Sitta von
Reden (1997a: 156) stresses "the ideological constraints of money-use created by the ethical frame of the polis and the uneasy fit of coinage with
honour, the body and 'Self', which were part of that frame," while Leslie
Kurke (1999: 12, 35) sees "an alternative narrative behind the development
of various money forms in Greece: an ongoing struggle over the constitution of value and who controlled the highest spheres of exchange, between
the traditional elite and the emerging city-state," adding that this "argument
about political and economic contestation . . . is strangely foreshadowed by
the tropes and troubles of identity-formation."

Kurke explains the methodological implications of her questions:

Because coinage is a polyvalent symbol within a complex symbolic
system, the struggle I endeavor to reconstruct is a struggle *over* and *in*
representation. At issue is who controls signification and who has the
power to constitute the culture's fundamental hierarchies of value.
While these issues have "real life" implications—for example, in the
sociological basis of citizenship and relative status of citizens—such a
struggle over fundamental hierarchies of value can only be a discursive
one, fought out in the codes of our texts, visual images, and signifying

practices over the constitution of the cultural imaginary. Thus, it is not as if there is some "reality" we are struggling to get to behind the texts, images, and practices, if we can just break through their screen by patient source criticism and sifting of "facts." In this "contest of paradigms," the discursive structures of our texts (literary and visual) *are* the facts at issue. (Kurke 1999: 23)

New historicism has brought new sophistication to our reading of the texts; but it has also aestheticized economic analysis, trapping it in a bloodless realm of competing discourses, disconnected from the brute realities of hunger, poverty, and the creation and distribution of goods. The new humanists have shown that moving from discursive structures to prediscursive economic facts is more difficult than historians conventionally assume, but not that it is impossible (I. Morris 2000: 12–17). Understanding ancient culture is vital to analysis of the economy, but it is not itself a sufficient account of the economy.

SOCIAL SCIENCE: ECONOMICS

While humanists tend to work from a specific body of texts and to focus on particulars, economists tend to begin from propositions, drawing out logical implications that can be operationalized and sometimes tested against selected bodies of data. The data are there to test the hypothesis, not to be enjoyed or understood in their own terms. The social scientist may rely on "stylized facts," which may or may not be true, but are assumed to be true for the sake of building a useful model; or may even dispense with evidence altogether, judging theories on their logical consistency, and particularly on their mathematical elegance (Reder 1999: 15–39).

Classical economics started from the assumption of material scarcity and asked how we can maximize material well being. The basic axiom was that exchanging goods in an open market was the most efficient solution. For Adam Smith, this simply meant recognizing human nature, our "propensity to truck, barter, and exchange one thing for another" (Smith 1970: 117 [1789: I.2]). As Smith saw it, "It is not from the benevolence of the butcher, the brewer, or the baker that we expect our dinner, but from their regard to their own interest" (1970: 119). If individuals do what they do best and then exchange the products with each other, everyone will be better off than if they each try to produce everything they need. In a free market, innumerable individual decisions will find an equilibrium between consumers' demand for a good and producers' willingness to supply it, which will set that good's price. In pursuit of continuing profits, producers will direct part of their profits toward increasing their capital stock. And depending on the returns, choices between investing in human capital, physical capital, and natural resources will also tend toward an equilibrium. For most of the twentieth century, economists theorized this process in terms of marginal utility, the value attached to an extra unit of consumption or investment, even though real people rarely calculated costs and benefits in this way. Since the 1950s economists have developed game theory as a better description of market behavior, imagining exchanges as games played between two or more rational actors whose moves influence each other and the rules of the game itself (Kreps 1990; Dixit and Nalebuff 1991).

Ancient historians have largely ignored economic theory. There are two obvious reasons for this. First, ancient historians seem to feel that they lack the data to test formal economic models. But this is only a partial explanation, given economists' propensity for "proofs" based on stylized facts or internal logic. Second, ancient historians seem to feel that economic models are no help for understanding a world of thin and discontinuous markets. This, in essence, was Finley's argument:

> The economic language and concepts we are all familiar with, even the laymen among us, the 'principles', whether they are Alfred Marshall's or Paul Samuelson's, the models we employ, tend to draw us into a false account . . . to speak of a 'labour market' or a 'money market' is immediately to falsify the situation. For the same reason, no modern investment model is applicable to the preferences of the men who dominated ancient society. (Finley 1985a: 23)

Finley probably exaggerated the weakness of factor markets in the Roman Empire (Temin 2001). He was clearly right to insist that markets were less integrated than those in the twentieth-century West, and those historians who write as if ancient economies worked just like modern ones can go seriously astray (for example, French 1964). But that is far from being the end of the story. Development economists have shown that formal models can make sense of economies in which markets are shallow and fragmented (see Ray 1998). Further, ancient historians who combine simple formal models with awareness of the peculiarities of antiquity have raised and answered important questions (see K. Hopkins 1980, 1995/96, 2000; von Freyberg 1989; Cohen 1992; Kehoe 1992; Andreau et al. 1994; Reger 1994; Ellickson and Thorland 1995; Warburton 1997). Their work is widely praised, but not widely emulated. We might say that they are models *to* the field, but not models *for* the field.

There are two reasons for this distinction. First is an ideological/ institutional problem. Most ancient historians are educated in humanistic university departments, studying under liberal humanists. They complete grueling doctoral programs overseen by these same professors and then seek jobs from like-minded employers. Usually they end up in Classics, Near Eastern, or History Departments, and sometimes in Religious Studies. Archaeologists will go to the same departments (but substituting Art History for History), sometimes Anthropology, and often museums. Only rarely do ancient historians end up among economists, political scientists, or sociologists. On balance, individuals predisposed to contribute to large questions about how markets work, in which the ancient Mediterranean is just one case among many, are less likely to persevere in humanistic environments than those who find particularism and empiricism congenial. To use the economists' phrase, they tend to exit the game early. Those who do not exit—whether because they misunderstand the discipline or become too obsessed with antiquity to give it up—may find the professional rewards for speaking the language of neoclassical economics meager by comparison with those for entering the fray in philology or cultural history.

Second, the opportunity costs are high for ancient historians to become economists and economists to become ancient historians. An economist wanting to work on antiquity needs to master a large and complex body of texts and archaeological data, the minutiae of source analysis, and several difficult dead languages. While there are striking exceptions (Temin 2001, 2002), few find the price worth paying, given the probably low payoff. History is tangential to most economics. North American ancient historians, on the other hand, rarely have training in economics beyond basic college courses; in Europe, few have even that. The costs of learning a whole new technical language and set of methods are high; those of unlearning the assumption that evidence always come first and details matter most may be even higher. Only a few economists and ancient historians are willing to pay these costs.

SOCIAL SCIENCE: SOCIOLOGY

Many social scientists find economists' assumptions too narrow. Where mainstream economists treat utility maximization as hardwired into the psyche, the starting point for analysis, a broad sociological tradition sees it instead as a problem to be analyzed. Sociological thought is somewhat harder to define, according to Andrew Abbott because "the discipline is not very good at excluding things from itself" (2001: 5). Some schools of sociology are sternly positivist, while others veer toward humanistic reflexivity. Neil

TABLE 1.1

The assumptions of economics and economic sociology (Smelser and Swedberg 1994: Table 1)

	Economic Sociology	Mainstream Economics
Concept of the actor	The actor is influenced by other actors and is part of groups and society	The actor is uninfluenced by other actors ("methodological individualism")
Economic action	Many different types of economic action are used, including rational ones; rationality as *variable*	All economic actions are assumed to be rational; rationality as *assumption*
Constraints on the action	Economic actions are constrained by the scarcity of resources, by the social structure, and by the meaning of structures	Economic actions are constrained by tastes and by the scarcity of resources, including technology
The economy in relation to society	The economy is seen as an integral part of society; society is always the basic reference	The market and the economy are the basic references; society is a "given"
Goals of the analysis	Description and explanation; rarely prediction	Prediction and explanation; rarely description
Methods used	Many different methods are used, including historical and comparative ones; the data are often produced by the analyst ("dirty hands")	Formal, especially mathematical model building; no data or official data are often used ("clean models")
Intellectual tradition	Marx-Weber-Durkheim-Schumpeter-Polanyi-Parsons/Smelser; the Classics are constantly reinterpreted and taught	Smith-Ricardo-Mill-Marshall-Keynes-Samuelson; the Classics belong to the past; emphasis is on current theory and achievements

Smelser and Richard Swedberg constructed a table of oppositions explaining the difference between economic and sociological thought (see Table 1.1).

Economics and economic sociology offer competing models for thinking about economic action within a generalizing social science framework (Granovetter 1990). Their protagonists use different terms, favor different methods and evidence, and have different discourses of the proof. Economists more often aim for lawlike propositions than sociologists, while sociologists prefer typologies. Weber argued that markets and profit maximization were driving forces in the world, but not always the primary driving forces. They are wrapped in larger networks of power relations, which constitute the primary explananda (Weber 1968: 63–211). His central question explored what caused the market and its associated forms of rationality to take over the nineteenth-century West. His favored methods were typology building and comparison of ideal types (Swedberg 1998). The focus on ideal types makes sociology less particularistic than most humanities but also makes reportage matter more than it does for economists (Runciman 1983: 57–144, 223–300).

One of the central issues in economic sociology is "embeddedness," the degree to which the Smithian propensity to truck, barter, and exchange dominates particular social situations (Granovetter 1985). Weber (1976a [1904/5]) argued that prior to the rise of Calvinism in sixteenth-century Western Europe, market relations were everywhere subordinated to other status considerations. As Mario Liverani and Peter Bedford explain in their contributions to this volume, Polanyi's adaptation of Weber had a massive influence on Near Eastern history. In Greco-Roman history, Finley's *Ancient Economy* was a more directly Weberian account (I. Morris 1999a). Finley insisted that status—"an admirably vague word with a considerable psychological element" (1985a: 51)—was the independent variable; it drove all else, including economics. He offered

> a highly schematic model of the history of ancient society. It moved from a society in which status ran along a continuum towards one in which statuses were bunched at the two ends, the slave and the free— a movement which was most nearly completed in the societies which most attract our attention for obvious reasons. And then, under the Roman Empire, the movement was reversed; ancient society gradually returned to a continuum of statuses and was transformed into what we call the medieval world. (Finley 1981 [1964]: 132)

This neo-Weberian framework holds together Finley's influential divided-Mediterranean model. As he saw it, Egypt and the Near East were characterized by continuous, finely graded status structures, while the citizen states of Greece and the Roman Republic broke down into free and slave. These status structures drove economic history, therefore we should keep the Greco-Roman and Egyptian–Near Eastern separate in our analyses.

CONCLUSION: SOCIAL-SCIENCE HISTORY

Neoclassical economics has never had much influence on ancient Mediterranean studies. Marxism dominated the field in East European communist countries until 1989 and had some impact in Western Europe from the 1920s onward (though hardly any in the United States). A larger minority of Western ancient historians embraced Weberian sociology from the 1950s onward, and some turned toward new historicism in the 1990s. But both the classical and biblical fields have always been overwhelmingly branches of liberal humanism.

We want to increase the diversity of approaches in ancient history by drawing more inspiration from the social sciences, and in particular from two schools of thought: the "new economic sociology" that has built on Weber's foundations (Granovetter 1990; Swedberg 1991), and the "new institutional economics" that has wedded key neoclassical principles to a concern for institutions, ideology, and demography (North 1981, 1990). We start from Douglass North's proposition that

> the task of economic history [is] to explain the structure and performance of economies through time. By 'performance' I have in mind the typical concerns of economists—for example, how much is produced, the distribution of costs and benefits, or the stability of production. The primary emphasis in explaining performance is on total output, output per capita, and the distribution of income of the society. By 'structure' I mean those characteristics of a society which we believe to be the basic determinants of performance. Here I include the political and economic institutions, technology, demography, and ideology of a society. 'Through time' means that economic history should explain temporal changes in structure and performance. Finally, 'explanation' means explicit theorizing and the potential of refutability. (North 1981: 3)

Liberal humanistic historians had little to say about any of these issues. Weber, Polanyi, Oppenheim, and Finley made structure a central concern, but there has been little emphasis on performance and explanation. Analyzing performance requires quantification, which, for the ancient Mediterranean, usually means estimating parameters from comparative expectations and turning to archaeology for empirical data; explanation calls for more clarity about falsification.

Most scholars make quantification and falsification the core criteria for distinguishing social-science history from other forms (see discussions in King et al. 1994; Gerring 2001). Summing up the arguments of Gary King, Robert Keohane, and Sidney Verba's *Designing Social Inquiry* (1994), Henry Brady (1995: 12) suggests that the most important requirements are to "construct falsifiable theories; build theories that are internally consistent; select dependent variables carefully; maximize concreteness; and state theories in as encompassing a way as possible." Likewise, the Social Science History Institute at Stanford defines its core goals as "logical consistency, the specification of falsifiable hypotheses, and the careful and unbiased examination of quantitative and qualitative evidence" (Haber 2001).

There is no generally agreed definition of what makes history socialscientific (for example, Monkkonen 1994; Baker 1999), but we suggest that ancient history needs to change in eight main ways if we are to explain the structure and performance of Mediterranean economies. We must:

1. Make the definition of key terms and underlying assumptions clearer;
2. Be more explicit about processes of model building;
3. Present clear propositions with testable implications;
4. Be explicit about methods and particularly about standards of falsification;
5. Break large problems down into smaller, more easily answerable questions;
6. Specify causal relationships;
7. Quantify whenever possible;
8. Formulate descriptions and explanations in ways that can be generalized to allow comparisons between different regions and periods.

Much preliminary work is necessary before we can achieve these goals. There is little agreement on what basic terms should mean, and still less on appropriate ways to build models and test them. In part, this is because our subject matter is so vast. A study of urbanism that defined "city" in such a way as to include both Rome and Amarna could end up being so broad as to lose all analytical power. As noted above, Horden and Purcell responded to this problem by rejecting typologies and explicit definitions altogether, dissolving the category of "city" into a shifting matrix of interactions (2000: 101). This is typical of the approach that we described as the new humanities. We suggest instead that taking on a problem as large as the economic unity of the ancient Mediterranean requires us to be *more* rigorous about definitions, assumptions, and methods, not less. Definitions in the social sciences always involve trade-offs between precision and generality; but the problems of these trade-offs are well known and have been thoroughly analyzed (Gerring 2001: 65–86).

Four Hypotheses

Building a social-science history of the ancient Mediterranean will take many years. This volume merely scratches the surface of a single problem: It asks how specialists in different parts of the Mediterranean have gone about model building, and explores the relationships between their models and the particular kinds of data surviving from each region and period. Each contributor considered four competing hypotheses about the divided-Mediterranean model. They have all explored whether these hypotheses—either taken singly or in combination—could account for the differences between the economic histories so far written of the four regions under review (the Near East, Greece, Egypt, and Rome).

WE ALREADY HAVE THE ANSWERS

The null hypothesis, as it were, is that some version of the divided-Mediterranean model is in fact more or less right: That is, there were clear differences between the structure and performance of economies in different parts of the basin. In the Finley/Polanyi version, economic activity was everywhere embedded in larger social concerns, but the concerns of the Greco-Roman world were very different from those of Egypt and the Near East. In Greece and Rome, egalitarian male citizenship mattered most, most people practiced subsistence agriculture on privately owned land, and for some fifteen hundred years the economy was largely cellular and static. In Egypt and the Near East, on the other hand, temples and palaces controlled land, labor, and credit until the Macedonian conquest and remained important long after it.

Depending on exactly how we express the hypothesis, we can specify certain observable consequences. If, as most Roman archaeologists now insist, there is compelling evidence for an improvement in economic performance between 200 BC and AD 200 (see Hitchner and Saller essays in this volume), then the Finleyan thesis in its simplest form cannot stand. Equally, if we find closely comparable institutions and structures in the Near East and the Greco-Roman world, or can show that formally different institutions were in fact functionally similar, we will again be forced to modify or reject Finley's model. Bedford shows good reasons for thinking that Greek and Babylonian ideas of citizenship were not as different as Finley believed. Substantivist historians of the Near East, Greece, and Rome have made great headway in understanding the structures of economic institutions and ideologies, but the general conclusion of the contributors to this volume is that this first hypothesis only accounts for part of the variance between the economic histories written about different regions.

WE ARE ASKING DIFFERENT QUESTIONS

Specialists in different fields simply bring different questions to their data and thus end up writing different accounts of the economic history of their regions of focus. Research programs experience evolution in the Darwinian sense of descent with modification; the stronger the institutional boundaries between them, the more they are likely to diverge over time until they acquire some of the force of what Kuhn called scientific paradigms. Anyone familiar with Mediterranean history and archaeology knows that Classics, Near Eastern studies, and Egyptology have their own questions, methods, and standards of proof. Scholars within each interpretive community tend to go to different conferences, write for and read different journals, and expect different standards of presentation and proof; in short, they virtually speak different languages. Ancient Mediterranean scholarship might be the victim of sunk-costs hysteresis (David 1985): Centuries of investment have locked each regional tradition into a particular path. In the absence of a severe shock to the system, the cost of breaking out is prohibitive.

One observable consequence of this hypothesis should be that specialists in the different regions will find that they do not agree on basic terms, questions, and standards. The eight substantive chapters that follow suggest that there is at least some truth to this. Romanists emphasize economic performance more than historians in other fields; Hellenists focus more on new historicism; Near Eastern historians discuss Marxism more; and Egyptologists prefer philology and publication of texts. Yet attempts like the Social Science History Institute's to reach across the disciplinary divides do seem to work, suggesting that this too is at best a partial explanation.

WE HAVE DIFFERENT KINDS OF EVIDENCE

All fields of ancient Mediterranean history are empiricist. It is easy to decry ancient historians' lack of imagination and the stifling effect of institutional constraints, but these failings are only part of the problem. Unlike historians of more modern periods, ancient historians who ask new questions rarely have the option of going back to the archives to pull out the data they need to answer them. Archaeology is the one area in which new data can be generated almost at will, although these data have problems every bit as complex as those of the texts (Morris, Chapter 5).

The core problem in thinking on a Mediterranean-wide scale is not just that so little survives from antiquity, but that there are very different kinds of evidence from different regions and time periods. Greek economic history has traditionally rested on "literary" texts, such as collections of courtroom speeches originally written on behalf of wealthy citizens and then revised and circulated as models of Greek prose style. Romanists also rely heavily on literary texts (like Cicero's letters) but have access to far more inscriptions than do Hellenists. Egyptologists have a completely different evidential base. There are many nonliterary papyri, such as household accounts and state documents. Where Hellenists tend to generalize about economic mentalities, and have been drawn strongly toward the cultural history of economic categories, Egyptologists privilege the nuts and bolts of estate

management or fiscal policy, or limit themselves to editing and publishing
"archives" (Manning, Chapter 8).

In the Near East the situation is different again. There is a bewildering
variety of texts. As Liverani and Bedford explain, in some periods most material comes from palaces; in others, from temples. When texts derive from
either of these two sources, historians tend to emphasize the central control
of trade and production. But when texts produced by traders far from the
palaces and temples are better represented, as in the large cache of Old Assyrian records from Kanesh in Anatolia, historians emphasize the indepen-
dence of individual traders (Kuhrt 1998). The published texts are scattered
across vast distances and periods, and our evidence may be systematically
skewed.

It is harder to specify observable implications of this hypothesis. On a
few occasions, unusual conditions have led to the survival or papyri and similar documents from parts of the Roman Empire outside Egypt (Bagnall,
Chapter 9), suggesting that this hypothesis explains some of the variability.
If the massive weighting of the documentary record in Egypt's favor is in fact
merely an artifact of the good survival of papyrus there, many theories about
the peculiarity of the Egyptian economy and its obsessive record keeping
must be rejected. Morris suggests that archaeology may allow historians to
make more direct comparisons between regions, perhaps circumventing the
cultural and environmental differences that have shaped the literary records
so heavily. But it may be that to test this third hypothesis, we need to develop different kinds of models, less data-driven than the old ones.

WE ARE BUILDING THE WRONG KINDS OF MODELS

As Manning emphasizes, ancient historians usually build models inductively,
generalizing from a mass of texts or artifacts. Some of the major advances
have come when historians reverse this process, beginning from general
propositions and using them to establish the parameters of the possible. Keith
Hopkins's treatment of Roman revenue flows (1980, 1995/96, 2000) and
the recent debates over the demography of Roman slavery (Scheidel 1997,
W. V. Harris 1999) are probably the best known examples. Ed Cohen's
analysis (1992) of Athenian banking works in a similar way. In important earlier papers, John Davies (1998, 2001) has drawn attention to the inadequacy
of the kind of economic models ancient historians have normally tried to
construct. He suggests that we should seek to describe economic flows,
rather than patterns of exchange, aiming for "a long-range (indeed
indefinitely extensible) map on which flows can be traced" (Davies 1998:
243). This calls for diagrammatic rather than descriptive modeling, and for

"separat[ing] the mapping and the measurements of such flows from the assessment of whatever incompatible *mélange* of ideologies which may have stimulated or inhibited such flows" (251). This challenge requires ancient historians to think more abstractly than their humanistic intellectual traditions normally encourage. We may need to experiment with new forms of representation and narrative.

The only way to test this hypothesis will be by trying out new models and approaches; the proof of the pudding will be in the eating. In their chapters in this volume, Davies and Saller work with very different models from those conventionally found in ancient economic history.

The Structure of the Book

We have grouped the chapters along conventional lines to highlight the contrasts between the forms of ancient economic history pursued in different areas of the Mediterranean. Part I focuses on the Near East, spanning the third through first millennia BC; Part II is on Greece, concentrating on the middle of the first millennium BC; Part III is on Egypt in the half-millennium from roughly 300 BC through AD 200, under the political control of the Ptolemies and the early Roman Empire; and Part IV is on the Roman Empire in the first two centuries AD.

In Part I, Mario Liverani provides a panoramic review of the history of interpretations of the ancient Near Eastern economies of the third and second millennia BC. He divides this history into three phases, which are only partly chronological but do overlap. In the first phase, roughly spanning the 1920s through the 1960s, debates polarized around one model emphasizing state centralization and a second privileging private property. Broadly speaking, German and Russian scholars dominated the first school of thought, and English-speaking scholars the second. From the 1960s through the 1980s, Liverani's second phase, new models emerged in Western Europe and North America, influenced by Polanyi, neo-Marxists like Karl Wittfogel, and comparative anthropologists. In the third (continuing) phase, a more complex picture has been built up using multifactorial analysis and some modern economic theory. Liverani is skeptical about much recent scholarship and continues to believe that "cultural forms" must be brought to bear in any model of economic behavior.

In Chapter 3, Peter Bedford surveys the Near East in the first millennium BC. This is a shorter time period but one with fuller and more complicated evidence. The Neo-Assyrian, Neo-Babylonian, and Persian empires successively dominated Western Asia militarily, but there were many continuities from earlier periods. Bedford argues that some of the categories that Finley used to describe the Greco-Roman economy also apply to first-millennium economic activity in the Near East. Bedford examines Marx's and Weber's work on Near Eastern social structures before continuing with the two most significant scholars of the ancient Near Eastern economies, Leo Oppenheim and Igor Diakonoff. Bedford concludes by discussing more recent developments, including Morris Silver's reaction against Polanyi, and Ellickson and Thorland's legal, rational-actor approach to land tenure in the ancient Near East. In his concluding section, he addresses the problems of the preserved written record. In Chapter 4, Mark Granovetter, a leading economic sociologist, responds to Liverani and Bedford. He emphasizes the one-sidedness of both Polanyian and rational-choice interpretations of the fragmentary Near Eastern data, and the need for more complex models, allowing room for the diversity of historically attested responses.

Part II moves on to societies in the mid-first millennium BC and shifts the focus to Greece. In Chapter 5, Ian Morris examines the contributions of archaeology to Greek economic history in the first millennium BC. He argues against Finley's skepticism and against the general trend in archaeological theory toward culturalism, suggesting that we can use archaeological data to quantify standards of living. Finley paid almost no attention to the standard of living, but from many perspectives this is the whole point of doing economic history. Morris identifies significant and sustained improvement in living standards and argues that this provides proxy data for another question that Finley avoided—the performance of the Greek economy, in the sense of increases in per capita economic output through time. Finally, he suggests that if we start asking new questions about economic growth and standards of living, this archaeological approach can be transferred from Greece to other parts of the Mediterranean, allowing us to create a comparative ancient economic history. In Chapter 6, John Davies extends the arguments of his "Models and Muddles" essay (1998) to show some of the possibilities for representing ancient economies diagrammatically, rather than in what he calls "the soggy descriptive mode" that has characterized ancient economic historiography. In Chapter 7, Takeshi Amemiya, a leading econometrician with a strong interest in ancient Greece, responds to Davies's arguments, suggesting that ancient historians still do not fully understand the limits or possibilities of mainstream economic theory.

The two chapters on Egypt both focus on post-pharaonic periods. In Chapter 8, J. G. Manning argues that continuities from the Saite and Persian periods are essential for understanding the Ptolemaic situation. Impressed by the large number of surviving Greek government records, the

Russian émigré Michael Rostovtzeff developed a highly influential model of a state-centralized economy. In building a new model of the Ptolemaic economy, Manning argues for a regional approach, suggesting that Ptolemaic state power relied, as it did historically, on the loyalty and cooperation of local elite, no matter how despotic the Ptolemies' aims may have been. While new military settlements were an important means of asserting state aims, Manning stresses local power alongside state power, and basic institutional continuity with previous regimes, with temple estates guaranteeing traditional Egyptian property rights.

Roger Bagnall's chapter on Roman Egypt criticizes Finley's tendency to see Egypt as unique in the ancient world and to claim that the Egyptian papyri have no relevance for other parts of the Mediterranean. Bagnall discusses recent discoveries of papyri outside Egypt, particularly in the Near East, which imply that late-period Egypt was increasingly integrated into a larger world. Bagnall notes that in contrast with the Ptolemaic and Byzantine periods, no one has yet written a grand synthesis of the Roman history of Egypt. He suggests that the sheer bulk of Roman papyri discourages such approaches. Bagnall sketches the development of scholarship, stressing the advances in economic studies that integrate large groups of papyri from one region (Oxyrhynchus) or the operations of one large estate (Appianus) and studies driven by economic theory using inscriptions as well as papyri. The urban economy and social status, including the institution of slavery—both subjects that Finley studied outside Egypt—have recently received intense study. Bagnall concludes with a prospectus for future research. Among the most pressing needs, Bagnall suggests, is a systematic study of taxation.

In Part IV, Bruce Hitchner and Richard Saller address the vexed question of economic growth in the early Roman Empire. Hitchner suggests that the environmental conditions and institutional frameworks present in the early empire were conducive to economic growth and seeks direct evidence in the archaeological record. He identifies large-scale investment in agriculture in the western Mediterranean, particularly in water mills and olive presses, manuring and terracing, and iron tools. Along with this went an infilling of the rural landscape. Hitchner concludes that in the second century AD agriculture and manufacturing both reached levels that Europe would not see again until the eighteenth century, and that the challenge facing historians is to produce models of a premodern economy that can incorporate such growth.

Saller begins his chapter by showing just how casual ancient historians have been in their thinking about models of the Roman economy. Rostovtzeff and Finley are usually opposed as representing, respectively, modernist and

primitivist visions; Saller shows that in fact the relationships between their visions are far more complex. He then builds on recent arguments by Chicago
School economists to estimate the parameters of economic growth in the
early Roman Empire. Once this is done, he suggests, the whole nature of the
questions we need to ask about ancient Mediterranean economies changes.
The response to Hitchner and Saller comes from Avner Greif, an economic
historian specializing in game-theoretic approaches to medieval Italian economies. He suggests that instead of looking for crucial variables that the Roman world lacked, we should look at its positive contributions to the gradual accumulation of institutions, ideologies, and technologies that, by the
sixteenth century, pushed Europe across a critical threshold that no society
had reached before.

Conclusion

This volume is a response to recent debates about the long-established practice of drawing a line through the map of the ancient Mediterranean world,
with Greco-Roman societies on one side of it and Egypt and the Near East
on the other. In this introduction we have made two arguments: First, this
opposition is the product of eighteenth- and nineteenth-century debates
that need to be reconsidered in the early twenty-first century; and second,
the approaches that currently dominate ancient history are not adequate to
this task. We have suggested a more explicitly social-science history as the
best response to both problems. The papers in this volume are a first step toward developing such a history. Only some of them explicitly ground ancient economic history in economics and economic sociology, but collec-
tively they move toward three goals. First, they bring together specialists in
periods and regions normally treated separately, aiding the process of developing shared methods; second, they set out core issues in each area that will
need to be addressed before a proper comparative history can develop; and
third, they bring together social scientists' commentaries with expert studies by ancient historians. Our overall goal is to illuminate the intrinsic connections of detailed knowledge of the evidence and its problems, sophistication about building and testing models, and awareness of the metanarratives
that frame our most basic questions. By engaging in all these activities simultaneously, we may be able to resolve old questions and above all to frame
new, more pressing, ones.

The divided-Mediterranean model comes in for severe criticism in this
book. Some of the contributors openly reject it, while others provide new
forms of evidence or ways to build models that may make it irrelevant. Some

readers will doubtlessly interpret this as yet another attack on Moses Finley's work. But this is not our goal. Given that Finley made some of his most important contributions as much as fifty years ago, and his larger Weberian theoretical framework had already been around for fifty years at that point, it is hardly surprising that we now know more and ask different questions. But in another way, we have yet to live up to the standards that Finley set. In *The Ancient Economy* he sketched the first explicitly theorized framework for ancient economic history, and in his final book, *Ancient History: Evidence and Models* (1985b), he drove home the need to link empirical and conceptual issues. Hence the title of our volume, borrowing from both these classic texts. In closing, we can do no better than to quote the last words in Finley's last book: "The objective, in the final analysis, is the paradoxical one of achieving a more complex picture by the employment of simplifying models" (Finley 1985b: 108).

Notes

1. Cohen (2001: 1–3) reviews some of these claims.

2. There is a huge literature on the history of the scholarship. We have found the following works particularly useful: F. M. Turner 1981; Clarke 1989; Grafton 1991; Gunter 1992; Kuklick 1996; Larsen 1996; Marchand 1996; Schnapp 1996; Stray 1998; Dyson 1998; Edwards 1999; Hingley 2000; Payne et al. 2000; Winterer 2002.

3. Blaut (2000) and Stokes (2001) discuss some of the most influential work.

4. Both the editors of this volume taught in the University of Chicago's year-long undergraduate History of Western Civilization program in the late 1980s and early 1990s. The course was much less homogeneous than Gress suggests; each year ten to fifteen completely autonomous sections were offered, taught by faculty and postdoctoral fellows, nearly all from the History Department. Not surprisingly, the contents of the Western Civilization curricula tended to follow broader trends in contemporary historiography. But as a statement of the program's original rationale, Gress's claims may have more merit. The Chicago program was redesigned in 2001 as a two-quarter sequence, omitting the ancient Mediterranean. Since Richard Saller's arrival at Chicago in 1984, an Ancient Mediterranean World Civilization track had been offered in (increasingly successful) competition with Western Civilization. Columbia closed its Contemporary Civilization program in 1998.

5. We have adapted this definition from Giddens's introduction (1976: xi) to *The Protestant Ethic and the Spirit of Capitalism* (Weber 1976a [1904/5]). Neither in this book nor in the generally clearer *General Economic History*

(Weber 1950 [1919/20]) did Weber provide concise definitions. Swedberg (1998: 7–21) has a convenient summary.

6. The whole of the *Journal of Modern History* 44 (1972) was devoted to the book; see also Parker 1974; Kellner 1979; Kinser 1981.

7. The literature on globalization is vast. We draw particularly on the very diverse perspectives of Harvey 1989; Appadurai 1996, 2001; Castells 1996–98; Giddens 1999; Sen 1999; de Soto 2000; Friedman 2000; Soros 2002; and Kugler and Frost 2001.

8. In this section, we summarize arguments originally presented in I. Morris 2001.

Part I

The Near East

Chapter 2

The Near East: The Bronze Age

MARIO LIVERANI

A Necessarily Simplified Overview

The topic of interpretive models of the economy of the ancient Near East is so large that most historians would evaluate as foolish or useless any attempt to deal with two millennia (circa 3000 through 1000 BC) as a unit in an area as large as the Near East. Not only is the time span long indeed, but it is also covered by an enormous (albeit discontinuous) set of data. And not only is the area very large, but it is also differentiated into various ecological and cultural units—from steppe and true desert to forested mountains, from Mediterranean to arid climates, from rain-fed agriculture to irrigation networks, from urban centers to pastoral encampments, from bureaucratic states to loose tribes, and so on.

Moreover, the story of modern interpretations is by now long enough— let us say one century—to make sense and deserve a study of its own. Unlike classical historians dealing with the Greek and Roman world, who have a well-established tradition of considering a thorough survey of older theories as a necessary prerequisite for a new discussion, historians dealing with the ancient Near East, busy as they are with absorbing continuous inputs of new data, tend to forget (or better, remove) older theories and find satisfaction with the latest one. This is probably the mark of a historiography too strictly linked to the philological treatment of texts—where obviously the latest reading of a line or sign renders previous readings obsolete and useless—and not interested enough in the evolution of approaches and models as a meaningful topic in itself, and especially as a welcome tool in the difficult task of historicizing our own approach and our own models, or at least of setting our studies in the larger frame of the history of modern culture and thought.

On the one hand, therefore, this chapter is necessarily simplified, with too few hints at regional variability and chronological developments. However, such a unified treatment of the subject matter is partly justified (or at least, made less arbitrary) by the fact that the basic structures of the ancient Near Eastern economies had been established in the frame of the so-called urban revolution at the end of the fourth millennium BC and remained rather stable until the major crisis at the end of the second millennium BC (Liverani 1998). The "Bronze Age," invented as a classificatory device for tools and weapons, can still be used as a large historical label, encompassing similarly structured socioeconomic systems and quite sharply opposed to the (differently labeled) preceding and succeeding periods.

On the other hand, I will try to make sense out of a story in which the very actors were in most cases unaware of the roles they were playing, or of the positions they were occupying in the long-run evolution of historiographical theories. In order to anticipate the guidelines for my presentation, I see a basic and progressive movement from highly ideologized and strongly counterposed models toward more complex and flexible models. This movement has to do with the end (or death) of ideologies, with the availability of more sophisticated tools for economic analysis, and even with a more sophisticated mastery of the textual data. It is welcome in its major outlines, although not devoid of problems.

Land Property and Land Management

We have to start with the problem of land tenure, both because it is a basic issue in most agrarian societies like those of the ancient Near East, and because the first clear model for the economy of the ancient Near East is the model of the "temple-city" as advanced by the Assyriologist Anton Deimel (1931, based on earlier studies) and by the economic historian Anna Schneider (1920), and kept almost unchallenged up to the mid-fifties (Falkenstein 1954). I want first of all to point out that Deimel's and Schneider's positions were not at all the same. Deimel emphasized the facts (the presumed facts, of course) that in Sumerian city-states, all agricultural land belonged to the temple, and the whole population worked under temple management. Schneider, on the contrary, emphasized the (presumed) fact that the Sumerian economy was mixed, including features of a statist economy side by side with features of feudal relationships and features of the free market—so that the case of the Sumerian city-states does not fit into the evolutionist trajectory theorized by Karl Bücher (1893), to whose school Schneider herself belonged.

A first critique of the "temple-city" theory came from the Marxist Assyriologist and ancient historian Igor Diakonoff (1954, and more generally 1982), who recalculated the technical data in order to show that the temple properties covered only a part of the city's entire territory. In Diakonoff's view, the space left free (so to speak) was occupied by the local communities, that is, the villages and the extended families. The existence of two sectors in the ancient Near Eastern socioeconomic structure was shaped in a way not too different from the so-called Asiatic Mode of Production (Zaccagnini 1981; Zamora 1997), even if Diakonoff did not use that term, which was taboo in the Soviet Union at the time. The two sectors are in a sense parallel, since lands of the temple/palace sector are managed differently and kept separate from those in the local communities; but in another sense they are linked by subordination, since the local communities are "tributary" to the temple or palace, where the unifying political power is located.

Among Western Assyriologists, Diakonoff's criticism was appreciated and countered at the same time (see especially Gelb 1969). On the one hand, it was appreciated because it provided a more variegated picture than the simplistic "temple-city" model as conceived in the statist theories of early-twentieth-century Germany. On the other hand, according to Western scholars, the space left free had to be occupied not by local communities or enlarged families but by private property and private management.

In any case, the dismissal of the totalizing model brought about the dismissal of its label as well—so that it has become common today to deny the very existence of a temple-based economy for the third and second millennia BC, with the possible exception of the Third Dynasty of Ur (Foster 1981; Postgate 1972; Powell 1978). Besides, the very existence of village communities, supported by neo-Marxist scholars in Western Europe, was strongly put in doubt, since the specific features defining a "village community" in medieval Europe are not to be found in the ancient Near East (Leemans 1983). Finally, the role of irrigation in producing centralized agricultural management—already present in Deimel's model, and which became the basis of the totalizing views of Karl Wittfogel (1957)—was discarded as a major factor following Robert McC. Adams's more precise analysis (1966: 66–71; 1981).

With the temple reduced to a secondary role and quite modest agency, and the local communities removed as figments of the imaginations of

Marxist historians, the space is left completely free for private (and personal) property, for private management of the irrigation network, for a free market in land, and so on. A recent book titled *Privatization in the Ancient Near East and Classical World* (Hudson and Levine 1996) is merely the latest result of this trend.

In order to arrive at a more balanced model (Neumann 1987a; Renger 1995), based on today's available evidence, we can advance some observations. First of all, when we state that Manchester in the nineteenth century was an "industrial city," or that Venice in the sixteenth century was a "merchant city," we certainly do not mean that the entire population of Manchester was engaged in textile or mechanical production, or that the entire resources of Venice came from long-distance trade. We want simply to emphasize that a specific sector had a paramount relevance in shaping the entire economy of that city or state. A given sector was the most important in comparison to the others, so that it influenced in various ways and degrees the other sectors as well. In general terms: If we want to put together a working model of an economy, we have to evaluate the quantitative assessment of its component parts and understand the inner functioning of the city as a "temple-city," certainly not because the temple was the only economic agency, but because it was by far the biggest agent, capable of influencing the other, minor, agents.

A second point that is worthy of note concerns the concept of "private" ownership. To my mind, the concept is meaningful if contrasted with that of "public" (temple/palace) ownership, thereby defining the two basic sectors in the economy of the ancient Near East. On the contrary, the identification of "private" with "personal" ownership (of property) seems to me to be grossly misleading. Every society has its own rules (or habits) in property ownership and management, and in the Bronze Age private property was owned by the family rather than by individual persons—as demonstrated by the restrictions in selling land outside the family. Personal ownership emerges in the temple/palace and in the family sectors, especially during the Late Bronze Age, through processes of usucapion (Liverani 1984).

A third point, also worthy of note, concerns the relationships between the temple (and palace) agencies and the local communities (villages or enlarged families). The often-repeated statement that the local communities were "tributaries" of the temple or palace, in the sense that they had to deliver a quota of their product, is inaccurate. The most important flux of resources was not about products but about labor. Here Witold Kula's model of the "feudal" economy of early-modern Poland is to be recommended.[1] The temple/palace agencies had a positive economic balance because they used cheap compulsory labor coming from the villages, only in the period of major work, thereby charging most of the social costs to the local communities. In a tremendously simplified way, I would suggest that the direct delivery of product (Figs. 2.1a and 2.1b) is characteristic of chiefdoms, while the triangular pattern (Fig. 2.2) is characteristic of early states (Liverani 1998).

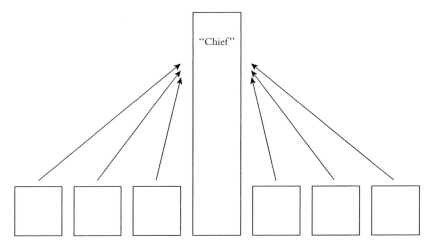

Figure 2.1a.   Direct delivery of product/characteristic of chiefdoms (stage 1) (after Liverani 1998)

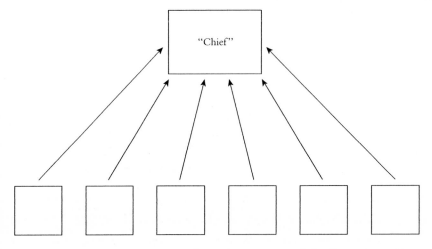

Figure 2.1b.   Direct delivery of product/characteristic of chiefdoms (stage 2) (after Liverani 1998)

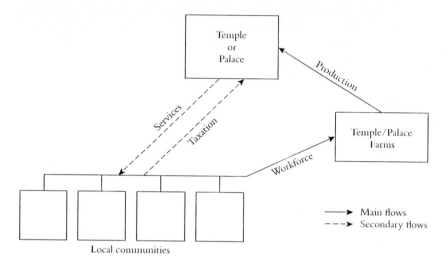

Figure 2.2. Triangular delivery of product/characteristic of early states (after Liverani 1998)

Finally, land tenure is a subject in which regional variations cannot be ignored. Attention has been concentrated on lower Mesopotamia, but the "peripheral" areas are equally relevant to an overall assessment. The conditions of rain-fed agriculture are quite different from those of irrigated agriculture; but even inside lower Mesopotamia the different technical functions of "basin irrigation" (prevailing in the Akkadian area) and of "furrow irrigation" (prevailing in Sumer) stem from different geomorphological situations and generate different socioeconomic management structures (Liverani 1997, 1999).

Administered Trade versus Private Enterprise

Debates about trade have been as lively and important in the development of scholarship as those about land ownership. The topic of Near Eastern trade passed almost unscathed through the debate between "primitivism" and "modernism" in Greek and Roman economies but was brought to center stage by Karl Polanyi's work (Polanyi et al. 1957; for the Near East, see Renger 1994; van de Mieroop 1999: 109–11). Polanyi's thesis is well known: Trade in the early empires was an activity administered by the temple/palace, carried on by trade-agents and not by free merchants, based on fixed prices, without market places and without market mechanisms.

Because Polanyi used Assyriological data, especially from the Old Assyrian and Old Babylonian periods, a reaction from Assyriologists was unavoidable, and generally quite negative. For sure, the examples selected by Polanyi fit his theory badly, and the rebuttal by Assyriologists was quite easy (Gledhill and Larsen 1982). Old Assyrian trade, the best-known trade network in the whole of ancient history before Roman times, was apparently a private affair, in the hands of private entrepreneurs, aiming at private profits, and reinvesting the profits in further trade (Larsen 1967; Veenhof 1972). The palace at Ashur is almost entirely missing from the picture provided by the documents. Textual attestations revealed the relevant terms regarding prices and marketplaces.[2] Assyriologists and historians of ancient Mesopotamia therefore seem happy with the idea that Polanyi's proposals about trade were in error (Powell 1978)—although Polanyi's other major proposition, about the redistributive nature of the ancient Near Eastern economy, got a better audience.[3] And of course administered trade and a redistributive economy were strictly linked together.

I am not happy with such a dismissal of administered trade. First of all, the assessment of administered versus private trade is a matter of quantity and quality. What I mean is that the local exchange of lettuce and vegetables certainly existed but as a minor part of our overall evaluation of Mesopotamian trade. Such an evaluation should also be differentiated according to period. The role of the temple was especially relevant during the Early Bronze Age, and administered trade culminated under the Third Dynasty of Ur, as demonstrated by its "balanced accounts" (Snell 1982). The role of private enterprise was especially relevant during the Middle Bronze Age, with the activity of the Old Assyrian and Old Babylonian merchants. Finally, palace-administered trade underwent a renewed increase during the Late Bronze Age, especially in the form of ceremonial exchange between royal courts.

A second, and more important, point is that trade can be subdivided into two basic segments.[4] The first of these concerns the relationship between the temple or palace and its trade agents; the second segment (or set of segments) is related to the merchants' activities once they left their home country and ventured into foreign lands; the final segment is related to the settling of accounts between merchants and central agencies at the end of the (yearly) process. The administered relationship, using fixed values and pursuing materials unavailable at home, was limited to the starting move and the closing move: trade agents got silver and/or processed materials (that is, mainly metals and textiles) from the central agency and had to bring back after six months or a year the equivalent in exotic products or raw materials. The economic balance between central agency and trade agents could not but be regulated by fixed exchange values. But the merchants' activity once they left the palace was completely different: They could freely trade, playing on the different prices of the various items in various countries, even using their money in financial activities (such as loans) in the time span at their disposal, and making the maximum possible personal profit. Documents pertaining to the first and final segments will of course give us the impression of an administered trade, while documents pertaining to the intermediate segments will give us the impression of free trade. The two impressions are both correct and do not contradict each other.

An additional complication is that merchants carrying on a "public" activity of gathering products can also engage in personal activities during the same trip, using the same "money" or additional "money" entrusted to them by private persons. The amount of such side-activity is difficult to evaluate but could have been significant.

Craftsmanship: Concentrated or Dispersed?

The relationship between crafts and central agencies is also the subject of a similar (although less intensive) debate, which can be solved along the same lines. In the old model of the temple-city, craftsmen were enrolled into the ranks of the central agency, processing raw materials provided by the agency itself. They delivered their finished products to the agency, which in turn supported the craftsmen through the ration system (in the early stages) or through land allotments (in later stages). In its extreme formulation, this model represents the central agency as the sole "customer" of the craftsmen and represents all the craftsmen as inner (full-time) dependents of the central agency, leaving to the "free" population in the villages only the task of producing food.

V. Gordon Childe (1950) formulated a similar model of urban concentration of the specialized labor (as against the dispersal of food production in the villages) on archaeological grounds. But when fuller evidence became available, the correlation between the size of settlements and the presence or absence of specialized activities turned out to be far from consistent: markers of specialized crafts (metal slags, pottery discards, lithic débitage, and so on) are in fact also present in minor sites (Tosi 1984), and this holds true even for administrative or ceremonial markers, like the Late Uruk clay cones, assumed to belong to administrative centers, yet also found in small settlements.

The obvious objection against the "totalitarian" view of urban concentration is the attestation of crafts (perhaps mostly part-time crafts) in the villages and in family environments (Liverani 1999: 46); crafts had a plurality of customers, since their products were not only destined for luxury activities (or conspicuous consumption) by the elite, or for storage as treasure in palaces or temples, but also for the normal and widespread needs of the entire population.

Piotr Steinkeller (1996) has made a good point about the dispersion of potters across the entire territory and society rather than being concentrated under temple direction. This contribution makes it possible to formulate a more general picture of craftsmanship in the ancient Near East (Renger 1996), a picture whereby the dilemma about centralization versus dispersion does not receive a yes or no answer but can receive a differentiated assessment. Among the factors that influence the degree of centralization, we can include at least the following: (1) Destination of the finished products, whether widespread or selected (or monopolized by the central agency); (2) Technical skill required; (3) Value and provenance of the raw materials; and (4) Size of work-force. These factors (and perhaps others too) interact in determining the most fitting location and juridical status of the various crafts.

To give a few examples: Pottery making requires a ubiquitous raw material (clay) and low technical skill, and has a variety of "customers" (both central agencies and families). It therefore tends to be rather widespread. Jewelry (van de Mieroop 1987) is aimed at a more selective market, requires higher levels of technical skill, and the necessary raw materials are expensive and mostly exotic; it is therefore produced more efficiently in centralized workshops. Textile production (Waetzoldt 1972; McCorristen 1997) has a wide potential market and an easily available raw material (wool), but large-scale production is only possible with a sizeable concentration of cheap labor. From the technical point of view it can be practiced both by families and by temple or palace workshops, but from the economic point of view centralized workshops are more convenient and likely displaced family production from the market.

The partition into sequential episodes in trade was also present in many crafts. For instance, the production of textiles is the final stage of a complicated sequence: sheep breeding, shearing, spinning, weaving, and the production of clothes have very different characters and require different forms of management. A central agency may find it convenient to entrust flocks to "free" shepherds (in a manner not too different from that used for trade agents) but use corvée labor for shearing (in a manner not too different from that used for harvesting) and workshops for spinning and weaving (with high numbers of female and juvenile personnel, paid through food rations; see Gelb 1972; Maekawa 1980). They would then sell textile rolls to be tailored into finished cloths locally.

The variety of customers can be managed in two basic ways: first, by duplication, that is, the parallel existence of two sectors, one private for family consumption, and one public for the needs of the central agency; and second, by complimentarity, that is, by the side activity of "public" craftsmen in order to satisfy private needs.

Does this analysis falsify the model of urban concentration of specialized crafts? Certainly not. Once again, the final evaluation must take into account both quantity and quality. While some crafts were dispersed in villages and carried on by individual families, the most important and most complex were located inside, around, or in connection with the central agency (Neumann 1987b)—in itself the largest consumer of finished products, the biggest concentration of working personnel, and by far the most effective gatherer of raw materials (local and exotic alike).

A Short Sketch of the History of Scholarship

While a detailed history of the study of the economy of the ancient Near East would be a difficult task, and cannot be provided in the framework of this short chapter, I can summarize a few basic points here.

A first phase lasts from roughly 1920 (when the first models were advanced) to about 1960. This phase was marked by an opposition between state-centered views and "liberal" views, the former dominating. The state-centered views were especially prevalent in Germany and also in the Soviet Union (in the form of the Slave-Owning Mode of Production, then officially adopted for the entire ancient world). The "liberal" views prevailed in the English-speaking world.

A second phase lasted from about 1960 through about 1980 and was marked by the impact of substantivism (Polanyi et al. 1957) and neo-Marxism (with the Asiatic Mode of Production), by more explicit use of anthropological models and parallels, by the abandonment of universalizing evolutionary patterns, and by the search for properly Near Eastern features.

A third phase, still going on, is marked by the criticism of substantivism and neo-Marxism by the introduction of multifactorial analyses (sometimes influenced by systems theory) and the keyword (and key concept) of "complexity," with the related abandonment of general theories and of a general historical framework in favor of permanent values and behavioral laws.

Of course, a few exponents of the second phase still survive, I myself am one of them. I have to confess that I do not feel at ease with present-day deconstructionist trends, according to which every case can be studied on its own, with no concern for its setting in a meaningful historical context. I still think that economic activities—not only in the ancient world, but in every period—depend on social and cultural conditions, and not only on economic laws. Although some basic principles, such as the search for personal profit, or the exploitation of the weak by the strong, are permanent factors in human activities, the task of the historian (including the economic historian) is to look for the specific cultural forms that every society and every technological phase developed in order to organize and manage the economic relationships between contrasting interests. The old models can still be revisited, certainly with a critical attitude (pointing out the political preconditions of those models), but also with an attentive eye, in order to catch their heuristic value in an attempt to provide with historical meaning a story that otherwise could run the risk of ending in senseless chaos.

Notes

1. Kula 1976 [1962]; for a Near Eastern case, see Liverani 1979.
2. Especially the term *mahiru*; see Röllig 1976.
3. On "staple finance," see Polanyi 1960, revived by D'Altroy and Earle 1985.
4. See the patterns sketched by Snell 1977.

Chapter 3

The Economy of the Near East in the First Millennium BC

PETER R. BEDFORD

Introduction

In fundamental ways the economic life of the Near East in the first millennium BC stood in continuity with earlier periods. Agriculture and animal husbandry remained the mainstays of the economy. Agricultural techniques differed according to climate and terrain—in Babylonia (southern Mesopotamia) irrigation agriculture continued to be practiced, while in northern Mesopotamia and along the Syro-Palestinian coast rain-fed agriculture was the norm, with hillside terracing and desert farming in practice in southern Palestine. Different regions continued to specialize in certain produce; for example, dates in Babylonia, and olives in Syria-Palestine. Although the evidence is contestable, it is thought that the climate of the region was slowly getting wetter from around 900 BC, after a dry spell beginning around 1200 BC that may have contributed to both the collapse of Late Bronze Age polities in the eastern Mediterranean and the political, military, and economic decline of Assyria and Babylonia (Neumann and Parpola 1987).

Politically the Bronze Age (third and second millennia BC) was largely characterized by city-states and, from the mid-second millennium, territorial states of more or less equal power (Hatti, Mitanni, Assyria, Babylonia, Egypt). The first millennium came to be characterized by the development and reproduction of empire, which dominated all other forms of political organization and eradicated such polities as the independent kingdoms that had developed in Syria-Palestine (Israel, Judah, and the Aramaean states). The succession of empires—Assyrian, Babylonian, Achaemenid Persian, Hellenistic, Parthian / Roman / Sassanian—each incorporated an ever-increasing territory under its control. In this chapter, I briefly explore aspects of the social and economic organization of the first three of these empires, the Neo-Assyrian (circa 1000 – 612 BC; termed "Neo-" to distinguish it from earlier periods of Assyrian history); the Neo-Babylonian (circa 625 – 539 BC), and the Achaemenid Persian (539 – 331 BC). In doing so I touch on two issues relevant to Moses Finley's understanding of the ancient economy. The first is the issue of land ownership, since Finley contended that the essential difference between the economy of the Greco-Roman world and that of the ancient Near East was that the former "was essentially and precisely one of private ownership" (Finley 1985a: 29), whereas the latter was dominated by palace or temple ownership. The second, as noted by Morris and Manning in their introduction, is the notion of citizenship, particularly as it pertains to urban contexts. I also make some very modest suggestions for the study of the economy of the ancient Mediterranean world.

Finley, Models, and the Assyriologists

I begin by relating Finley's understanding of the ancient Near Eastern economy to the views of two leading Assyriologists, A. Leo Oppenheim, on whom Finley acknowledges dependence, and I. M. Diakonoff, whose Marxian view Finley notes but does not engage (Finley 1985a: 214 n. 39). Given Finley's indebtedness to categories borrowed from Weberian sociology, Weber's own remarks on the ancient economy, including the ancient Near East, are significant and will also be briefly touched on below.

As is well known, Finley considered the economies and societies of the ancient Near East to be organized quite differently from what he termed "the Graeco-Roman world." He wrote:

> The Near Eastern economies were dominated by large palace- or temple-complexes, who owned the greater part of the arable land, virtually monopolized anything that can be called "industrial production" as well as foreign trade (which includes inter-city trade, not merely trade with foreign parts), and organized the economic, military, political and religious life of the society through a single, complicated, bureaucratic, record keeping operation for which the word "rationing", taken very broadly, is as good a one-word description I can think of. (Finley 1985a: 28)

As a result, he confessed, "Were I to define 'ancient' to embrace both worlds, there is not a single topic I could discuss without resorting to disconnected sections, employing different concepts and models" (Finley 1985a: 29). From this one assumes, since Finley is not explicit, that where there are apparent similarities between the ancient Near East and the Greco-Roman world— significant private ownership of land, status groups, forms of dependent labor, urban citizenship—they must be modeled differently in each case since they are located in different socioeconomic systems.

Finley draws on Oppenheim as his only source for understanding ancient Near Eastern economy and society. The intellectual relationship between Finley and Oppenheim is quite interesting. Oppenheim was invited by Karl Polanyi to participate in his Columbia project as the Assyriological expert around 1953, and Oppenheim contributed a brief chapter in Polanyi's *Trade and Market* (Oppenheim 1957, in Polanyi et al. 1957). Although influenced by Polanyi (not that his name appears in Oppenheim's seminal *Ancient Mesopotamia* [1964]), Oppenheim was critical of Polanyi's view of Mesopotamian society as dominated by a single redistributive organization (temple or palace), as well as his notion of "marketless trade." For Oppenheim, the city was the most important aspect of Mesopotamian economy and society since it exhibited a "pattern of integration" (terminology directly borrowed from Polanyi, but unacknowledged) that "maintained its effectiveness through three millennia of history" (Oppenheim 1977 [1964]: 95). He contended for two "closed-circuit organizations in which goods and services were channeled into a circulation system" (Oppenheim 1977: 95), namely, the palace or temple, and the urban community of "citizens" (on which see below), the difference between them being that the temple and palace were redistributive systems, whereas members of the citizen community held private land and determined their own political and economic affairs. Thus, a sizable private economy flourished alongside the redistributive economy so that it is incorrect to speak of the latter as the characteristic transactional mode (Finley's "dominant types, the characteristic modes of behaviour" [1985a: 29]). Polanyi had a static view of ancient Near Eastern society and economy, one that took no account of change over the region's three-thousand-year history. While Oppenheim's understanding is hardly dynamic, he does take into account historical change and regional differences in economic organization, whereas Finley's view of the ancient Near Eastern economy is static, recognizes no regional difference, and emphasizes the single component (palace or temple) ideal-type redistributive economy. Finley thus represents Polanyi's view, not Oppenheim's.

How these two components—the temple/palace and citizen community—related to each other is obviously of central importance, yet Oppenheim does not successfully address this (he speaks of a "symbiosis" on pp. 113–14, which is not particularly helpful). Also, their relative size economically is difficult to judge from the available evidence. It apparently sufficed for Oppenheim that he could show to his own satisfaction the existence of both components and that the citizen community was not dominated by the temple/palace, the two being separate from, yet in a relationship with, each other. Oppenheim's understanding of the urban citizen community bears further discussion since it confronts another aspect of Finley's view of ancient Near Eastern economy and society. While Finley cites Oppenheim in support of his views, he does not seem to have accorded Oppenheim's opinions serious attention.

According to Oppenheim, the citizen body was "a community of persons of equal status bound together by a consciousness of belonging, realized by directing their communal affairs by means of an assembly, in which, under a presiding officer, some measure of consensus was reached as it was the case in the rich and quasi-independent old cities of Babylonia" (Oppenheim 1977: 95). They were of "equal status" because they were all "owners of landed property, fields, gardens, and manorial estates" (Oppenheim 1977: 113), and so, although living in the city their economic means was landed property outside the city. The idea of an urban citizen community, even when another layer of power such as a king or emperor may be above it, might have given Finley pause to consider possible relationships between Greek and Near Eastern (here, Babylonian at least) forms of social organization. Even more so, the following exposition should have caught Finley's eye and demanded comment. The long passage is worth quoting in full.

> The new city-dwellers went on relying primarily on their out-of-town farms for food and supplies, so that the market place as a means of economic integration was very slow to gain what little importance it eventually assumed in Mesopotamia. Since each household produced its own needs (in its manor), it was profitless to engage in home manufacture of goods for sale to other households, for which reason the number of slaves was kept low. Being of the same status—differing only in individual wealth—the city people rather easily achieved a *modus vivendi* in dealing with affairs that affected them as a community. Their commercial activities centered in the management of their rural holdings and, if capital was at their disposal—either accumulated through partnership or borrowed from the temples—they concerned themselves with intercity

trade, managed, curiously enough, from a special locality, the harbor, outside the city proper. It is as if the intracity and intercity economies had to be kept apart either for status reasons or in order to maintain the specific economic and social climate of the community. The latter is especially worthy of note when one contrasts it with the deeply agonistic mood of the Greek city where an ever-enlarging arsenal of complex and elaborate practices was needed to keep city government functioning in the face of the ambition of certain individuals, who wished to assume control and to exercise power over their fellow citizens. The very presence of the great organizations [that is, temple and palace] in the Mesopotamian city seems to have created an equilibrium of forces and an over-all harmony that endowed the city with the longevity which the Greek *polis* could not achieve. (Oppenheim 1977: 114)

Oppenheim is here writing about the rise of urbanism in southern Mesopotamia, but it is clear that he sees this as the pattern of urban life throughout much of Babylonian history. He admits indebtedness to the history of Greek cities in the fifth and fourth centuries in his portrayal of the Babylonian city and recognizes the polis and the Mesopotamian city as unique city types. I draw attention to four points raised in the above quotation that could have engaged Finley in his consideration of the character of Near Eastern economy and society:

1. The market was not important since city dwellers' households were economically self-sufficient (see Finley [1985a: 109–10], on self-sufficiency and markets).
2. Urban dwellers who were landowners, and thus of equal status, formed a group that dealt with affairs that affected them as a community. This became the "citizen community" and was juridically defined (see Finley [1985a: 45], on "orders").
3. Intercity trade, and investment generally, was embedded in status concerns (Finley 1985a: 35–61).
4. Organizing city government and maintaining the rule of citizens was apparently resolved in Mesopotamia in concert with the great urban institutions.

Finley had a keen interest in the city and its place in the ancient economy (1981: 3–23; 1985a). It is unfortunate that he ignored these four points touched on by Oppenheim (but never treated by him in depth) rather than explore the possibilities for a study of the ancient city that included both Greco-Roman and Near Eastern examples. After all, Weber had already in

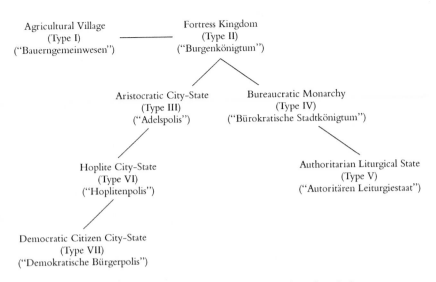

Figure 3.1.   Stages of the social organization of agricultural societies

his *Agrarverhältnisse* (1976b [1909]) argued for a common origin for Near Eastern and Greco-Roman cities based on the practice of agriculture and the development of agricultural communities. In his discussion of the characteristic ancient forms of economic organization, to be strictly differentiated from medieval and modern forms, Weber outlined "certain stages of [the social] organization [of agricultural societies], [which] were recapitulated by all the peoples in Antiquity from the Seine to the Euphrates among whom urban cities developed" (Weber 1976b: 69; see Fig. 3.1):

> *Type I*: Walled settlement, with household and (unwalled) village continuing as the centers of economic life; all free members of the community had a share in ownership of the land, and where slaves were not numerous they also did part of the field work; chiefs with transient function and status.
>
> *Type II*: King elevated above subjects and possessing land, slaves, and herds; king could demand tribute, performance of labor service. Development of Type II predicated on productive land able to support rent payments and profit from commerce. Richest fortress-king could force other kings to become vassals, leading to the development of large realms.
>
> *Type III*: Developed from Type II in Mediterranean. Formed from a league of great "clans"; dominant class possessed lands and serfs (or debt-slaves) that enabled members to train themselves for war and ob-

tain costly arms; typical form of labor-power was the debt-slave; open
land outside the city came to be divided, part of it being farmed by
independent peasants outside the aristocratic families, the rest being
worked by a large class of debt-slaves.

Type IV: Developed from Type II in Mesopotamia (Babylonia and
    Assyria) and Egypt. The king created a bureaucracy entirely subordi-
    nate to himself and organized hierarchically; the king could thus
    govern subjects directly, and the city became no more than a royal
    capital; needs of the royal household met either by forced labor or
    tribute/taxes, the former generally developing out of the latter.

Type V: Developed from Type IV in the Near East. State's necessities
    were met by a carefully contrived system of duties imposed on the
    state's subjects, now treated purely as fiscal units—corvée labor ser-
    vices, state monopolies, taxes. It fostered commerce.

Type VI: Developed from Type III in Mediterranean. Domination of
    aristocratic clans legally abolished; cities military institutions rela-
    tively democratized with military service and citizenship dependent
    on ownership of land.

Type VII: Developed from Type VI in Mediterranean. Army service
    and citizenship rights no longer dependent on ownership of land; all
    citizens could become eligible for office without regard to property
    qualifications (Weber 1976b [1909]: 69–79).

Although I do not want to discuss here these various "stages" (on which see
Deininger 1985), or debate their validity (see Finley [1985b: 88–103] on the
Greek city-state), Weber's approach offers another possible way of bringing
together the study of Greco-Roman and Near Eastern economy and society.
The two regions do not belong to completely separate and unrelated worlds;
they have produced distinct yet historically and typologically related forms
of social organization.

Weber's work has not attracted much attention from historians of the
ancient Near East. Much more interest has been generated by the work of
Marx, that other great "stage" theorist, with significant modeling done by
scholars interacting with the idea of the "Asiatic Mode of Production."
Their approach is historical or evolutionary in its outlook, identifying and
explaining stages in the changing structure of ancient Near Eastern economy
and society. These studies explicate both the character of changing forms of
landed property and control over land and the structure of socioeconomic
relations between the palace and/or temple and the communities of free
people organized in extended family groups that controlled community

land. Most attention has focused on the third and second millennia (Bronze Age), but there has been work undertaken on the first millennium, particularly the Persian and Hellenistic periods (Diakonoff 1969, 1974, 1982, 1991; Liverani 1975, 1984; Briant 1982a, 1982b; Zaccagnini 1989). I want to touch briefly on the work of Diakonoff, since Finley cites him in *The Ancient Economy*, and because he has modeled the relationship between Greek and Near Eastern socioeconomic organization.

Diakonoff (1991) identifies three related ways in which society developed in early antiquity represented by (Type I) southern Mesopotamia (Sumer, Babylonia) in the Bronze Age (third through mid-second millennium), (Type II) Egypt, and (Type III) northern Mesopotamia, Syria-Palestine, Asia Minor, and Aegean (generally second-millennium). All three types shared a common structure to their socioeconomic organization. There were two sectors: a private/communal sector and a state sector. The three types can be distinguished both in terms of agricultural practices (different forms of irrigation agriculture in Type I and Type II; rain-fed agriculture in Type III), which had repercussions for the rate at which socioeconomic organization took place (Type III slower to develop than Types II and III, and as a result southern Mesopotamia and Egypt exerted a powerful cultural influence over these areas), and in the relative prominence of the two sectors. In Type I the state was dominant, whereas in Type III the private/communal sector sometimes gained prominence over the state sector. Since Diakonoff holds that the same "laws" governed the development of both Types I and III (Type II also, but Egypt is outside my brief here), they developed similar forms of socioeconomic organization. Here I briefly recount Diakonoff's view taken from his discussion of Type I as a counterpoint to both Finley and Oppenheim. According to Diakonoff (1991), Babylonia was divided into two sectors: One, the temple, later state, economies, which included persons related to these organizations; and two, lands settled by free inhabitants who participated in the self-government of the community. The supreme proprietor of these lands was the territorial community, but the lands were held by extended family households (see Oppenheim 1977, who differs on identifying landownership; he promotes private ownership).

Society was divided into several "social estates" (equivalent to Finley's "orders," I think, as they are juridically defined):

1. *Upper*: Members of the communities who participated in the communal ownership of property in land and had the right to participate in communal self-government (there was wealth differentiation in this group);

2. *Lower*: Temple- or state-economy personnel who owned no land outright but either possessed land only in return for their services or possessed no land and were allocated rations;
3. *Slaves*: Treated as possessions, deprived of rights.

There was another, more profound, socioeconomic division, namely, social classes occupying different positions within the production process and differing in their relationship to property in the means of production and to exploitation:

1. *Upper Class*: Those who did not engage in productive work and who exploited the labor of others. They managed the economy of the state sector in the interest of the ruling class as a whole.
2. *Middle Class*: Agriculturists and craftspeople who engaged in productive labor but, as a rule, did not exploit the labor of others. This consists of the less well-to-do landowning community members and lower echelon state sector personnel.
3. *Lower Class*: Slavelike dependents who owned no property within the economy and who were also subject to extraeconomic exploitation (physical and ideological coercion). Slaves, whose number was considerably less than the dependents, are also included here.

Small households did not require many dependent workers, but temple lands and the state sector did, since no free agriculturists would plow and sow temple lands. Because these workers were bound to the estate that employed them (they were not allowed to leave it), they have been frequently classified as serfs. But since they were subject to slave-type exploitation, the Greek term "helots" should be used for state slavelike dependents who were settled on land and who maintained the members of the ruling class with their labor (Diakonoff 1974).

This Bronze Age Near Eastern form of socioeconomic organization, as represented in Type III in particular, gave rise to two forms of socioeconomic development in the first millennium BC ("Late Antiquity" for Diakonoff), namely, the polis and the Near Eastern empire. Leaving aside the latter for discussion below, it is noteworthy that Diakonoff views the polis not as something wholly unlike any earlier form of socioeconomic organization, but rather as a polity closely related to the Near Eastern types outlined above, except that it has only one sector, the "private/communal." He writes:

> The classical European *polis* . . . developed (albeit on new lines) in the framework of the ancient society that existed in the 3rd and 2nd millennia BC. We must not forget that the classical type of ancient society

emerged in the process of the decline of the hierarchic agnatic structures which were so typical of all early ancient societies without exceptions. . . . The societies of these classic Graeco-Roman *poleis*—and of those succeeding them—were characterized by an ancient type "one sector" economy, where the state economic sector after the destruction of the state economies at the end of the Creto-Mycenean civilization, was reduced to a minimum if not to nil. But the non-state economic sector (the "communal and private" one) was of course well known in Asia as well. . . . *[T]he existence of a "one-sector" structure of economy (with only the "communal and private" sector!) does by no means prove that Pericles' Athens belonged to another and "higher" formation in comparison with the societies which alongside of a private-communal one also had a state sector.* Such societies were not limited to Asia, but existed earlier in Greece itself, compare Cnossos, Pylos, Mycenae, etc. One should also note that the Western antiquity itself also knew another type of "one-sector" economy where the state sector had nearly totally ousted the "communal and private" one. Such an economy was Sparta which in this respect more resembles not only the Hittite society but even Egypt. *The Asiatic states of the 3rd and 2nd millennia B.C., especially the city states, just because of their "two-sector economy," belong to an early stage of a society type which, as it were, was intermediary between Sparta and Doric Crete on the one hand, and Athens, Corinth, Republican Rome, etc., on the other.* (Diakonoff 1982: 93–94; my emphasis)

Finley was quite familiar with Marxian approaches to the study of antiquity, certainly of the Greco-Roman world, and his work shared with scholars such as Diakonoff an interest in dependent labor, the need for which he recognized existed in all the societies of the wider Mediterranean world from the third millennium to the end of the Roman Empire. On this matter Finley himself saw possibilities for the study of the Near East informing an understanding of the Greco-Roman world while still retaining the clear distinction between the two, specifically for the period after the collapse of Bronze Age civilizations (Finley 1964). The earlier period of Greek history (Bronze Age) did have clear parallels with the Near East—Mycenaean palace economies and the palace/temple economies of Near Eastern cities—but the Greeks emerged after the "Dark Age" to form radically different modes of social and political organization, whereas the Near East, one has to assume from Finley, reproduced forms of its traditional centralized palace/temple organization. This must be why Finley chose to begin his study in *The Ancient Economy* at 1000 BC and why, beginning at that time, the Near East and the Greco-Roman world cannot be studied in tandem.

Diakonoff, however, bridges the divide that Finley wants to put in place between the Bronze Age and the first millennium. In the above quotation from Diakonoff, Finley would agree with comparing Bronze Age Near Eastern and Bronze Age Aegean polities, yet Diakonoff claims that Aegean and Near Eastern polities of the Bronze Age are not something completely different from what appears in the Aegean in the first millennium. In fact, the Near Eastern polities of the third and second millennia are "intermediary between" various types of Aegean polity of the first millennium ("two-sector" economies are between "one-sector state" and "one-sector private-communal" economies). Near Eastern forms of socioeconomic organization are far from being completely different from the Greco-Roman world in the first millennium BC; they are typologically connected and so can be studied in an integrated fashion. Diakonoff's analysis is one with which Finley should have had some empathy since it sets up a continuum or spectrum of forms of socioeconomic organization that relates the Near East to the Greco-Roman world rather than segregating them.

In summary, two points can be reiterated. First, Oppenheim and Diakonoff agree, against Finley, that the Near Eastern economy cannot be typified as a state-run enterprise in which private or communal ownership of land has but an inconsequential role. The economy must be recognized as always having two components—temple/palace and private/communal. Second, Weber, Oppenheim, and Diakonoff all offer ways of integrating the study of the socioeconomic organization of the Near East with the Greco-Roman world. Oppenheim and Diakonoff at least relate the Bronze Age Near East to the first-millennium Aegean (how the first-millennium Near East relates to the Greco-Roman world needs more explicit treatment). I am not here to advocate any of the above approaches but simply to point out that Finley ignored the challenge to his division between the two regions offered by these works.

Despite their differences, Finley, Polanyi, Weber, Oppenheim, and Diakonoff all share the view that ancient economy and society are to be distinguished from later periods, particularly the modern world. There have been a few recent voices attempting to articulate modernist approaches to the economy of the ancient Near East. I will mention only in passing the work of the economist Morris Silver, who has published three books on the economy of the ancient Near East (Silver 1983, 1985, 1994), because his work has been subject recently to a thorough evaluation by Renger (1994). Silver's work is fundamentally a critique of Polanyi's substantivist understanding of the ancient economy from a modernist perspective. It is not a sustained critique, however, but a series of notes on the main tenets of

Polanyi's view—redistributive mode of integration, markets, trade—selecting evidence from primary texts across the historical length and geographical breadth of the Near East and drawing on relevant secondary literature to disprove Polanyi. I cannot speak for specialists in economic theory or economic history, but if the books were written for specialists of the ancient Near East in order to warn them off Polanyi (since, apparently, "his influence among ancient Near Eastern specialists is far more pervasive than they admit or, perhaps, are aware" [Silver 1985: 2]), I believe he has seriously misjudged his audience. Most students of the ancient Near East, including those cited by Silver such as Adams (1974), Oppenheim (1977, as outlined above), and Gledhill and Larsen (1982), are ambivalent about Polanyi's work, even when they are in sympathy with his substantivist position. On markets, for example, Polanyi has for some time been considered to represent an extreme position. Even Renger (1984, 1994), who is particularly sympathetic to the later Polanyi, is critically engaged with his work. Finally, Silver's critique of Polanyi is not the same as a positive argument for a modernist interpretation of the ancient economy. That argument still waits to be made.

More substantial to my mind is the contribution of Ellickson and Thorland (1995), who from a "law-and-economics" perspective have employed a "rational-actor-optimist" model of human behavior to account for the pattern of landholding in the ancient Near East (Mesopotamia, Egypt, Israel). This model "anticipates that an individual will estimate the expected utility of alternate actions, and then choose the action that promises to maximize his personal expected utility, which may, of course, reflect a concern for others' welfare" (Ellickson and Thorland 1995: 327). In regard to patterns of landholding, the model "forecasts, with some caveats, that changes in economic conditions will prompt residents of a society to alter their property institutions so as to minimize the sum of: (1) transaction costs; and (2) the costs of coordination failures" (Ellickson and Thorland 1995: 324–25). As rational actors the ancients were no different from us and, as a result, the law-and-economics approach is "despite its many limitations . . . a fruitful prism in all social contexts" (327) and "can be a timelessly valuable heuristic for analysing human affairs" (411). In comparison, cultural pluralists (dominating history, anthropology, and sociology) give too much weight to the influence of ideology, language, class structure, and other cultural factors on institutions, including land regimes.

After reviewing evidence covering four millennia and topics such as private property in land, kinship groups and organizations as landowners, time spans of standard land interests, the role of land in the system of public finance, land transfer, land finance, and the politics and economics

of legal restrictions of land transactions, Ellickson and Thorland
conclude:

> Much of the evidence adduced seems consistent with our initial
> hypothesis that a small, close-knit social group will typically succeed in
> devising land-tenure institutions that maximize the welfare of the
> group's members. When free from outside coercion, ancient villagers
> appear to have adopted the marble-cakes of land-tenure arrangements
> that law-and-economics theory predicts: private ownership of houses,
> gardens, and small arable lands plots; communal or institutional owner-
> ship of arable and grazing lands where that arrangement was necessary
> to exploit efficiencies of scale or spread risks; and network of open-
> access lands. The record suggests that the social impetus toward these
> arrangements was universal—i.e., present regardless of a society's
> religion, ethnic make-up, and other cultural features. (Ellickson and
> Thorland 1995: 408–9)

This is a necessarily brief and oversimplified outline of their work. Intel-
lectually it is more powerful than Silver's attack on Polanyi and deserves close
attention. An explicit assumption of this approach is that it can also be used
to examine landholding patterns in the Greco-Roman world, since members
of those societies were also "rational actors," thus uniting the wider Mediterranean world. Unfortunately, the constraints of space and my lack of detailed knowledge of the model precludes further discussion in this chapter
(although see the sections regarding landed property in the Neo-Assyrian
and Neo-Babylonian periods, below). By including it here I hope to elicit
input from economists who may be more familiar with it, and to provoke a
response from my ancient history colleagues.

The First Millennium: Sources, Problems, Prospects

The study of the economy of the ancient Near East in the first millennium
BC is still in its infancy. This is in part a result of the scholarly effort
demanded to translate and edit the tens of thousands of cuneiform texts from
this period, many thousands of which even now, after 150 years' work, remain to be published. Understandably, this task has dominated the attention
of Assyriologists and has generally shaped their training, which has coupled
philological expertise with the study of single archives or discrete topics,
usually in isolation from broader considerations. Modeling of the economy,
as well as of much else, is commonly eschewed in favor of description. This
predilection for description over modeling no doubt reflects a general

commitment to history as a humanities discipline rather than as a social science. It also arises out of the belief that before any modeling of the economy can be undertaken, much more preliminary work—such as preparing reliable text editions, establishing a reliable chronology, and writing political history—needs to be completed. Even though considerable advances have been made on these fronts, doubts are commonly voiced that our sources will not yield the types of information that will permit proper economic analysis, and that the project should be abandoned at the outset.

Regarding Finley's characterization of the Near Eastern economy, it is not difficult to show that private/communal ownership of land continued in the first millennium alongside palace and temple economies and that, as a result, his view is inaccurate for this period as well. More problematic is determining first, how the development and reproduction of empire affected economic structures in the first millennium; second, model(s) for the Near Eastern economy(ies) in this millennium; and third, how such models might view the Near East and Greco-Roman worlds in an integrated fashion rather than as completely separate.

These issues are problematic basically due to the fragmentary picture of the economy derived from the extant sources. Sources for the Neo-Assyrian empire are concentrated in the latter period of the empire (mainly the eighth and seventh centuries) and come largely from northern Mesopotamia, with only a relatively few texts from Babylonia and elsewhere. In contrast, sources for the Babylonian, Persian, and Hellenistic empires come largely from southern Babylonia, supplemented in the Persian period by administrative records of payments to workers and officials from Persepolis (Iran). All these are from a later period (sixth through third centuries). Clearly there is no possibility of fusing the information derived from texts in the northern region from earlier in the first millennium with those from the south in the later first millennium to obtain the "whole picture." This contention is further supported by the quite different provenances of the Mesopotamian sources. In the north the texts come from, or are basically related to, the palace and government. In the south the texts come from the temples, and there is considerably less information about the government. Again, it is not simply a matter of collapsing these two "great institutions" into a single sector. In the late first millennium the Babylonian temples were not an arm of the state, nor were they run by the state (Dandamaev 1979). In Assyria, temples were closely connected to the state, but from the available sources they seem to play a different role in the economy than the Babylonian temples. More work needs to be done on the Assyrian temple to supplement past research (Menzel 1981). Also, because there is an overrepresentation of

72   PETER R. BEDFORD

texts connected with either the palace or temple, our perspective on the
economy may be biased by these sources. For Babylonia in the Neo-
Babylonian and Persian periods there are family business archives such as the
Egibi archive from Babylon, the Murashû archive from Nippur, and the
Ea-ilūta-bāni archive from Borsippa, among others. From the Assyrian period there are archives connected to the government officials in Assyria and
Babylonia, but very little overall on the private sector of the economy. These
archives offer some insight into forms of land tenure and land use, business
organization, and trade. However, they represent activities of people who
belong to the highest strata of society: those with important political ap-
pointments or connections. It is very difficult to understand the economic
life of the "ordinary people." Further, since the texts come from cities, we
know relatively little about those living in the countryside.

    This regional difference is also borne out in patterns of landholding. Land
in the south was held "either by the great organizations or by private absentee landlords who lived in cities and usually rented it out to poor tenant farmers. Farmers who lived on their own fields were the exception." In the north
(Assyria/Syria), "farmers seemed to have lived mainly in villages which were
held either in feudal tenure or in private possession by the lord of the
manor—the king, his high officials, members of his family"—who formed
a thin layer of a ruling class that could be replaced by newcomers without
affecting the economic structure of the region (Oppenheim 1977: 86).

    There is a third region beyond Mesopotamia to consider in any modeling:
the Syro-Palestinian coast. Coastal regions, led by the Phoenician cities Tyre
and Sidon, had a different climate and therefore produced different agricultural products. Most significant, however, was the role of the Phoenician
cities as trade centers, which was promoted by the Assyrians' demand for exotic goods and then exploited by the ensuing empires. Via these centers the
eastern empire could control Mediterranean commerce (Frankenstein 1979;
Sherratt and Sherratt 1993). Phoenicia was not the only area of the Levant
whose economic activity was stimulated by Assyrian imperialism. According
to Hopkins:

    The luxury goods demanded as tribute payments held more conse-
    quences for agricultural economics than short-term impoverishment;
    they incited the search for high value materials. These commodities had
    to be procured on the international trade network. To enter this net-
    work demanded intensive investments in exportable agricultural prod-
    ucts. Thus Assyrian power pushed dependent polities to produce more
    and pulled them towards specific products. These influences were joined

by increasing population densities, urbanization, and political centralization in spurring agricultural industrialization and commercialization. In
Israel and Judah, the intensification of olive and wine production stands
out. Terrace technology advanced, reclaiming denuded hillside slopes.
The terraces were accompanied by hundreds of rock-cut presses
throughout highland regions where wine production progressed at both
industrial sites . . . and dispersed farmsteads. (D. Hopkins 1997: 29)

This is an aspect of the impact of imperialism that deserves closer attention.

One prospect for a longer-term institutional study is offered by
Babylonian sources covering temples in the Neo-Babylonian, Persian, and
Hellenistic periods. This work has begun, but there is still opportunity for
much more to be undertaken. The study of Babylonia also provides an
opportunity to relate the Near East to the Greco-Roman world. If the
Hellenistic Near East can be integrated into the study of the Greco-Roman
world (as even Finley admitted), and given that it can be shown that there is
strong continuity between the Hellenistic periods and Achaemenid Persian
periods in the roles and organization of Babylonian temples and cities
(Oelsner 1984, 1987; van der Spek 1987), and that certain of these continuities reach back into the Neo-Babylonian and Neo-Assyrian periods, then it
may be possible to imagine ways of relating the Near Eastern empires to the
Hellenistic and Roman empires. Continuity with change rather than radical
disjunction between Hellenistic-Roman empires and earlier Near Eastern
empires needs to be explored more closely, including modes of extracting
wealth from the empire, landholding and exploitation, and administrative
organization. Near Eastern empires should not be unlike Hellenistic and
Roman empires because the former influenced the latter.

What of the Near Eastern empires and classical Greece? Perhaps
Diakonoff is right, and the correct modeling is the Bronze Age Near East
with the classical Aegean. From the first-millennium polities, it is probably
the Phoenician cities that might be modeled with the Greek cities in certain
respects, together with first-millennium Babylonian cities with their citizens
and rights generally recognized by imperial governments (*kidinnūtu* [divine
protection] status, on which see below).

The textual sources can be categorized as follows (for further details see
Kuhrt 1995: 473–78, 501–5 [Neo-Assyrian]; 573–75 [Neo-Babylonian];
647–52 [Achaemenid Persian]):

1. *Royal inscriptions*: Royal inscriptions from Babylonia do not contain
   much in the way of economic information beyond the refurbishment
   of temples and the institution of regular temple offerings. Assyrian

royal inscriptions recounting the military exploits of Assyrian kings include information about the territories conquered, reorganized, and resettled as well as lists of tribute and booty. They also contain information on how the upper echelons of the palace/government were integrated into the land and labor economy, with further information in this regard coming from royal grants. Royal inscriptions are literary in character and highly charged ideologically. Part of the ideology is the opening up of new agricultural lands, the implementation of which is reflected in legal and administrative texts. Royal inscriptions are the closest one gets in the Near East to the types of texts Finley used to uncover the "economic mentality" of the Greco-Roman world. These texts are not nearly as helpful as Xenophon, Cato, or Cicero, however. There are no ancient Near Eastern treatises on the economy or literary commentary on society or politics. This is a clear example of what Morris and Manning note in the introduction regarding the difference in types of sources available for the study of the Near East and the Greco-Roman world.

As for literary texts, one should mention the Hebrew Bible (Old Testament) as a source for information on the social and economic organization of Palestine in the first millennium. The Hebrew Bible is, possibly apart from a few chapters of early poetry, a body of texts from the first millennium, much of it written in reaction to or in the context of Assyrian, Babylonian, and Persian imperialism. These texts do not address the economy directly, but they include snippets of information such as Solomon's state-run foreign trading ventures (I Kings 10), the utopian debt releases of Leviticus chapter 25 (Jubilee year), the prophet Amos railing against the appropriation of the lands of the poor by the rich, the Naboth's vineyard story (I Kings 21), and Ezekiel chapter 27 on Tyre's trading network. As with Assyria and Babylonia, there is no text devoted to commenting on the economy or economic organization.

2. *Legal, economic, and administrative texts from state and temple archives*: These include documents written for high-ranking officials, not just the crown. There are examples of conveyances (real estate sales, sales of persons), contracts (which include interest clauses), rental agreements, receipts, judicial documents, taxation documents (lists of incomings, lists of out-goings, accounts, assessments, "census"/cadastral texts), and ration lists.

3. *Legal, economic, and administrative texts from private archives*: Includes business archives from private firms.

4. *Correspondence, both state and private*: There is a sizable corpus of letters written between the Assyrian king and various officials involved in the running of the empire. The king does not address economic policies directly, but the letters do make mention of economic matters. Information can be gleaned about agriculture, labor, and administration. Parpola (1995), for example, has gathered the scattered references in correspondence to the building of Dur-Sharrukin, a new royal city (Sargon II; built circa 715–705 BC). Among the matters addressed, including the planning, organization and supervision of the works, and the procurement of materials and labor, is the financing of the project. Building expenses were apparently financed by loans taken from private money lenders.

Postgate's assessment of the relative value of the sources for information about various aspects of the Assyrian economy and society is still accurate almost twenty-five years after he wrote (Postgate 1979: 195):

Good—palace sector;
Fair—army, state labor, administration, tribute, taxation, landholding;
Poor—social structure, city economy, village economy, prices and currency;
Bad—non-state labor, crafts and industries, trade (the latter may be pushed up a category or so).

Even allowing for the qualitative nature of his assessment, the prospect of modeling the economy is not good. The problems with sources are compounded by the lack of any useful figures. Many texts are full of numbers, but they commonly lack context. Too often we can read a text, but not really know what it is about. Scribes did not normally put headings on texts to identify them. Economists and some other historians may complain that Near Eastern specialists are being too timid, displaying the innate conservatism of the field. Maybe so. But it is very difficult to judge the scale of an economy when one is unsure of the significance of many of the figures or suspicious of their accuracy. For example, the Assyrian royal inscriptions note the number of persons deported from subjugated lands; we might be able to estimate the population of the Near East at that time if we could accurately estimate the percentage of the conquered population they represented. It could also offer a rough guide to the size of the population brought into northern Mesopotamia to work on newly expanded agricultural areas. Should the figure of approximately 1.5 million deportees be taken seriously? The important study by Adams (1981) on settlement patterns in southern

Babylonia has shown a positive demographic trend during the first millennium, but I do not believe that he or anyone else has ventured a figure for the population of the region.

The lack of useful figures means that it is impossible to do a balance sheet for these empires. We do not have sufficiently explicit statements in the texts to enable us to determine how the listed quantities relate to the internal production or consumption of the empire. We have figures on imports, tribute, taxation, and the like, but we are unable to assess their significance.

The Neo-Assyrian Empire

Postgate's assessment of the value of the Assyrian sources for an understanding of the economy has been mentioned above. Here I sketch some aspects of socio-economic organization. It is possible to speak of two phases of the Assyrian empire, a conquest phase and an imperial phase. The first phase is characterized by the expansion of the empire's borders and acquisition of wealth for the crown via tribute and booty. Much of this wealth went into various forms of display—palaces, refurbishment of temples and cities in the homeland, building of new royal cities. Conquests were consolidated with an essentially military administration whose purpose was to exact regular taxation from the subjugated territory. Over time, provincialization emerged from the concentration of the administration of a region in one center. Whether it was a deliberate policy of the Assyrians is unknown, but it is a form of organization that is adopted and developed by ensuing empires. There are rational economic reasons for such a development. Rather than all taxes, labor service, and other incomes going into the center and then back out to the provinces, provincial heads organized their own local regions to use the incomes, to accumulate wealth in the provincial capital, and to send only a certain amount back to the center.

This is not the only example of the crown/government acting rationally to reduce transaction costs. Administration procedures were streamlined in the provision of *ilku* (the "performance of military or civilian service for the state, or the payment of contributions as a commuted version of that service" [Postgate 1974: 91], incumbent on landowners and probably all "Assyrians"). The government would determine a man's *ilku* obligation and then leave it to the individual to make the relevant payment directly to its eventual recipient. This system relieved the government of the physical burden of collecting and distributing the items and enabled it, in theory at least, to calculate exactly how many soldiers and animals could be supported, without ever handling the relevant materials itself (Postgate 1979: 203–4).

The *iškaru* system is another example. In this system craftsmen converted raw materials under the direct control of the government into finished products. Instead of maintaining a large body of ration-drawing personnel, requiring considerable supervision, the policy seems to have been to allocate quantities of raw material to craftsmen and to define their obligation to supply finished products with a commercial-style debt note. The system worked more on the principle of commercial, or rather fiscal, obligations (Postgate 1979: 205). This can be compared with Neo-Babylonian temples where credit/loan documents were also used when entrusting valuable materials (gold, jewelry) to craftsmen. These men were, however, on the payroll of the temples as shown by ration lists (Renger 1971).

In comparison to the above examples of rational economic action, villages display elements of economic activity embedded in social conventions; for example, communal restraint on the private sale of land (Postgate 1989). There are also instances of the crown acting on the basis of such conventions, although the impact on economic life is difficult to judge: (*an*)*durāru* is a royal edict canceling the enslavement of free citizens for private debt; *kidinnūtu* status of certain Babylonian cities recognized the long-standing rights of their citizens, including curtailment of the king's authority to exact taxes, fines, labor service and army service (Kuhrt 1995: 610–17). Neither of these would have been driven by an economic policy. Both probably reflected the traditional role of the Assyrian king and had important legitimating value.

Postgate (1979) sees three sectors of the economy: palace sector, government sector, and private sector. This tripartite division has not convinced everyone, including Liverani (see Chapter 2). The government sector seems to overlap both the other sectors rather than being completely discrete. For example, when a high government official is involved in trading activities for personal gain, one must assume that he operates in the private sector, not the government sector, even though it may be his government position that affords him opportunity to trade (Cole 1996: 56–68; I should point out that much of the evidence for private traders points to not very high-volume trade, an exception being Oppenheim 1967). However, an official trader sent out by the crown to undertake trading activities should be categorized as part of the palace sector (Elat 1987).

Palace Sector: All things owned by the royal family. Included in this sector as consumers are the royal palaces, royal family, domestic staff, administrators and military, and court officials. Income was in the form of booty, tribute, "gifts," produce and rents from lands owned, credit activities, slave sales, appropriations, and confiscations. Expenditures were on subsistence of palace residents and staff, equipment of military staff, luxuries, gifts, regular temple offerings, building operations. *Government Sector* (including the army): Drew on the private sector to provide resources for civil and military operations via taxation and conscription, *ilku*, and *iškaru*. The backbone of the government sector was the provincial system. The government subordinates were responsible for the collection of payments of all kinds from their province, and for conscription and supply of soldiers and civil laborers. Village inspectors were responsible to the provincial administration for the assessment of taxation. There is no evidence of a conscious effort by the crown to control or monopolize trade, although both the crown and government officials were involved in it via agents. *Private Sector*: Hard to document because of scarcity of sources.

Liverani (1984) has used a two-sector model of "palace" and "family" to examine trends in land tenure and inheritance from the mid-third through mid-first millennium. He sees two processes at work in the first millennium that I believe are apt particularly for the Neo-Assyrian period (at least in the Assyrian homeland and northern Mesopotamia) (see also Fales 1984a, 1984b; but compare to Postgate 1989). First, the palace sector directed to members of the palace organization (high officials at court and in the provinces) land, labor, and surpluses as it decentralized control of its lands (Liverani 1984: 39–40). Some (most?) of these lands may well have been prebendary holdings accompanying the office, rather than actually "owned" by the officials (Postgate 1989: 147). Much of the labor on these estates would have been deportees from elsewhere in the empire, some of whom were put to work in (new) royal cities. The agricultural land around these cities was not sufficiently large to feed the population, so new agricultural lands, including some in quite marginal areas (successful crops in two out of five years), were opened up. The legal status of these deportees was not "slave" but "dependent labor," since they were tied to a particular estate. Postgate views them as "helots," borrowing Diakonoff's category.

One way to interpret this development is as a risk-management strategy on the part of the crown. In order to increase land under cultivation, officials are "granted" lands and workers and manage the risk. In return the state draws an income in the form of taxes. Temples in Babylonia might have filled a similar role. These institutions can also pass the risk along, and that is what we see with firms such as the Murashûs in Babylonia in the Achaemenid Persian period. They managed royal and temple lands and leased them out

to others. They also offered a service to look after the military and other obligations that were attendant on the land. In return they sent rents back to
the landowners.

The second process noted by Liverani is the erosion of the connection
between the land lot and a family or kinship group, which had characterized earlier periods. Eventually land becomes freely alienable. The upshot of
this is that "some families are completely deprived of landed property (and
enslaved for debts), while other families accumulate large extensions of land
which in the 'free' sector come to be the exact counterpart to the large
landed properties belonging to the high officials in the Palace sector"
(Liverani 1984: 42).

Both processes led to landed property being concentrated in the hands of
only some individuals or families, in comparison with the second millennium when landed properties were equally distributed among different family units in the family sector, and centralized by the great organization in the
Palace sector (Liverani 1984: 40).

Neo-Babylonian and Achaemenid Persian Periods

Finally, to address briefly the issue of landholding and citizenship in Babylonian cities during the Neo-Babylonian and Persian periods, which was
touched on above when outlining the views of Oppenheim and Diakonoff
against Finley.

We know from texts that land (that is, arable land, not house or building
plots) was owned, in the sense of exclusive dominion, by private individuals
or families, by the crown, and by temples. There is no doubt that there was
privately held land in Babylonia in the Neo-Babylonian and Achaemenid
Persian periods, apparently without any limitation on its control. This land
could be used as surety, sold, inherited, and passed on in dowries. There are
numerous field sales, but almost exclusively of small plots, most not larger
than 1.35 hectares. From the available evidence it appears that there were
few large private estates, but we must be careful in what we surmise. An important and still unknown aspect of privately owned land is its quantity—
the percentage of all cultivable land that was privately owned remains unclear. The documents informing us of privately held land come mostly from
large urban sites and tend to offer insight into the more substantial and
better connected families. Although it is not unusual to find references to
villages and small settlements, private landholding in these locations remains
to be studied, but it may not prove possible to elucidate the situation there
from the available documents. Interesting, particularly when considering

Finley's view of private landholding in the ancient Near East, is Dandamaev's contention that "long before the period under consideration [Neo-Babylonian and Achaemenid Persian periods], much of Babylonia's land had been privatized nearly to the same degree as occurred in the classical Mediterranean realms. The land had become truly private property held by those who cultivated it, unless they were tenants or military soldiers settled on state lands" (Dandamaev 1996: 207).

The House of Ea-ilūta-bāni (Joannès 1989) left sources spanning six generations and can be taken as an example of a reasonably well-to-do urban family. From the city of Borsippa, the family owned several hectares (about 2.5 acres) of land in the immediate environs of the city, some slaves, and a certain number of claims in silver and gold. To best maintain and manage land, property was not divided among heirs. Another partial solution to this problem was to marry a close relative, such as a niece, in order to keep land in the family.

Royal land is the second category of land and is mentioned more frequently in the documents from Babylonia than privately held land, but to my knowledge no comprehensive study of the scattered references has been undertaken. Much of the royal land was probably acquired via canal building activities that opened up or maintained arable land, rather than by means of confiscation. It was made available for exploitation in basically two ways:

1. To members of the ruling elite—that is, members of the extended royal family, the nobility, and senior bureaucrats in the administration (they were commonly overlapping groups). These either cultivated the land using slaves or other agricultural workers, or leased the land to others and received rental payments.

2. By leasing the land to tenants, who were obligated to undertake military service or to outfit a chariot, or to make an equivalent payment, usually in silver—these are the so-called fiefs, such as the "bow fief," "horse fief," and "chariot fief," which are best attested in the late Achaemenid-period Murashû texts. These lands "were occupied by groups of agnatic relatives. The properties could be leased or pawned, and shares in them were transmitted by inheritance, but they were not normally alienable" (Stolper 1994: 245). There are other fiefs such as "hand land" (*bīt ritti*), which do not seem to have carried military obligations. Fiefs could be allotted to corporate groups of royal dependents, sometimes organized by profession or by ethnic group, or by place of origin—these are called *ḫaṭrus* (Stolper 1985: 70–103). The organization of the various types of fiefs and their modes of

landholding have been studied by Stolper (1985) and others and cannot detain us here. Again it remains unclear as to what percentage of cultivable land belonged to the crown.

The temple was the third landowner and, if our sources are anything to go by, the largest. Temple lands had been acquired by means of land grants from the crown, through the development and maintenance of canals, and through the appropriation of the privately owned land of indebted small holders. These temples, in large cities such as Uruk, Sippar, Babylon, Borsippa, Nippur, and Ur, were the center of their respective urban communities. Much of the land owned by the temple was not exploited directly by temple agricultural workers, rather it was leased to entrepreneurs and other families who were members of the urban elite. They then leased the land to others for rents or organized the temple land using indentured or other agricultural labor. Temples granted bow fiefs, but it is unclear that they carried obligations similar to the royal fiefs. However, the nexus of the urban elite, the temple administration, and the exploitation of temple land has given rise to the notion of the citizen-temple community. It is true to say that economically prominent urban families were in close connection with the temple and occupied leading positions in the city and temple administration (Kümmel 1979; Frame 1984) because they were integrated into the economic interests and activities of the temples. They were extended families who spread the wealth and positions among their members (that is, relatives). But not all "citizens" of these cities were so economically advantaged, and there was not equal access to temple holdings nor equal opportunity to exploit them.

According to Dandamaev, who has written most extensively on this, the citizen-temple community (although he does not use this explicit terminology) of Babylonian cities was the highest level of a three- (sometimes described as four-) tiered social structure (Dandamaev 1982, 1988; compare to Diakonoff's discussion on third- to second-millennium organization of Babylonia):

1. *Fully Fledged Citizens*: This group is designated by the Akkadian term *mār banî*, which is usually translated as "free person," "citizen," or "nobleman," and taken to refer to persons with full citizen rights, including a seat on the city's governing council (Akk. *puḫru*).

2. *Free Born Persons Deprived of Civic Rights*: For example, aliens who lived in Babylonia for various reasons and who did not possess land within the city's common fund. They were settled, in some cases, in separate and distinct communities with their own self-government (Eph'al 1978; Dandamaev 1983).

3. *Various Dependent Social Groups*: For example, fief holders. One part
   of this category consisted of slaves, so on occasion Dandamaev divides
   this category into two—category 3 becomes dependent social groups
   such as fief holders; category 4 comprises slaves.

This view of the social structure of Babylonian cities is generally accepted
(see, for example, Kuhrt 1995: 618–21). Dandamaev describes the *mār banîs*
as "citizens with full rights [who] were members of the city or village assembly (*puḫru*), which had a certain judicial authority in the resolution of
family and property matters" and who "possessed immovable property
within the communal land district which came under the jurisdiction of the
popular assembly. Many of them were holders of certain shares of income
from the temple. Such citizens included persons of high rank (upper echelons of the state, and temple officials, merchants, prosperous scribes, etc.) as
well as craftsmen and peasants" (Dandamaev 1982: 40–41).

When Dandamaev writes that citizens of Babylonian cities "possessed
immovable property within the communal land district which came under
the jurisdiction of the popular assembly," this "communal land district" is
not land belonging to the citizen-temple community (contra Weinberg
1976). Rather, Dandamaev means that the citizens held private land within
the legal jurisdiction of the city and that the *puḫru* could make decisions in
such matters as disputes over boundaries or inheritance. (Even here one
needs to review the evidence for the assembly's authority over privately held
land; for example, judges making rulings over land). The Babylonian
citizen-temple communities had authority over temple lands, and even here
the nature of that authority is complicated by the internal administrative
structures of the temples. It is clear, however, that the integration of the private and the communal or temple economies in the first millennium BC, a
fundamental development in the appearance of the citizen-temple community according to its proponents, did not mean the abolition of privately
owned land in favor of community-owned land.

While not economically equal, all citizens were, theoretically, legally
equal. All citizens may have been entitled to a determined part of the temple
revenue, but this did not necessarily mean that all were entitled to usufruct
of a portion of temple land. As mentioned earlier, entrepreneurs and leading families exploited the land via leases, or the temple cultivated the land
directly by means of its laborers.

There are gaps in our understanding of the *mār banî*, or the citizen stratum of society. Martha Roth has collected evidence showing that some individuals were slaves or dedicated to a temple and *mār banîs* simultaneously.

She notes that "there is no evidence to suggest that a person's status as *mār banî* was determined by birth; rather the status is one that can be conferred on a former slave[3] such translations as 'free-(born) person' or 'citizen' imply a social and political structure inappropriate for Neo-Babylonian society" (Roth 1989: 487). There is further evidence (cited in van Driel 1989: 206) for the descendants of foreigners being designated as *mār banîs*. This might suggest that persons could move from status level 2, alien without civic rights, to status 1, fully fledged citizens.

Conclusion

This chapter has been written with Finley's characterization of the ancient Near Eastern economy foremost in mind. In focusing on landholding and urban citizenship while reviewing some models and evidence relevant for both Finley's view and the first millennium more generally, I hope I have not diverted us too far from the task we as a group have set for ourselves. While Finley's view can be set aside, there is obviously much work to be done in modeling the ancient Near Eastern economy and in integrating those models within the economy of the wider Mediterranean world. Those of us working on the ancient Near East (well, speaking for myself at least) need to develop a higher level of methodological sophistication in our economic analysis. One of the central debates will have to do with determining which tools are the most appropriate. I have touched on only in passing the "primitivist/modernist" debate, but it is clearly one to which we will have to return.

Note

I prepared the first version of this paper while I was a Research Fellow at the Stanford Humanities Center, Stanford University, for the 1997–98 academic year. My thanks to members of the center, the Social Science History Institute, and the Stanford Department of Classics for their hospitality and collegiality.

Chapter 4

Comment on Liverani and Bedford

MARK GRANOVETTER

My first reaction to these two excellent chapters is surprise at how much the question of ancient economies has been framed by broad theoretical debates, and then alarm at the extent to which these debates seamlessly meld ideology and argument. Although there have been numerous positions staked out over the twentieth century, as noted in the volume's introduction by Morris and Manning, the two mainly invoked in these chapters are, on the one side, that of Weber/Polanyi/Finley, and on the other, a rational actor/ optimal outcome argument of the sort made in law and economics.

In my view, the extraordinary historical variability of human institutions and motives means that any assumption of invariable and informed rationality is fundamentally a matter of faith and can only be sustained by hidden tautologies and highly selective use of evidence. This proposition is all the more true when theorists join to the reductionist rational-actor model a further assumption that such actors successfully maximize some communal objectives. An excellent example is the assertion of Ellickson and Thorland (1995: 408–9, cited by Bedford) that evidence from the ancient Near East confirms the argument that "a small close-knit social group will typically succeed in devising land-tenure institutions that maximize the welfare of the group's members."

Let us pause for a moment to imagine the mass of evidence and the additional reasoning that would be required to sustain this Panglossian conclusion. To confirm that individuals indeed acted rationally and responded

84

to changes in economic conditions in just the precise ways required to "minimize the sum of (1) transaction costs; and (2) the costs of coordination failures" (Ellickson and Thorland 1995: 324–25, cited by Bedford) would require us to have rather detailed evidence on what individuals did, and to what stimuli they were responding. We would, moreover, need to understand how self-seeking individuals overcame the usual difficult problems of coordination, and indeed did so in a way that optimized some agreed-upon set of objectives. The innocent phrase "close-knit social group" tacitly assumes an extraordinary degree of social solidarity and absence of conflicting interests of the sort that midcentury sociologists like Talcott Parsons were savagely (but appropriately) criticized for assuming. The argument requires further that individuals be sufficiently clever and farsighted to coordinate their individual behavior in such a way as to achieve the desired optimum, even though such calculations require the use of advanced calculus when carried out in modern microeconomics. Finally, the assumption that group welfare is successfully maximized blithely elides the daunting theoretical problem of what it can mean to measure the welfare of a group—the subject of centuries of dispute in political philosophy and more recently in welfare economics.

On the evidence side alone the case looks open and shut, or perhaps merely shut. Bedford tells us that the "study of the economy of the ancient Near East in the first millennium BC is still in its infancy," given that many thousands of cuneiform texts from this period remain unpublished even after 150 years of work, and that many experts doubt that we will ever have the information needed to do any proper economic analysis. What can such an evidentiary situation imply for an argument that requires massive empirical support before it can be taken seriously? In the absence of hard evidence on the costs of transactions or of coordination, it is all too tempting to examine the data at hand and assert that they show such costs to have been minimized. This can only be argued after the fact, by stretching the definitions of such costs, or of social welfare, to fit what has been found. Such hidden tautology is the only way to preserve what is more an article of faith than an empirical hypothesis.

But in the Polanyi/Finley argument, that individual rational behavior rarely characterizes the ancient Near East, ideology, though an opposite one, intrudes as well. Though Max Weber was famously "value-neutral," the same cannot be said for Polanyi, whose thought so strongly influenced Finley. We must deal with three Karl Polanyis: Polanyi the ideologist, Polanyi the theorist, and Polanyi the empirical analyst. Just as devotion to free markets and laissez-faire lurks behind the arguments of law and

economics, a socialist distaste for the excesses of capitalism propels Polanyi's
dismissal of markets and market exchange as the universal mode of meeting
human needs. This is clear in Polanyi's polemical writings, beginning with
The Great Transformation (1944) and especially in "Our Obsolete Market
Mentality" (1947). Polanyi the theorist, however, offered a far more nuanced approach. In his 1944 and especially his 1957 work, supplemented
by his posthumous (1977) writings, he argued that human societies had
three fundamental ways to provide the material goods and services that
their members desired, and that each could be defined by individual behaviors, but only succeeded in any widespread way if these behaviors were
supported by correlated social institutions. Thus, exchange had to be supported by market institutions, redistribution by centralized political structures, and reciprocity by institutions of kinship and friendship. He argued
quite explicitly that while some societies might be dominated by one or
another such mode of economic integration, there was no reason why
societies could not have both dominant and subordinate modes, and indeed that exchange, redistribution, and reciprocity might well support one
another in important ways. In Polanyi the empirical analyst, however,
Polanyi the polemicist pushed aside Polanyi the theorist. Though his theory
should have told him that real economies are complex mixtures of economic modes, his distaste for modern markets and his apocalyptic vision of
nineteenth-century societies being utterly and totally dominated, and all but
destroyed, by such markets, led him to draw sharp and unwarranted distinctions between early and modern economies, in which exchange and
markets typified only the latter.

Both Liverani and Bedford review the accumulation of evidence that in
the ancient Near East, this picture, produced by Polanyi and partially en-
dorsed by Finley, cannot be sustained. Liverani shows that trade and craft
work in the Bronze Age were complex activities, and that some parts of
these were controlled by temples and/or palaces, and other parts were more
marketlike. Because of this, partisans of totalizing views can assert their arguments for the exclusive presence of state control or of private property by
carefully selecting evidence that supports their position and dismissing evidence for the other view as minor and inconsequential. In the imperial
period of the first millennium BC discussed by Bedford, it would be implausible to dismiss the significance of centralized redistribution, but his discussion shows that a substantial private economy flourished alongside the
state-run operations. Thus Finley's argument that redistribution is the characteristic model is exaggerated. Indeed, toward the latter part of this period,
privately held land may have become more typical. For Polanyi the theorist,

the simultaneous presence in these societies of redistribution and market exchange should not have been surprising, nor a target for disproof. Indeed, the more subtle parts of Polanyi's argument would lead us to wonder in what way these elements related to one another; Bedford correctly notes that this articulation is of central importance, but not successfully addressed by A. L. Oppenheim, a key student of this period. Here we have a theme of quite general importance in economic history, which Polanyi's framework points us to: How do political and economic structures mesh with and support or undermine one another? Ideologists of all persuasions push us to analyze the economic and the political as separate and unrelated entities, but effective social actors know better than to make this separation. New studies of twentieth-century state socialist economies, such as those of Eastern Europe, make clear, for example, that the redistributive apparatus of "scientific socialism" made selective and strategic use of market exchange to support its overall political enterprise, in part by reducing the rigidities and inequalities that a pure redistributive system imposes—much as predominantly marketized systems introduce elements of redistribution for the same purpose (Szelenyi and Costello 1998).

Our habit of analyzing politics and economics as separate spheres can lead to highly inappropriate conclusions. Partisans of a rational-action view might, for example, view Bedford's findings for the Neo-Babylonian and Achaemenid Persian periods—of a market in privately owned land—as evidence for the ubiquity of instrumentally rational economic actors. But political entrepreneurs benefit from liquidity of resources like land, and have many reasons to support it. Eisenstadt, in his account of the sources of power in centralized bureaucratic empires (1963), noted that would-be rulers, no matter how ambitious or skilled, are stymied in their attempts to extend their domain if land, labor, and other resources are bound up in primordial social units that prevent their alienation. Following in the tradition of Max Weber, who also had as a central concern how political actors could assemble effective administrative structures, Eisenstadt posited the necessity of sufficient social specialization to loosen the hold of kinship units on resources, before rulers could accumulate the rewards they offered to followers.

Thus, temples and palaces may have viewed free markets and exchange as opportunities to extend their domain rather than threats to their hegemony. Rulers who understood these issues best should have encouraged alienability of resources, while simultaneously moving as best they could to accumulate and monopolize them as they came on the market.

To say this is not to make any specific claim about events or patterns in these societies, but rather to suggest that debates about whether politics or rational economic action dominated a society are unproductive. What is really most interesting for any society is to understand how political, economic, and social activities and institutions fit together and produce the great variability of outcomes we see in history. People seek goods and services not merely for consumption, but also to achieve their political, social, and cultural goals. Models and understanding of how people produce goods and services cannot achieve theoretical sophistication if they neglect this fundamental fact of human life.

Part II

The Aegean

Chapter 5

Archaeology, Standards of Living, and Greek Economic History

IAN MORRIS

Greek economic historians work mainly with texts, which were mostly produced and read in contexts that have few close parallels in other parts of the
ancient Mediterranean world. There were certainly similarities between the
literary cultures of Athens and Rome, but the differences often seem even
more striking (compare Ober [1998] and Fantham [1994]). The Near East
and Egypt were too varied for us to make the kind of sweeping generalizations that Finley often favored (see Liverani and Bedford, Chapters 2 and 3,
respectively), but even a casual review of scholarship on cultures of reading
and writing indicates major differences from both Athens and Rome (for
example, Bottéro 1992; Roccati 1997; Berlev 1997). The palaces, temples,
scribal schools, and private trading firms that provided the contexts of production and consumption for much of the extant Near Eastern and Egyptian
textual records are very different from the legal and aristocratic settings so
important for Athenian and Roman literary activity. These contrasts between
literary cultures pose real problems for historians interested in systematic
economic comparisons across regions and through time. Demosthenes'
twists and turns lead us into a demimonde of shifty moneylenders and swin-
dling guardians, with few obvious points of contact with the mountains
of paperwork with which Zenon or the Murashûs buttressed their enterprises (see Manning and Bedford in this volume). Small wonder, then, that
Hellenists have imagined the ancient economy in very different ways than
historians of other parts of the ancient Mediterranean. The fourth-century

91

Athenian orators' carefully wrought literary texts made citizen status a central consideration, and Finley followed them in seeing status as the overriding preoccupation in Athenian life (Finley 1985a: 35–61). In his view this set Greece and Rome apart from Egypt and the Near East, where very different status structures existed. In the 1990s some scholars went further still, relating the Greek texts to a specifically Hellenic "economic imaginary," driven by ideological conflicts peculiar to the archaic and classical poleis (von Reden 1995, 1997a; Carson 1999; Kurke 1999). But if the contexts of production and performance of the literature that survives from Athens were so radically different from those of the surviving texts from Babylon, Memphis, Susa, or (to a lesser extent) Rome, are we justified in assuming that the Athenian economy was structured by unique ideological principles?

The main issue in this book is whether the differences between the accounts that historians now write of economics in different parts of the ancient Mediterranean accurately reflect real differences in antiquity. One way to try to answer this question would be to relate the textual evidence that we actually have to the textual evidence that we do not have: that is, to ask whether the difference between, say, Greek and Babylonian economic texts is more an artifact of differences in literary production, consumption, and preservation than one of differences in the forms of economic activity. After all, unlike the situation in Egypt and the Near East, most Greek and Roman literature survives only because monks and scholars thought it was worth copying. Their criteria for selection determine the shape of our evidence; had some truly eccentric monastic order preferred agricultural accounts to rhetoric—or if the Greek climate had preserved different materials—we might have an Athenian version of the Kellis Account Book (see Bagnall, Chapter 9). An assumption that is rarely made explicit underlies all text-based comparative work on ancient Mediterranean economics: The texts that survive are a sample that more-or-less accurately reflects the larger population of texts that were originally produced, and therefore the extant documents reflect the nature of economic activity in different regions.

I see two ways to test this assumption. One is through arguments from silence: If, for example, the ancient Greeks had had institutions that functioned like the Assyrian palaces or Ptolemaic temples, we would hear about them in the extant sources. If a substantial amount of fourth-century Athenian foreign trade was organized by officials working for the Priestess of Athena, the practice would surely come up somewhere in Demosthenes. It does not, so we can probably argue from silence that there really were huge institutional differences between fourth-century Athens, Babylon, and Egypt. But there are many other questions, such as whether the fourth-century Athenian economy performed better than that of fourth-century Babylon, or did a better job of fairly distributing the fruits of economic activity, for which arguments from silence are much harder to make. This is where a second way of addressing the implied assumption comes in. We need to look for new kinds of data that all the regions under consideration have in common. That means, of course, archaeological evidence.

By archaeological evidence, I mean all artifacts surviving from antiquity. Coins, inscriptions, papyri, and other objects with writing on them fall under this heading, as well as house walls, graves, and broken pottery. Artifacts with writing on them have their own interpretive problems, which have been ably discussed in Routledge's recent series of handbooks (Bagnall 1995; Howgego 1995; van de Mieroop 1999; Bodel 2001). But there are also problems and possibilities that inscribed and illustrated artifacts share with all categories of material remains from antiquity, whether excavated or found on the ground's surface.

I make five arguments:

1. Using archaeological evidence as a source for economic history is considerably more complicated than historians have generally recognized;
2. Despite the difficulties, we can still base economic analysis on archaeological data, although it will have to be analysis of a very different kind either from that advocated by Finley or most of his critics;
3. In the case of first-millennium BC Greece, we will need to construct new kinds of models, focusing on new questions;
4. These new questions are mostly about standards of living and, indirectly, economic growth;
5. These methods and model-building procedures can be transferred from Greece to other parts of the ancient Mediterranean, thereby providing the basis for a much broader, comparative economic history.

The Formation Processes of the Archaeological Record

Archaeologists gather the detritus of ancient life. That means that archaeologists never get direct access to ancient economic activities. They find washeries where Athenians separated silver from rock and lead, amphoras that once contained wine, and wrecks of the ships that transported these commodities from one end of the Mediterranean to the other. But they do not find the actual processes of production, exchange, and consumption. Consequently, archaeological data are always proxy data. In the process of excavating we actually create a static archaeological record that exists in the present. Then we try to figure out what dynamic processes in the past might have produced it. In doing this, we face severe problems of ambiguity and equifinality.

The links between contemporary material and ancient life are the formation processes of the archaeological record. All inference depends on understanding these processes, so, not surprisingly, archaeologists have devoted tremendous energy to theorizing them.[1] But just as nonhistorians rarely understand the technical dimensions of historical source analysis, nonarchaeologists rarely grasp the range of issues involved in formation processes. Elton (1967: 30) made a famous distinction between professional and amateur historians, saying that "the hallmark of the amateur is . . . a readiness to see the exceptional in the commonplace, and to find the unusual ordinary." The professional, steeped in the sources and the methods developed by generations of other professionals, "knows the 'right' questions—those capable of being answered and those that lead to further questions" (1967: 32). In archaeology, formation processes occupy much the same place that source criticism does for the text-based historian. Here we reach the heart of the professional/amateur distinction: Most ancient historians have approached archaeology in a spirit of high amateurism.

To some extent, analysis of formation processes is a matter of common sense; but it is a *refined* common sense, and historians who fail to take advantage of professional archaeologists' refinements are likely to misinterpret the evidence seriously. For example, it should be obvious that the people who lived in the past did not leave behind on their sites examples of everything that they used. If we forget this, and assume that we are digging up a constant cross section of past material culture, we will go awry. Prehistorians (for example, Binford 1981a; Schiffer 1985) usually call this fallacy the "Pompeii premise" (even though Penelope Allison [1997] shows that it is as misleading at Pompeii as anywhere else). But how are we to move from the remains that we do recover to the activities of people in the past? Archaeologists sometimes like to say that their craft is like assembling a jigsaw puzzle without the benefit of a picture on the box lid and with 99 percent of the pieces missing. To make it worse, we do not know in advance whether the loss of pieces is caused by random or systematic distortion—that is, whether the loss of evidence is the equivalent of most of the pieces of the puzzle falling down the back of the couch or of someone carefully removing every piece with the color red on it. The answers to these questions set the limits for what we can infer from the material record.

Most archaeologists find it useful to break formation processes down into two types, depositional and postdepositional. Michael Schiffer (1976) speaks instead of *C-transforms*, meaning cultural processes that cause people to use some objects in ways that make them enter the archaeological record while using others in ways that mean that they probably will not survive; and *N-transforms*, or natural processes that alter the material record between the time of its original deposition and its recovery by modern scholars. As Binford (1981a) insisted, Schiffer's assumption that the archaeological record is fundamentally a distortion of some preexisting neutral state is illogical. Further, some of the most important postdepositional processes are just as much C-transforms as the activities that originally produced deposits. Particularly when dealing with classical antiquities, this is a decisive advantage for the depositional/postdepositional classification, although its disadvantage is that the distinction between these processes sometimes has to be more arbitrary than that between Schiffer's C- and N-transforms.

POSTDEPOSITIONAL PROCESSES

I begin with postdepositional processes because the problems that they pose are often more obvious and commonsensical than some of those raised by depositional factors. Objects and traces of ancient activities survive in two main ways: by remaining in use (for example, a building like Hadrian's Pantheon in Rome) or through burial (usually under the earth, but also under the sea). The boundary between these processes is permeable, of course. An object may be buried, then returned to circulation through either natural processes or human activity. Some objects have very complex histories: they may get buried (say, as a cadaver), then be returned to circulation (as holy relics), then get discarded again (in the destruction of a monastery by Vikings), then return to the world of the living again (as museum exhibits). But most of the time, the basic categories of burial and continuous use remain useful.

Burial can be deliberate or accidental. Once an object or context of activity has been discarded, abandoned, or deliberately buried, it may survive more or less unchanged until an archaeologist unearths it, or—as virtually always happens—its situation may be significantly altered by postdepositional forces. Erosion may destroy entire sites or new construction may disperse the original depositional context, effectively destroying the ancient object. The rapid expansion of Greek cities and holiday resorts since the 1960s has devastated the archaeological record in some areas while leaving others virtually untouched. Even without human intervention, certain soil conditions may destroy all traces of pottery or iron; in Greece, wood, papyrus, cloth, and other organic materials hardly ever survive. On the other hand, geological events like the deposition of "Younger Fill" soils in some parts of Greece in late Roman times may bury the ancient landscape so deeply that archaeologists rarely reach it (see Sbonias [1999] for a general discussion). Alternatively, artifacts that lie exposed on the surface may gradually disintegrate, with the result that more recent periods of the past are better represented than more distant ones (Bintliff et al. 1999).

After a century of collaboration with geophysicists and geomorphologists, archaeologists understand well the stratigraphic processes that have buried artifacts (E. Harris et al. 1993), and Mediterraneanists have made particular contributions to the study of how once-buried objects return to the surface (Francovich and Patterson 2000). Scientific advances allowing us to examine subsurface remains without destructive excavation have been widely applied in the Mediterranean (Pasquinucci and Trément 2000). Serious attention to soil science is more common on surface surveys than on excavations, but the tools are available, and attention to micromorphology and systematic sampling can clarify our understanding of the physical processes that have intervened between deposition and recovery (Courty et al. 1989; Orton 2000).

The processes of recovery are themselves part of the postdepositional transformation of the archaeological record. Recovery is incomplete; we know that we have not excavated every archaeological deposit in Greece, and that we have not published every deposit that has been excavated. For many purposes, this does not matter. But for economic historians who want to quantify their data, it can matter a great deal. For example, several million Greek pots have been found. But if we ask how pottery production worked, we often need to know what proportion of the pots originally made have been found so that we can extrapolate to the original output. For one category, the prize amphoras given out at the Panathenaic games every four years, we have rough estimates of the original numbers and thus can calculate a recovery rate. In a classic paper, Robert Cook (1959) argued for a recovery rate of 0.2 percent, which he applied to Athenian ceramic production generally. He concluded that pottery production employed so few people that it was basically a household craft, not an "industry" in any meaningful sense of the term (Arafat and Morgan 1989). But problems abound, even when we have such a well-known category of finds as the amphoras. Using a slightly different sample, T. B. L. Webster (1972: 3) calculated a 0.3 percent recovery rate; M. Bentz (1998: 17–18) puts it as high as 1 percent. Further, archaeologists do not agree on how to relate the Panathenaic amphoras to other categories of pots. Webster (1972: 4, 6) argued that probably about 1 percent of all Greek pottery had been found as of the time of his writing; Ingeborg Scheibler (1983: 9) estimated 3 percent, and M. Eisman (1974: 52) no less than 10 percent. Vladimir Stissi (1999: 405 n. 4), on the other hand, taking a more rigorous approach to quantification, concludes that even the 1 percent recovery rate "is far too high, especially for less finely decorated pots." These arguments have enormous implications for our understanding of ancient industry.

Stissi (1999) draws attention to a second major problem for quantification: the attitudes and ideologies of the archaeologists themselves. Alluviation, erosion, and natural decay are not the only filters between archaeologists and ancient behavior. At the most general level, the belief that classical archaeology should aim to illuminate a particular Greco-Roman ethos, which stands at the origins of European culture (see I. Morris 2004), means that many classical archaeologists see little to gain from careful quantification, or even saving sherds of plain pottery. Further, there are important differences among national traditions in the archaeology of Greece, which must be factored in to any study combining evidence from different research teams. European prehistorians have given much thought to such differences (Hodder 1991), but classical archaeologists have neglected this topic. Detailed histories of particular projects (for example, Fotiadis 1995) or of the guiding assumptions behind fieldwork in a particular period (I. Morris 2000: 77–106) can also help us control for variations in data collection and quality.

A final factor is the cultural history of the long time span between deposition and the beginning of professional archaeology in the late nineteenth century (Schnapp 1996). The Pantheon is still standing because in 609 Pope Boniface IV consecrated it as a church. If such activities had occurred more often, the archaeological record would be very different. Postdepositional cultural history is as important as natural processes in deciding what survives. It means that different kinds of objects have different chances of being preserved in constant use or through burial. Bronze, gold, and silver can easily be melted down and turned into new objects; they are inherently less likely to enter the archaeological record than pottery. Once broken, pottery is practically worthless and is hard to destroy completely. We can safely assume that a far higher proportion of ancient Greek pottery survives than of ancient Greek gold work—but how much higher?

We might draw three main conclusions about the role of postdepositional factors in the formation of the archaeological record. First, we know far more about some categories of evidence than others; second, the distribution of our evidence in time and space may not reflect the ancient activities that we are most interested in; and third, arguments from silence are even more problematic when we are dealing with artifacts than when we are dealing with texts.

Arguments from silence and quantitative claims based on inadequately controlled samples bedevil economic archaeology. Finding Athenian pottery in an Iron Age village in Sicily definitely tells us that such pottery reached this site. But unless the sample is large, drawn from different activity areas within the site, and accurately quantified, it will reveal little more than this. And unless all these conditions are met, the absence of Athenian pottery from the site will indicate nothing at all. An abundance of Athenian pottery in one location may indicate the house of a trader, or an émigré Athenian, or a collector; or it may mean that Athenian wares were particularly popular at this site. Unless we can quantify the entire range of our evidence and test theories against a null hypothesis, we simply cannot say. The normalization problem can only be addressed through massive statistical syntheses and more systematic attention to sampling (Orton 2000). Otherwise, attempts to interpret pottery (or other artifacts) as evidence for trade are highly vulnerable. For example, in a well-known article, Colin Renfrew (1975) proposed a series of models correlating the fall-off in frequency of finds of a given provenance as distance from the source increases with different exchange mechanisms. But in practice, archaeologists have not been able to control both depositional and postdepositional factors across a wide range of sites and to specify the level of background noise with sufficient accuracy to use such quantitative tools. As Ian Hodder and Clive Orton (1976) put it, archaeological formation processes are often equifinal: Radically different activities in the past can produce much the same archaeological record in the present.

Generally, the fuller the data, the less susceptible they are to postdepositional processes. One of classical archaeology's greatest strengths is the sheer quantity of evidence available (Snodgrass 1987: 14–35; Stissi 1999: fig. 156), although this benefit is partly canceled out by biases in collection strategies. Greek archaeologists have often used painted pottery to make claims about the history of trade, but insofar as these are quantitative claims, they are generally undermined by failure to think hard enough about postdepositional processes (see Snodgrass 1980: 126–29). The constraints of paper publication mean that even with the best will in the world, archaeologists cannot include everything they recover in their catalogues of finds. A few archaeologists understand the need for quantifiable data sufficiently well that they explain the relationship between the excavated record and the published record, and the criteria by which they decide which parts of the former end up in the latter; but most do not. The result is that the data are systematically skewed, but in unpredictable ways. Nor is it even possible in all cases to go back to the primary data, the finds themselves. Many archaeologists in

Greece discard all pottery but the "diagnostic" sherds (rims, handles, bases, decorated fragments, and other pieces that can be dated), often keeping no records of the undiagnostic finds. Human bones are routinely thrown away, and few digs systematically collect animal bones or pollen samples. The situation has improved in the last twenty years, but the postdepositional distortion of much of the record is still large and unpredictable.

DEPOSITIONAL PROCESSES

Archaeologists know a great deal about postdepositional processes. But even in a situation with the best imaginable preservation and the most up-to-date recovery techniques, and controlling for as many postdepositional factors as humanly possible, archaeologists still face problems in moving from a static, contemporary material record to the dynamics of past behavior (Binford 1983). In the 1960s, the self-styled "New" or "processual" archaeologists (so-called because they felt that they studied universal behavioral processes, as opposed to the particularistic details that 1950s culture historians had worked on) began taking this problem very seriously. They tried using ethnoarchaeology (the study of the material culture of contemporary populations) to build up "middle-range theory," linking the material fragments that archaeologists recovered with the activities that would have produced them. This important work put the study of archaeological formation processes on a firmer and more systematic footing.

But critics in the 1980s (Hodder 1982a, 1982b) pointed out that the New Archaeologists approached deposition as if all people in all places thought and behaved in the same ways, effacing the role of culture. In searching for cross-culturally valid laws of the behavior behind the archaeological record, New Archaeologists were simply ignoring human agency, at the very moment when cultural anthropologists were focusing more and more on meaning, culture, and representation (for example, Geertz 1973; Bourdieu 1977 [1972]). For Lewis Binford (1981b), ethnoarchaeology was the royal road to middle-range theory; for Ian Hodder (1982a), it was a way to reveal the complexity and cultural specificity of the ways people use material culture.

The critics of the New Archaeology, who called themselves "postprocessualists," shared in the widespread anthropological turn toward linguistic and constructivist theories of meaning (Hodder 1986). Claude Lévi-Strauss (1949) had drawn on structural linguistics to interpret kinship as a communication system, and French theorists went on to demonstrate that material culture also functioned as a kind of language (Baudrillard 1981 [1972]; Bourdieu 1984 [1979]). The postprocessualists agreed with the New Archaeologists that understanding postdepositional factors does not give us direct access to the past. But the postprocessualists went further, arguing that understanding deposition is not a matter of formulating a general middle-range theory but of reaching historical understandings of particular cultures. Material culture is a text (Shanks and Tilley 1987a, 1987b; Tilley 1990, 1991), just as heavily implicated in language games as is verbal culture (Lyotard 1984). The material text is there to be read and interpreted, not explained through reduction to underlying principles (Tilley 1993). Where New Archaeologists had looked to the natural sciences for models, post-processualists turned first toward history and later toward literary theory. Metaphor, experience, and performance seemed like more useful analytical categories than causation (Shanks 1992; Tilley 1993, 1994, 1999; Hodder et al. 1995; Hodder 2001; Pearson and Shanks 2001).

Hodder (1986: 3) suggests that "in archaeology *all* inference is via material culture. If material culture, all of it, has a symbolic dimension such that the relationship between people and things is affected, then *all* of archaeology, economic and social, is implicated." That is, we do not simply add post-processual archaeology to New Archaeology to get a fuller picture. Rather, it undermines the central assumption of the New Archaeology, that a general middle-range theory will allow us to interpret depositional processes.

The more complex the societies we deal with, the more obvious the post-processualists' point seems. For example, no gold cups have been found in archaeological deposits in classical Athens, even though we know from examples excavated in Bulgaria that classical Athenian workshops were making such cups (Filow 1934; Vickers and Gill 1994). Further, classical texts mention gold cups, and make clear—as the postprocessualists insist—that the meanings of such cups were contingent, context-dependent, and negotiable. Thucydides (6.32) tells how patriotic Athenians poured libations from gold cups in 415 BC as the fleet sailed for Sicily. Demosthenes (22.75) also mentions gold cups, but only to imply that any man who took pride in owning gold cups lacked the qualities of a true citizen. To say that Meidias went around positively bragging about his gold cups was to hint that he harbored antisocial hubris, posing a threat to democratic society (Demosthenes 21.133, 158). And when pseudo-Andocides (4.29) told a jury that Alcibiades not only bragged about having such cups but even pretended that cups belonging to a state embassy were in fact his own, he represented him as living beyond the pale of civilized society.

Given this cultural milieu, it is hardly surprising that we find no gold cups in the three thousand or so graves known from fifth- and fourth-century Athens. Athenian expectations about the use of material culture were complex and restrictive. It seems that there was no single meaning to a gold cup.

Depending on who used it, and how, and who was interpreting that use, it could demonstrate a person's piety or hubris. By focusing on the active role of culture and the importance of beliefs, postprocessual archaeology in a sense requires us to know what was going on in people's heads before we can draw conclusions from the material record. This largely accounts for the common criticism that it is an "anything goes" method. Archaeologists weave different stories about prehistoric values from their meager materials, then use these stories to interpret the data to fit with their initial assumptions. This is not a problem if we start from the poststructuralist position going back to Hayden White's classic *Metahistory* (1973) that there are no grounds other than political or aesthetic ones for choosing between competing historical accounts. It is no longer unusual to find archaeologists, including those interested in Greece, arguing that the only way to judge an archaeological interpretation is by its political implications (for example, Hamilakis 1999). But if we accept Douglass North's proposition (quoted in Chapter 1) that in economic history, "'explanation' means explicit theorizing and the potential of refutability," then postprocessual archaeology poses a serious challenge to economic archaeology.

I have argued elsewhere (I. Morris 2000: 3–17) that it is possible to take poststructuralist arguments seriously yet still evaluate interpretations, regardless of their political implications, by using the standard historical methods of contrasting different kinds of sources and varying the geographical or temporal scale of analysis. If we find that texts (whether literary or material) seem to tell the same story, even though they were generated out of entirely different language games, or that very similar patterns recur in otherwise very different cultural zones, we know we are onto something deeper than the linguistic and nonlinguistic structures within which historical actors constructed and contested meaning. Close analysis of the evidence is likely to tell us a great deal about the peculiarities of each community and struggles over meaning within them; but that does not mean that readings that move past form to content are necessarily false. There will always be problems with moving from a discursively constituted material record to nondiscursive economic phenomena, but the problems are of well-known types, and historians and archaeologists have methods for dealing with them. On some occasions the complexities of discursive conflicts may indeed rule out such attempts to go beyond form, but that needs to be demonstrated empirically, not simply asserted.

Classical Greek archaeologists have three tremendous advantages over prehistorians. First, as noted above, their evidence is extremely rich and varied; second, its absolute chronology is fixed unusually well; and third, it includes written sources. This density and variety of data points constrains interpretation far more than in the study of the European Neolithic, where much of the most imaginative postprocessual work has been done (Hodder 1990; Tilley 1996; Thomas 1996, 1999; Bradley 1997, 1998). It seems to me that archaeology is, in the first instance, always a form of cultural history. As the postprocessualists insist, all inference is via material culture, and all material culture and depositional practice is implicated in representational strategies. We must always begin analysis by trying to understand these strategies. But where the data are dense enough and varied enough, we can narrow the range of plausible interpretations to the point that we can move beyond the realm of discourse to prediscursive economic phenomena (I. Morris 2000). Few postprocessual archaeologists explicitly deny this, but their near-total focus on the construction and contestation of meaning, at the expense of ecology, demography, and economics, suggests that economic history in the sense defined in Chapter 1 (Morris and Manning) has been stricken from most postprocessual research agendas.

Archaeology and Greek Economic History

Most Greek economic historians have not known enough about archaeological theory and method to grasp the significance of the formation processes of the material record. They have tended either to underestimate or overestimate the problems involved. The best example of the former is still Mikhail Rostovtzeff's magnificent *Social and Economic History of the Hellenistic World* (1941). Classicists regularly hold this work up as a model for the integration of objects and texts. Rostovtzeff knew what was involved in field archaeology, having been involved with large-scale excavations at Dura Europus in Syria, and he filled his three-volume study with references to and illustrations of artifacts. But the reader will search in vain for any systematic analysis of archaeological sources and formation processes, statistical summaries of artifact distributions, or even close arguments over the interpretation of specific finds. Rostovtzeff made the bold claim—one well established among Greek historians since the 1890s, though Rostovtzeff gave it its strongest form—that from the age of Alexander onward, the east Mediterranean world was a realm of interlocked markets (see particularly Rostovtzeff's 1935/36 summary essay; and Reger's detailed response [1994]). Rostovtzeff produced careful textual editions of Egyptian papyri and was sometimes explicit about how he deduced economic patterns from estate accounts (Manning, Chapter 8); but he did not apply the same high analytical standards to the evidence of things as to that of words. His use of

material culture was a classic example of what I have called the ⌐"bits-and-
pieces" approach to using archaeological data as historical sources (I. Morris
1992: 1–2, 200–204). Eschewing systematic quantification and analysis of
formation processes, he selected data that he thought were either exception-
ally interesting or wholly typical and used them to illustrate a story founded
on the texts.

The second tendency is best illustrated by Moses Finley's use of archaeology. In principle, Finley strongly advocated archaeological history, arguing that

> it is false to speak of the relationship between history and archaeology.
> At issue are not two qualitatively different disciplines but two kinds of
> evidence about the past, two kinds of historical evidence. There can
> thus be no question of the priority in general or of the superiority of
> one type of evidence over the other; it all depends in each case on the
> evidence available and the particular questions to be answered. (Finley
> 1985b: 20)

His main programmatic essay on archaeology (1975: 87–101) raised some
of the same issues that I outlined above, but in practice, he virtually ignored
archaeological data. Noting the complexity of the arrangements for pottery
production described in a third-century AD papyrus from Oxyrhynchus, he
very sensibly concluded that "archaeological evidence or archaeological
analysis *by itself* cannot possibly uncover the legal or economic structure revealed by the Oxyrhynchus papyri or the alternative structures in Arezzo,
Puteoli, Lezoux or North Africa" (1985b: 25). Few archaeologists would
dispute this. But whereas archaeologists would then presumably ask how we
might combine excavated kiln sites with the texts, or what questions the archaeological remains *could* answer, Finley simply dropped the subject. Similarly, he was much impressed by Mortimer Wheeler's cautionary tale about
how reports of Roman sherds found in Gotland grew in archaeologists'
minds into significant Roman trade with Sweden. In fact, all thirty-nine
fragments came from a single pot (Finley 1985a: 33). An archaeologist might
conclude from this that distribution maps rarely tell the whole story, and
that we need more detailed work on the precise types, quantities, and contexts of Roman artifacts in the Baltic. Michael Dietler (1995, 1997) has done
just this, undermining world-systems models of archaic colonial encounters
in southern France. Finley, however, seems to have taken Wheeler's tale as
a demonstration of the limitations of archaeological data. His longest discussion of Roman pottery (1985b: 23–24) emphasizes how little it tells the
historian, even though the 1980s saw spectacular advances in economic

interpretations of amphora data (Tchernia 1986; *Amphores romaines* 1989; Laubenheimer 1992).

 Finley was reacting against the excesses of earlier generations of economic historians, for whom archaeology was often just grist for the mill of crudely modernist speculation. But by avoiding this whole class of data he did just as much damage to ancient economic history. While archaeological formation processes raise more serious issues than most economic historians seem to realize, this is not a counsel of despair. It just means that we must think very carefully about how we use the data. The archaeological data have the potential to transform radically the questions we ask about Greek economic history and our ability to answer them. Like many Roman archaeologists (see Hitchner, Chapter 10), I suggest that had Finley taken the material record more seriously, he might have developed a different model in *The Ancient Economy*. If we combine archaeological and textual data, we may be able to compare the different regions in the ancient Mediterranean far more rigorously and systematically than when using texts alone.

Archaeology and Standards of Living

But how do we do all this? Only, I suggest, by shifting the focus of our inquiries. Using the archaeological data appropriately calls for theoretical as well as empirical reformulations. In our introduction (Chapter 1), J. G. Manning and I quoted Douglass North's brief definition of the task of economic history: "To explain the structure and performance of economies through time." Finley concentrated almost exclusively on structure at the expense of performance. Economic historians of most other periods have emphasized economic growth (either in the sense of increasing total output or increasing per capita output; see Saller, Chapter 11) as the central issue. Finley was very clear that growth was not a useful concept in Greek economic history, and Paul Millett has recently claimed that "scope for sustained growth in the centuries BC was elusive or non-existent" (2001: 35).

I see three likely reasons for Finley's position (and Millett's elaboration of it): first, a reaction against the excesses and sloppy scholarship of the modernist historians of the 1890s–1950s; second, the nature of the literary sources, which prevented discussion of economic growth in any serious way; and third, his political position within a tradition going back to Polanyi and the Frankfurt School's critiques of Marxism. Given these factors, Finley's arguments make a great deal of sense and were certainly more consistent with the textual data than their precursors, even if this came at the cost of giving up even the fragments of archaeological data that Rostovtzeff had pursued. What makes far less sense is the failure of those many classical historians who have rejected Finley's claims out of hand either to pursue the economic theory and methods that they implicitly claimed were superior to Finley's substantivism, or to seek out new forms of evidence that would allow them to refute him.

We can perhaps explain why Finley and the substantivists spent so little time on economic growth; but why do economic historians of nonancient periods spend so much time on it? In the most widely read economics text of the twentieth century, Paul Samuelson and William Nordhaus spelled out the answer, under the upbeat heading "Cool Heads at the Service of Warm Hearts":

> You might well ask, What is the purpose of this army of economists measuring, analyzing, and calculating? The ultimate goal of economic science is to improve the living conditions of people in their everyday lives. Increasing the gross domestic product is not just a numbers game. Higher incomes mean good food, warm houses, and hot water. They mean safe drinking water and inoculations against the perennial plagues of humanity. . . . Although there is no single pattern of economic development, and the evolution of culture will differ around the world, freedom from hunger, disease, and the elements is a universal aspiration. (Samuelson and Nordhaus 1998: 7)

The history of economic growth explains differing standards of living in the past; and if we can explain why standards of living differed in the past, we may be in a better position to create institutions that foster continuing improvements in the future. As the economist Dan Usher asks, "Why, after all, would we want to measure economic growth, why is public policy directed to the promotion of economic growth, if we are not better off after economic growth than we were before?" (Usher 1980: 2).

No direct data for economic growth survive from antiquity, and Finley was probably right to argue (1985a: 23–26) that no such data were collected in the first place. However, direct data for standards of living *do* exist, if we examine the archaeological record against the textual record in appropriate ways. We might take our lead from the ways in which historians of the Industrial Revolution have worked.

For fifty years historians and economists have argued fiercely over whether English workers' living standards rose or fell between 1780 and 1850. This debate often came to stand in for the larger question of whether capitalism as a whole was a good or a bad thing (Taylor 1975; Cannadine 1984), and—hardly surprisingly in light of the high stakes—the protagonists developed rigorous methods and penetrating polemics. The standard of living, or "the material side of happiness," as Peter Lindert puts it (1994: 359), can mean many things. Some historians focus on real income, calculated by estimating the output of the country's agricultural, manufacturing, and service sectors and then comparing these figures with changing prices of consumption goods. Others put more faith in real wages, comparing evidence for the changing incomes of specific groups of workers with weighted price indices for bundles of consumption goods. Ferocious debates can develop over the weighting of different commodities: In the case of the English Industrial Revolution, slight changes in the importance attached to clothing prices can completely alter our perception of whether workers' material lives were getting better or worse (Lindert and Williamson 1983, 1985; Crafts 1985; Mokyr 1987; Feinstein 1998; R. C. Allen 2001). Concerned by the fragility of these measures, some historians have turned to direct measurements of diet, mortality rates, and morbidity (that is, patterns of health and sickness), while others have looked to evidence for age-specific heights as proxy data for all of these factors. Housing has attracted much attention, as have pollution and the amount of time people spent working. The variety of ways of looking at standards of living creates its own problems. If, for example, we think of the increasing life expectancy of nineteenth-century British workers as something exogenous to the workers' own households, created by government regulations, we should use it as a multiplier in calculating living standards on the basis of the real wage. By some estimates, this would mean that economic growth was as much as 25 percent higher than is normally thought. On the other hand, if workers effectively purchased longer lives by spending more of their income on nutritious food, fuel, or medical care by cutting consumption or saving somewhere else, it would be a mistake to use longevity as a multiplier (Williamson 1984). Roderick Floud, K. Wachter, and A. Gregory conclude that "each way [of estimating standards of living]—mortality, morbidity, diet or housing conditions—presents only a partial view of reality, while attempts at combining them give rise to the problems of double counting" (Floud et al. 1990: 286).

But for all the difficulties of the exercise,[2] a consensus has emerged that after stagnating between 1750 and 1820, English workers' living standards did increase significantly in the later nineteenth century (Feinstein 1998; Voth 2001). There is even some agreement on how to evaluate workers' perceptions of a declining quality of life relative to this material improvement (Lindert 1994: 375–78). Most important of all for the ancient historian, archaeologists are at much less of a disadvantage relative to modernists than they are in most areas of economic history. The indices that received most attention in the 1990s—stature, nutrition, mortality, morbidity, and housing (see Floud et al. 1990; Komlos 1996; Steckel and Floud 1997; Steckel 1999; Haines and Steckel 2000)—are archaeologically observable. There is some evidence that age-specific stature and the real wage moved together in early modern Europe (Floud 1994; Steckel 1995).

A few economic historians have recognized the huge potential of excavated skeletons for charting very long-term trends on standards of living (for example, Steckel and Rose 2002), but in practice, of course, the archaeological data present even more problems than modern textual ones. All the depositional and postdepositional factors described above apply. And the most severe difficulty is of our own making: Classical archaeologists rarely submit human bones, with all their potential as evidence for stature, mortality rates, and morbidity, to systematic analysis; and they rarely collect floral, faunal, and pollen remains at all, even though these are the most important information for food preparation and consumption.

In the final part of this chapter, I focus on the one category of evidence that is relatively abundant and well documented: housing conditions. This index of the standard of living points to substantial gains all around Greece in the half-millennium between 800 and 300 BC—so substantial, in fact, that they cannot be reconciled with the Finleyan model of essentially static economic performance. The gains are also hard to reconcile with the common assumption that prior to about AD 1750, improvements in productivity always triggered Malthusian cycles in which population expanded to outrun resources. Some economic historians even use preindustrial population sizes as a direct measure of economic output (De Long and Shleifer 1993). Recent work on early modern China—Malthus's classic case of the "positive check" of starvation and disease—has shown that its demographic history was much more like that of Western Europe than Malthus had realized (Lee and Wang 1999). Walter Scheidel has also revealed unsuspected complexities in Roman demography (Scheidel 2001a, 2001b, 2001c). I suggest that ancient Greece also defied simple expectations. In the language of economists, we might say that the Greeks not only widened capital to keep pace with population growth but also deepened it. An archaeological history of living standards has the potential not only to allow more systematic comparisons between different regions of the ancient Mediterranean than is possible with a purely textual approach but also to make a contribution to debates among economists on the conditions of economic growth.

Figure 5.1 shows the trend in median house sizes between 800 and 300 BC, based on a database of more than three hundred examples.[3] This

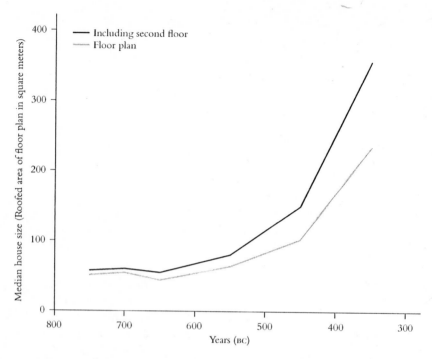

Figure 5.1.   Median house sizes in the Aegean, 800 to 300 BC

catalogue is not complete, and a more thorough collection may require revision of the values shown in the provisional estimate in Figure 5.1, but the
graph is unlikely to need serious changes.

The curves shown in Figure 5.1 require some explanation. First, the
lower line is based on the floor plans of the fully or almost fully excavated
houses. I have counted only those parts of the house that were probably
roofed. Counting the entire floor plans would increase the median sizes for
the sixth-, fifth-, and fourth-century houses by between 15 and 30 percent
but would have less impact on the seventh-century houses, when courtyards
were less common, and very little impact on eighth-century houses, when
courtyards were rare. Finally, I use the median rather than the mean size because the fourth-century mean is skewed by a few massive houses, such as
House IV at Eretria (1,950 square meters) and the House of Dionysus (3,183
square meters) and the House of the Rape of Helen (1,700 square meters) at
Pella (see Fig. 5.2). These houses stand at the beginning of the tradition of
Hellenistic palaces (Kiderlen 1995; Hoepfner and Brands 1996: 2–6). The
mean value for the cluster of houses dated around 700 BC is also significantly

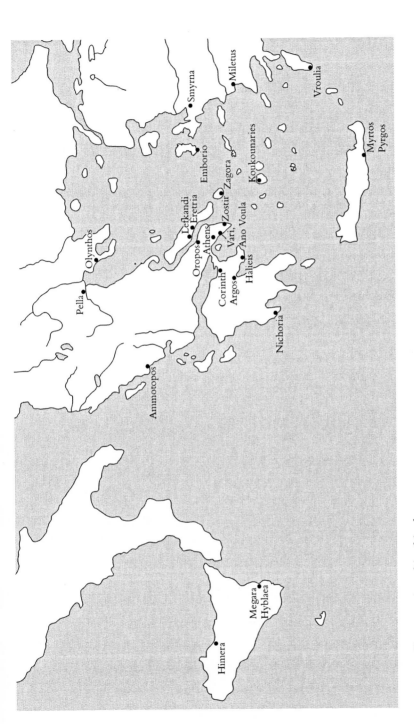

Figure 5.2. Sites mentioned in this chapter

TABLE 5.1
Mean and median house sizes, 800-300 BC, in m²

Period	Mean	Median
800–700	53	51
c. 700	69	56
700–600	53	45
600–500	92	67
500–400	122	106
400–300	325	240

higher (23 percent) than the median, because of the "Great House" (H 19/22/23/28/29; 256 square meters) at Zagora on Andros.[4] Table 5.1 shows the differences between the mean and median values.

Focusing on median values and the probable roofed area of the floor plan minimizes the differences between the eighth- and fourth-century houses, but there is still a very strong upward trend. The floor plan of the typical fifth-century house included more than twice as much roofed space as that of its eighth-century predecessor; that of the typical fourth-century house, nearly five times as much.

House Sizes: Postdepositional Problems

The whole range of depositional and postdepositional factors discussed above bear on these simple calculations. I discuss five particularly serious ones in this section.

First is the obvious problems of preservation. We know from literary sources (Lysias 1.9–10) and vase paintings that some houses had two floors, and on occasion parts of staircases have been found. The bottom line in Figure 5.1 accurately represents the state of our archaeological knowledge but not the realities of life in ancient Greece. But we are able to control for the distortion created by the disappearance of upper floors. The most extreme counterargument against the trend represented by the bottom line in Figure 5.1 would be to assume that all eighth- and seventh-century houses had second floors, as did many (let us say 50 percent) sixth-century houses, but no fifth- or fourth-century examples. But this was obviously not the case. The foundations of the Great House at Zagora and the peculiar apsidal room L (following the lettering system in Mazarakis Ainian's plan [1997: fig. 321]) at Koukounaries, both dating around 700, could have supported an upper floor, and there is some actual evidence for such a floor in the seventh-century Double Megaron at Smyrna. But very few of the flimsy eighth- and

TABLE 5.2

Estimated percentage of houses with second floors, 800–300 BC. Column (a) makes realistic assumptions, based on surviving data; column (b) makes assumptions that weaken the pattern visible in Table 5.1 and Fig. 5.1 as much as possible

Period	a	b
800–700	10	100
c. 700	10	100
700–600	25	100
600–500	25	50
500–400	50	25
400–300	50	0

even seventh-century foundations could have carried this much weight. Nearly all of our direct evidence comes from the fifth and especially the fourth century. At Ammotopos in Epirus, much of the second floor of fourth-century House I is actually preserved (Hoepfner and Schwandner 1994: 147–50). But even making this patently false assumption that all eighth- and seventh-century houses had second floors, and no fifth- and fourth-century houses did, would mean that instead of doubling between the eighth century and the fifth, house sizes stayed more or less the same; then after 400 BC they suddenly increased by a factor of 2.4. This assumption would discount any growth until the end of the Peloponnesian War, creating even more striking expansion thereafter. This would be the extreme case of biasing the data against the hypothesis. If instead of these implausible assumptions we make any reasonable estimate of the frequency of second floors, the rate of increase in house size between the eighth and the fourth century will only increase. The upper line in Figure 5.1 represents changes in the median house size if we assume that 10 percent of the eighth-century houses had second floors, 25 percent of those of the seventh and sixth centuries, and 50 percent in the fifth and fourth centuries (Table 5.2). While these guesses no doubt miss the mark, the upward curve in Figure 5.1 is probably as accurate an estimate of changes in house size as we can get.

A second problem is how we decide which rooms belong to which house. Most eighth-century structures are single-roomed, but Mazarakis Ainian (forthcoming) argues convincingly that at Oropos, Eretria, and Lefkandi, two or more small oval or apsidal structures would typically be grouped together in family compounds. This, he suggests, was an intermediate stage between single-roomed Dark Age houses and multiroom archaic and classical courtyard houses. It may be a typically Euboean pattern, with freestanding single-room structures preferred in other parts of Greece. But after 700, interpreting the boundaries of multiroom rectilinear houses is increasingly an issue. At some classical sites, like Himera and Olynthos, the dividing walls are fairly obvious, but some earlier cases, such as Zagora and particularly Vroulia, are less clear. My own suggestions for Vroulia (I. Morris 1992: 193–96) differ somewhat from Franziska Lang's (1996: 101 and fig. 65), though not enough to have a measurable impact on the seventh-century median figure. Overall, ambiguities about classification are not a major concern.

Third, the developmental cycle of the household raises a related problem. As Tom Gallant (1991: 11–33) has illustrated with a series of computer simulations, the size of any particular Greek family would have changed through time. When a family gets bigger, it may try to expand its house at the expense of a neighbor, if houses abut one another. When the family shrinks, it may sell off or rent parts of its house. Using a combination of house remains and texts, Elizabeth Stone (1987) has traced this process in a group of houses at Nippur in Iraq between 1742 and 1734 BC, and although no Greek site provides such detailed evidence, we must take this process into consideration. Overall, though, it does not seem to pose serious problems for interpreting long-term trends in house sizes. Where it is possible to trace the gradual expansion of houses, as at Zagora, Megara Hyblaea, and Himera, I have distinguished the different phases. On the whole, these phases all fall within the century-long chronological divisions I use. Where the standards of excavation or the quality of the report prevent such detailed analysis, I have concentrated on the houses' final plans (as at Vroulia: I. Morris 1992: 197–98).

Fourth, there may be problems of differential preservation from one period to another. For example, many Cycladic villages were abandoned in the seventh century. At Zagora, the final phase is quite well preserved, but virtually nothing survives of the early-eighth-century houses except scatters of pottery. At sites like Athens or Eretria, which remained in use for long periods, the tendency for fourth-century and Hellenistic houses to be larger and sturdier than earlier buildings means that sixth- and fifth-century houses suffer a disproportionate rate of disturbance. However, while these factors affect the relative numbers of houses surviving from each phase, they should not distort the typical size of the surviving houses.

Finally, the distribution of excavations may distort the pattern. If, for example, all the excavated eighth-century houses came from small village sites, and all the excavated classical houses from wealthy centers like Athens, Corinth, and Argos, the evidence would probably exaggerate the median size of classical houses relative to that of Late Geometric houses. However,

that does not seem to be the case. In the eighth century, Smyrna and
Eretria—surely two of Greece's major towns—are as prominent in the excavated record as Zagora; and in any case, the Zagora houses are among the
largest examples known. There may be more of a problem in the seventh
century, when Vroulia, Emborio, and Megara Hyblaea dominate the record,
although Miletus and Smyrna are also prominent. The sixth-century sample
is small, and no one site dominates, but in the fifth century Himera and (to
a lesser extent) Athens are prominent. However, the range of house sizes does
not vary strongly. In the fourth century, the relatively wealthy city of Olynthos dominates the record, although more and more houses are now coming
from Ano Voula and Stylida, and as in the fifth century, the typical house sizes
seem consistent from one site to another. In his recent attempt to document
the housing of the poor in classical Greece, Brad Ault (forthcoming a) was
able to find very few examples of small, squalid houses. The vagaries of excavation inevitably distort the record, but there is no obvious reason to think
that they have created a spurious pattern in Figure 5.1 and Table 5.1.

House Sizes: Depositional Problems

As always, matters become more complex when we move from postdepositional factors back to depositional ones. Decisions about the form and structure of houses are always ideological as well as economic. Home is where
the heart is, and few things are dearer to people than their houses. In a classic essay, Pierre Bourdieu (1990 [1970]: 271–83) showed how the normative house type of the Algerian Kabyle expresses deeply held cosmogonic
principles, and ethnographers have illustrated similar practices all around the
world (Blier 1987; Carsten and Hugh-Jones 1995). Richard Blanton (1994:
13–15) concluded from a cross-cultural survey that because houses embody
wealth as well as standing for it, they are "less subject to falsification" than
other indices of status. Blanton's claim is certainly valid if we limit our study
to the question of the standard of living, since the lavishness of housing is
itself a major part of that standard. However, to determine whether underlying economic growth made rising standards possible, we must factor
in belief systems, which influence the proportion of wealth invested in
housing. This raises many problems, but here I will concentrate on just two.

First, the most obvious way in which depositional factors might affect
interpretation of Figure 5.1 is if the buildings that I have cavalierly been
calling "houses" in fact changed functions in significant ways across these five
centuries. Alexandra Coucouzeli (1999) has argued that the fifty-meter-long
tenth-century apsidal house found at Lefkandi (Popham et al. 1993) was in

fact rather like the long houses common among native peoples in the Americas, and home to a dozen families. Comparing the size of this building with that of single-family, fourth-century homes would be a complex and potentially misleading exercise. Rival claims that the Lefkandi apsidal building was a chief's house (Crielaard and Driessen 1994; Mazarakis Ainian 1997: 48–57) seem more plausible to me, but Coucouzeli's argument nevertheless raises serious interpretive issues.

Changes in the crowding of houses are a major component of studies of living standards during the Industrial Revolution (Burnett 1986: 43–46, 61–69, 144–46, 326–27), but this is not archaeologically observable. As in the case of second floors, the most serious uncertainties concern ninth- and eighth-century houses. The literary evidence for residence strategies is largely anecdotal (Pomeroy 1997; Cox 1998; Patterson 1998), but it seems clear that the normative house in classical times was a single-family residence, and that families were typically nuclear. The precise size would vary according to the phase of the family's developmental cycle and the presence of dependents; and, as in modern case studies (McKinnon 1994: 277–78), we should imagine what scholars of urban blight since Seebohm Rowntree (1901) have called the "life cycle of poverty." Families with few income-earners and several young children face severe pressure on resources, which usually leads to the children going hungry so that the breadwinners can remain healthy enough to keep working. As the children grow up and begin to earn for themselves, the family should move out of poverty; but as the family's heads age and themselves become dependent on their children, they may slide back into dire need. The young and the old are always the most exposed to poverty, with devastating results for growth, morbidity, and mortality. Although it is not documented, the same was likely true in classical antiquity, along with the common consequence: Families in the grips of severe poverty would move into smaller and smaller accommodations, increasing the ratio of people to roofed space and creating unhygienic conditions.

Many classical households would have included some slaves, while fewer households would have done so in the eighth through sixth centuries. The data for the numbers and distribution of slaves are, however, poor. The enormous fourth-century houses at Eretria and Pella must have had staffs running into dozens, but the textual evidence—such as it is—suggests that few households had more than a handful of slaves (Garlan 1988: 55–60).

If we assume that before 700 the typical domestic residence was shared by several nuclear families, or by extended family groups, then the amount of roofed space per capita in the early periods was even smaller than is represented in Figure 5.1, and the subsequent increase in the standard of living was even more dramatic. Instead, we might extend Mazarakis Ainian's argument that before 700, nuclear families lived not in single houses but in compounds of several buildings, thereby increasing the amount of roofed space per person and reducing the sharp increase in Figure 5.1.

To some extent, these competing possibilities can be addressed empirically. In a critique of claims that the Early Bronze Age hamlet of Myrtos Pyrgos on Crete was the home of an undifferentiated "herd," sharing communal facilities, Todd Whitelaw (1983) showed that the distribution of hearths, storage, food preparation, and so on, suggested that the settlement was divided up between distinct families, each practicing the full range of domestic activities. Similarly, in Early Iron Age Greece—at all sites where the evidence is well enough published for analysis—we find that each structure has traces of spinning and weaving, preparation of food, storage, basic craft activities, and occasionally more specialized ones (I. Morris 1991: 31–32). We can probably conclude that eighth- and seventh-century settlements contained "houses"—permanent homes of nuclear families—in much the same sense as those of the sixth through fourth centuries.

The other obvious depositional problem is that house designs may tell us more about ideology than about economics. Down to 700 BC many houses in central Greece were simple, single-roomed, curvilinear structures, in which all activities went on within the same space or in the open air. At some sites, two or more huts of this kind were grouped together in family compounds. After 700, multiroomed, rectilinear structures became more popular, with clear evidence for functionally specific spaces. These new house styles, best seen at Zagora, were much more complicated and more expensive than the older styles. The question is whether we should see them as evidence that economic growth and increasing wealth raised the standard of living, or whether we should assume that ideological factors— a commitment to restraint and community homogeneity—had limited the scale of house building before 750, in which case the late eighth-century change reveals more about attitudes than economics. I have argued (I. Morris 2000: 280–86) that the shift was intimately linked to the creation of stronger gender distinctions. But did an increasing desire to separate male and female space dictate that people spent a higher proportion of their income on housing to create new spatial forms against an unchanging economic background, or did a rising standard of living present new opportunities for reinforcing gendered space? Or both?

Questions of this kind are central to postprocessual archaeology. We have no direct access to economic patterns, because all our evidence comes to us already implicated in strategies of self-representation. I suggested above, though, that standard historical methods of contrasting different kinds of sources do allow us to move beyond this impasse. In the case of eighth- and seventh-century houses, we might look at size against the background of building techniques. If people built small houses before 700 because they believed that simplicity and homogeneity were appropriate, and larger houses after this date because they wanted to engender space more rigidly, there is no particular reason why the methods of building should have changed. Yet we find that people not only built bigger after 700; they also built better. Drains and permanent, stone-lined hearths become quite common in the seventh century, and foundations were often more substantial. When houses really began to grow, around 500 BC, roof tiles (used on temples since the seventh century) replaced flat stone and clay roofs or pitched thatched roofs (Lang 1996: 108–17). This need not mean that increasing wealth was more important than changes in beliefs about gender or hierarchy in causing the expansion of house size around 700 BC; but it is hard to see why a new gender ideology would lead people to protect their homes better against water damage. The most plausible interpretation is that economics and ideology were inextricably linked. Growing wealth enabled typical citizen families to spend more on housing, producing more comfortable homes, and also homes that emphasized more strongly than before the distinctions between male and female spheres.

Median house sizes increased sharply between the sixth and fifth centuries. In an influential study, Wolfram Hoepfner and Ernst-Ludwig Schwandner (1994 [1986]) argued that a standardized "Typenhaus" appeared in the fifth century. Grouped into uniform blocks, these Typenhäuser were intimately involved with the egalitarian ideology of democracy. Although this thesis has its critics (Hoepfner et al. 1989; Etienne 1991; Nevett 1999: 27, 64), fifth-century houses were much more uniform in size than those of earlier times. This uniformity broke down in the fourth century. Olynthos is the only site where we have much evidence for the market value in drachmas of identifiable houses, but these data show that the fancier homes commanded significantly higher prices than the more typical ones (Nevett 2000). "Super houses" were built, like those at Eretria and Pella mentioned above; but more significantly for my arguments here, the median house size also increased by 128 percent. I have suggested (I. Morris 1992: 109-155; 1998) that the Hippodamian leveling ideology that Hoepfner and Schwandner see behind classical housing was part of a larger ideological system of restraint, involving burial, dress, private honorific monuments, and worship of the gods. This system was particularly rigid between about 500 and 425 BC, then relaxed, leaving more room for the rich to express their status in material forms. The civic egalitarianism that took hold in the fifth century and survived in attenuated form through most of the fourth was certainly a leveling ideology, but it is important to recognize that the selected level was higher than that of archaic times. Houses were much larger and much better built. As with the changes around 700, ideology and economics likely worked together. The fact that the general increase in wealth meant that fifth-century houses were spacious and comfortable probably made it easier to persuade would-be aristocrats to conform to the norms; and the fact that further increases in wealth allowed typical fourth-century families to live in grander houses than even the richest men of the eighth century may have made it easier to relax the constraints on contemporary noblemen.

Beliefs about the nature of the good society and economic realities worked together throughout this period, both constraining and enabling Greek home construction. We cannot hope to disentangle these factors. The very obvious role of beliefs in the great changes around 700, 500, and 400 mean that there was no simple and straightforward relationship between the curves in Figure 5.1 and per capita economic output. But on the other hand, the factors discussed above mean that we cannot cut these curves loose from prediscursive economic forces either. The richest fifth-century Greeks probably spent less on their houses than they could have afforded to do, while their fourth-century successors may have spent more than was prudent. But the five- or six-fold increase in the size of houses shown in Figure 5.1 still provides proxy data for a significant and sustained increase in per capita consumption across this half-millennium.

HOUSE CONTENTS: POSTDEPOSITIONAL PROBLEMS

Houses not only got bigger between 800 and 300: their contents also got richer. Anyone who has excavated first-millennium houses knows this, but documenting contents is even more difficult than tracking house sizes (Nevett 1999: 57–61).[5] First, most of the objects that were left behind have decayed in the intervening two or three millennia. The written sources suggest that some fourth-century houses had elaborate textiles and wall paintings (Walter-Karydi 1994: 32–52), but nothing survives of these.

Second, people took most things with them when they left their homes. Abandonment processes vary greatly through time and space and are driven largely by cultural concepts of cleanliness. Some people burn down houses when they abandon them, symbolically "killing" them, leaving excellent deposits for archaeologists; others sweep them thoroughly; others still simply walk away, leaving their last meal on the table. Even within a single cultural

context, houses that were deliberately abandoned and those destroyed by
sudden disasters leave very different deposits for excavators. Consequently,
abandonment processes are an excellent example of Schiffer's C-transforms
but straddle the line between depositional and postdepositional forces
(Cameron and Tomka 1993; Hodder 1982a: 190–93).

Abandoned first-millennium BC Greek houses generally have clean
floors. Even those houses destroyed suddenly by fire are relatively poor.
There is much debate over whether this means that Greeks really were poor,
as Herodotus repeatedly says by way of contrast with Persia (for example,
7.102), or whether they cleaned out their homes particularly thoroughly.
The texts are ambiguous. The "Attic stelai" (*IG* I³ 421–30), inscriptions
recording property seized from fifty or so Athenians condemned in 415,
mention one silver object and silver coins (*IG* I³ 427.93; 422.182) but no
other precious metals. There are plenty of bronze and iron tools, sold off for
quite high prices, and lots of pots, including 102 Panathenaic prize amphoras (422.41–60). The editor of the texts concluded that "our record of
the sale of confiscated property seems to show that there was little sense of
personal luxury in Athens in the last quarter of the fifth century, even among
men of wealth" (Pritchett 1956: 210). However, there is more to the evidence than this. David Lewis (1966: 183) pointed out that precious metals
would have been sold off by weight at the going price, and would thus not
show up in these texts, which are auction records; and Thucydides (6.60)
and Andocides (1.52) tell us that many of the suspects fled Athens, presumably taking their most valuable possessions with them. The Attic stelai are
the end products of abandonment processes every bit as complex as those of
the excavated houses. Against them, we may set the equally complicated
evidence of Aristophanes' comedy *Wealth*, produced in 388 BC. The slave
Karion describes Chremylos's household after the blind god Ploutos
(Wealth) has visited it: "Every pot in the house is crammed with silver and
gold—you'd be amazed. . . . Every bowl, every plate and vinegar cruet, has
turned to bronze, and all our rotting fish dishes are solid silver. Even our
lamps are suddenly turned into ivory" (*Wealth* 808–15). We have no way to
say which text evokes better the material experience of a rich Athenian
house. At least in fifth- and fourth-century Attica, abandonment and post-
abandonment cleaning were generally very thorough: At the Vari farmhouse
near Athens, abandoned around 275 BC, even the several tons of roof tiles
had been carried away (Jones et al. 1973: 361). Some inscribed house leases
specify that the renters had to provide their own tiles, suggesting that careful tile removal was common (*IG* II² 2499.11–14, 30–37; XII 5.872.52, 53,
63, 94); and when the departing occupants did not take their tiles and wood,

they could rely on looters to finish the job (Thucydides 2.14, 17; Lysias 19.31; *Hellenica Oxyrhynchia* 17 [12] 4–5).

That said, abandonment processes clearly affected different parts of the archaeological record in different ways (see also Pettegrew 2001). Broken pottery was virtually worthless, and no one would deliberately take it away from an abandoned house. Different attitudes toward cleanliness and garbage disposal will have had a huge influence on the quantities of pottery we recover from houses, but a pattern nevertheless emerges. At the Dema farmhouse near Athens, abandoned around 400 BC, red-figured pottery made up just 3 percent of the assemblage, and at the Vari farmhouse, just 2 percent (Jones et al. 1962: 89–100; 1972: 374–94). Ault meticulously published finds from five fourth-century houses from Halieis, where red-figured pottery averaged 3.9 percent of the minimum number of vessels, ranging from 1.6 percent in House C to 8.5 percent in House D (Ault, forthcoming b). But the garbage pits from a public building in the Athenian agora contained large quantities of red-figured pottery (Oakley and Rotroff 1992). We can probably conclude that red-figured wares were largely restricted to public and ceremonial contexts, with just a handful of sympotic vessels being used in most houses; and we can perhaps extrapolate from this conclusion to suggest that we can safely compare quantities of pottery found in different regions and periods, on the assumption that ceramics were far less vulnerable to abandonment processes than other categories of material.

But this is a very limited gain. When we turn from pottery to the base metals, we find enormous variation. The fourth-century "Priest's House" at Zostir held eighty-nine bronze coins, forty-eight bronze nails, fifty-six bronze fishhooks, nineteen bronze ornaments, and numerous lead fragments (Stavropoullos 1938), while most excavation reports mention no metal from houses. Some people are more careful than others, but can we really believe that there were houses where for centuries no one lost a coin or threw out a broken nail? There were, of course, variations in the richness of personal property; combined with different degrees of thoroughness in abandonment cleaning and reuse of the site, such variations might account for the observed differences. However, we probably need to introduce two further important sources of postdepositional distortion: the quality of excavation and publication. Fragments of broken metal tools and ornaments (particularly iron) can be hard to find, especially on salvage excavations under intense time pressure; and even if they are found, the excavator may not feel the need to provide exhaustive catalogues, especially in brief preliminary reports in journals like *Archaiologikon Deltion*.

The general impression from the site reports is that there was a massive increase in the numbers, variety, and expense of household goods between the eighth century and the fourth, but postdepositional factors interact in complex ways, undermining straightforward quantification. A thorough cleaning at or after the abandonment will leave only small scraps of pottery and metal. The less careful excavator may miss fragments of bronze and iron but will probably find most of the pottery. A brief publication will mention the more glamorous finds but will not discuss the rest of the assemblage. If we can safely assume that these factors randomly distort the relationships between the published record of excavations and the original material culture, then for the purposes of assessing overall change through time in the wealth of domestic goods, we can go ahead and make comparisons. If, on the other hand, we suspect that the distortions are nonrandom—for example, that some archaeologists dig and publish more thoroughly than others—we may not be able to address change in household goods at all. For instance, we may suspect that archaeologists working on small ninth- and eighth-century sites, where every excavated house is a significant addition to knowledge, will tend to work more carefully and publish their finds in more detail than those digging large fourth-century towns. Experiments have shown that systematic sieving not only increases the number of artifacts found but seriously changes the ratios between different types of artifacts (Payne 1972). We can expect to recover a larger proportion of the artifacts in use from sites destroyed violently than from sites abandoned peacefully, so we must be sure to compare like kinds of sites. If such destructions are more common in some periods or places than others, they may significantly bias our results.

For example, we might compare the total number of finds from Nichoria, at the beginning of our half-millennium, and Olynthos, at its end. These are among the best excavated and published sites of their respective periods, and both were dug by the same institution (the American School of Classical Studies at Athens). But even in these cases, digging and reporting styles changed so much between the work at Olynthos in the 1920–30s and that at Nichoria in the 1970s that we can make no simple comparison. At Nichoria, excavators recovered 125 metal fragments and 118 clay spindle whorls from an excavated area of roughly 1,700 square meters.[6] Unit IV-1 was abandoned peacefully and thoroughly cleaned out, but eighth-century Unit IV-5 burned down (McDonald et al. 1983: 32, 39, 49–50). Olynthos was also destroyed by fire, when Philip II of Macedon sacked it in 348. Several thousand square meters were cleared. The published lists of small finds fill eight large volumes, and include 4,402 bronze, silver, and gold coins, 1,278 terra-cottas, and 457 clay lamps, as well as many fragments of sculptures, worked stone basins, altars, millstones and querns, mortars, olive presses, and so on. Finds of iron, bronze, and lead included braziers, keys, figurines, weights, door knockers, meat hooks, and a whole range of other items (Robinson 1931–52; Robinson and Clement 1938; Robinson and Graham 1938). The 1928 season alone produced 25 spindle whorls, more than 200 spools, and 793 loom weights. These categories of artifacts were published in less detail (see Robinson and Graham 1938: 307–54). Styles of excavation and publication changed drastically between the 1920s and 1970s, adding to the difficulties of comparison, although we might note that the 1987–89 excavation in Olynthos House B.VII.1 produced finds very like those from the prewar digs (Drougou and Vokotopoulou 1989).

What should we make of this comparison? Despite the higher level of excavation technique at Nichoria, vastly more artifacts were recovered from Olynthos. Even after taking into consideration the full range of postdepositional factors, there is no way to avoid the conclusion that fourth-century Olynthians had far more things, and far more sophisticated things, than eighth-century Nichorians. But we cannot move on to make such a precise quantification of the differences as with the house sizes unless we are prepared to make a series of unjustified assumptions. I suggested above that typical fourth-century houses were five or six times as big as those of the eighth-century. Did the typical fourth-century house also have a collection of household goods five or six times as rich as that of the eighth century? Probably. Was it ten times as rich? Perhaps. Twenty times? Probably not. But these are only guesses, and the margin of error is compounded when we take depositional factors into account.

HOUSE CONTENTS: DEPOSITIONAL PROBLEMS

As noted above, beliefs about purity and dirt play a massive role in abandonment processes. They also influence what people do with refuse while they still occupy houses. If it was normal simply to throw garbage out of the back door, to lie around in the yard, we might find little of it; if, on the other hand, it was normal to dispose of it in carefully dug pits, we are likely to find far more. The literary sources suggest that purity beliefs hardened in Greece around 700 BC (R. Parker 1983); I link this to the widespread division of space into discrete domestic, funerary, and divine spheres at just this point (I. Morris 1987: 189–96). However, there is little indication that this practice had much impact on domestic garbage disposal. With the exception of dumps of sacrificial material in sanctuaries, garbage pits were rare throughout the first millennium. Abandoned wells and cisterns were popular dumps, as the Athenian Agora shows clearly (Brann 1962: 125–31; Sparkes and Talcott 1970: 383–99; and annual reports in *Hesperia*), but Brad Ault's (1999) publication of large groups of sherds from *koprones* (dung-storage bins) at Halieis suggests that much household debris was simply thrown out. Bintliff and Snodgrass (1988; Snodgrass 1994) suggest that great quantities of domestic refuse were carried out to the fields with manure, to form the "halos" of medium-density artifact scatters found around many settlements.

Changing ideas about purity may not have had much impact on the disposal of artifacts, but changing ideas about status may have been very important on the actual accumulation of household goods. Pritchett (see above) argued from the Attic stelai that fifth-century Athenian houses were modestly furnished, which certainly fits with the larger pattern of fifth-century restraint (I. Morris 1992: 118–27). The literary sources refer far more often to luxurious interiors in the fourth century than in earlier periods (Walter-Karydi 1994: 32–52), and nonportable luxury goods like mosaic floors only become common after 400 BC (I. Morris 1998: 69–70, 71, 73, 81). We might hypothesize that cultural factors restrained lavish consumption and display in the fifth and perhaps also the sixth century, before loosening in the fourth. The issues are much the same as with house size: After we have allowed for postdepositional factors, should we conclude that the increase in household goods between the eighth century and the fourth was caused by rising wealth, or by changes in beliefs against a stable economic background? It seems to me that ideological factors would be most important at the upper end of the scale. Pericles probably felt less comfortable than Alcibiades offering his guests wine from gold cups or having famous artists paint his house, and fifth-century values seem to have suppressed such activities. But would egalitarianism have discouraged a successful farmer from buying extra pottery, or perhaps replacing plain table ware with black-glaze? Or installing a stone drain to keep water away from his foundations? The attitudes in the literary sources that I have described as "middling" (I. Morris 2000: 113–85) seem perfectly consistent with a generally rising standard of living. There is no obvious reason to suppose that ideology had any significant impact on the kind of changes in household assemblages that we see when we compare Nichoria and Olynthos, and we can probably assume that the rise in living standards (however vague our quantification must be) was driven by increases in per capita economic output.

Conclusions

House sizes increased something like five- or six-fold between 800 and 300 BC. This represents a dramatic improvement in the standard of living, particularly when we factor in improvements in construction, drainage, and illumination. Fourth-century Greek houses were large and quite comfortable, even by the standards of developed countries in the early twenty-first century. It is hard to say how well furnished they were, but the impression (presently it can be little more than that) is that classical household goods were far richer than those of archaic times. Again, a five- or six-fold increase may not be far from the mark.

These observations are only a beginning; we need to compare the evidence for housing with that for changes in stature, nutrition, mortality, and morbidity. We also need to go beyond simply asking, "How well off was the average person?" (MacKinnon 1994: 265) to break down overall well being into subcategories such as children, the elderly, men and women, free and slave, rich and poor. Furthermore, we must look at the top and bottom quartiles as well as the mean and median figures. But the initial impression created by the data is that for most people in Greece, living standards increased substantially across this half-millennium. This increase is all the more remarkable when we bear in mind that population expanded enormously in just the same period. Table 5.3 shows the estimates reached by two of the most rigorously conducted settlement surveys of the 1990s: the Kea survey and the Argolid Exploration Project. Population increased roughly tenfold between the eighth century and the fourth. Economic historians commonly assume that prior to the Industrial Revolution, living standards improved only at a glacial rate, because any significant increases in per capita economic output were quickly converted into extra mouths to feed. Demographic expansion would outrun resource expansion, leading to famine and disease until a new equilibrium was established. But in Greece, across a long period of time (twice as long as the period that has elapsed since the Industrial Revolution began in earnest), population and living standards apparently increased together. As Saller notes in his discussion of Rome (Chapter 11), ancient economic expansion was trivial compared to the changes of the nineteenth and twentieth centuries. But compared to the expectations mainstream economists seem to have about premodern economic performance, and the expectations that the Finleyan model leads to, economic expansion was massive, sustained, and desperately in need of explanation.

The first step is to link increases in the standard of living to quantified changes in economic output per capita. This will be far from easy. If a

TABLE 5.3
Population estimates from the Kea survey and the Argolid Exploration Project

Period	Population	Relative Size[1]
Koressos on Kea		
900–700	100?	1.0
700–480	570–810	5.7–8.1
480–323	1020–1455	10.0–14.5
323–31	495–600	5.0–6.0
Southern Argolid		
750–650	1100	1.0
650–480	5880	5.3
480–c. 200	10,855	9.9
c. 200 BC–AD 100	4570	4.2

Sources: Cherry et al. 1991: 340; Jameson et al. 1994: 544–45.
[1]Treating first period as 1.0.

typical fourth-century house cost five or six times what one of the eighth-century cost, that does not mean that income per capita had expanded 500–600 percent.[7] Over time, consumption bundles change. If our income doubles, we probably would not spend twice as much on bread as we did before: Spending on certain goods is relatively income-inelastic, while spending on others (particularly luxuries) responds vigorously to changes in income. If we could draw up a cross-culturally valid table of income elasticities of demand, we could simply multiply the likely increases in Greek spending on housing to generate a figure for overall changes in per capita income. But we cannot. A huge variety of historically specific forces, both economic and cultural, shape what people will do with changes in income. Around 1800, English working-class families typically spent 4–5 percent of their income on housing (Horrell 1996: 580), but by 1900 the figure had risen to somewhere between 9 and 15 percent (Burnett 1986: 147). A hundred years later in California, 40 percent is not an uncommon figure. The only way to move from specific indices of changing standards of living to underlying trends in per capita economic output is by working out a macro-economic model including food, housing, ritual, and the complex ways in which wealth was siphoned off to pay for the state's building activities, sacrifices, and wars. This exercise will necessarily be largely speculative but can at least establish some basic parameters. Keith Hopkins's work on Rome (1980, 1995/96, 2000) and Daniel Jew's on fourth-century Athens (1999) might provide useful frameworks.

The second step is to try to explain what I suspect will turn out to be a surprisingly high level of economic growth. This calls for new models, probably owing more to economic historians like Douglass North (1981,

1990) and development economists like Debraj Ray (1998) than to Weber or Finley (or, for that matter, to the modernist ancient historians of the 1890s). Finley struggled to explain why there was no capitalist takeoff in the ancient world, and by extension why antiquity was so backward. The evidence for living standards seems to suggest that we should in fact explore why there was (by preindustrial standards) such sustained growth, and what it contributed to the very long-term economic development of Europe (see Greif, Chapter 12).

Finally, returning to the core questions of this book, such calculations make possible direct comparisons between the economic performance of ancient Greece and that of other regions of the Mediterranean. The depositional and postdepositional factors affecting the archaeological record in different periods and regions vary significantly, and much careful empirical work is still needed. But there is in principle no reason why archaeology should not provide a unified economic history of the Mediterranean, once we ask appropriate questions. In fact, the study of Greek standards of living and economic growth demands such a large-scale study, because without this comparative base, we have no way to know to evaluate the Greek experience. Did the Greeks expand their economy faster than other ancient peoples? Or were they in fact typical of a much larger pattern of cyclical economic growth and contraction (Wrigley 1988; E. L. Jones 2000; Goldstone 2002)? If the latter, then ancient economic historians will be challenging one of the fundamental orthodoxies of modern economic historians, that between the rise of the state in later prehistory and the Industrial Revolution after AD 1750, agrarian economies were essentially static (Lucas 1998). The ancient economy matters.

Notes

    1. Renfrew and Bahn (2001: 41–60) offer a good introduction; and Kristiansen (1985), Schiffer (1987), Nash and Petraglia (1987), and Lucas (2001: 146–99) give more advanced accounts.

    2. See the essays collected in *Explorations in Economic History* 24.3 (1987).

    3. Lang (1996), Mazarakis Ainian (1997), and Nevett (1999) provide catalogues of varying degrees of completeness for the period 1100–300 BC, with full references.

    4. Assuming that these rooms all belong to a single structure: see Mazarakis Ainian 1997: 171–74.

    5. I would like to thank Doctors Demetrius Schilardi and Petros Themelis for giving me the opportunity to excavate Dark Age, archaic, classical, and Hellenistic house deposits at Koukounaries and Eretria in the 1980s.

6. Measured from the plans of Areas III and IV in Coulson 1983: 10–11, 20–21, 45. I focus on excavated area rather than the volume of earth removed because the depth of the deposit is itself a function of the level of activity on site.

7. Our data for house prices are sketchy. Nevett (2000) reviews the inscriptions from Olynthos, documenting a range of prices from 230 to 5,300 drachmas. Also in the fourth century, Isaeus (2.35) refers to an *oikidion* being worth no more than 300 drachmas. If Olynthos House A.V.10 went for 5,300 drachmas, a typical fourth-century house must have cost at least 1,500 drachmas (Hoepfner and Schwandner [1994 (1986)] opt for 3,000 drachmas); and if the poorest fourth-century houses, like that from Block II at the Silen Gate on Thasos (Grandjean 1988), were the kinds of thing Isaeus had in mind as a 300-drachma *oikidion*, then the price (in Athenian fourth-century drachma equivalents) of typical eighth-century houses probably was in the 150-drachma range. As a very rough estimate, spending on housing probably increased tenfold across these five centuries.

Chapter 6

Linear and Nonlinear Flow Models
for Ancient Economies

JOHN K. DAVIES

This chapter, much revised from initial presentations, is the third of a triad. A first paper (Davies 1998) attempted to assess the problems and issues raised by a conference on "Trade, Traders, and the Ancient City" held in St. Andrews, Scotland, in September 1995. A second (Davies 2001), prepared as the keynote address to a colloquium on Hellenistic economies held in Liverpool in June 1998, outlines the conceptual and practical difficulties involved in creating any replacement for Michael Rostovtzeff's *Social and Economic History of the Hellenistic World* (1941) and attempts to plot a way forward. What follows here complements its partner papers, and conforms with the theme of the conference of the Social Science History Institute at Stanford, by focusing not so much on ancient economies as on ways of modeling them, especially on ways of representing them *visually*. It remains raw, a "think piece" rather than a map of directions.[1]

The Inapplicability of Classical Economic Analysis

I start from the position reached in my essay "Ancient Economies: Models and Muddles" (1998), which argued inter alia that though there are economic historians of antiquity who use the language, and share the assumptions, of the discipline of economics, in fact the standard discourse of economic analysis, whether classical or Keynesian or Marxist or neoclassical, has little to offer the economic historian of Mediterranean antiquity. It may

be helpful to spell out the reasons more fully than in 1998. They have nothing to do with the "absence of statistics," which is far from being a total absence in any case. They have far more to do with the range of practices and
institutions visible in antiquity that need to be incorporated in any realistic
model of economic interaction. First, and most obviously, an unquantifiable,
highly variable, but undoubtedly significant proportion of "production" and
"consumption" took place as a closed cycle within the physical or topological curtilage of family farms and estates, never reaching real markets. It does
not matter whether we follow the Chayanov tradition of identifying such
activity as a separate category, the "Domestic Mode of Production," or con-
versely grant some truth to Paterson's robust remark (1998: 158) that "the
concept of the self-sufficient peasant is a myth," or dogmatically push the
term "market" to its theoretical limit by asserting that the sum of production of a given commodity intrinsically forms a market even if no part of it
is perceived or activated as such; autarky, or at least semiautarky, as a practice (let alone as an ideological ideal) has to be part of the picture. It follows,
of course, that that picture cannot be composed entirely (indeed, maybe not
at all) of transactions to which concepts of "market" and of "price" are tidily
applicable.

Second, whereas standard economic discourse operates above all in terms
of two kinds of institutions, the "firm" and the "state," neither of them can
be mapped directly onto Mediterranean antiquity without serious distortion of reality. Each needs separate, albeit brief, consideration, since the case
for so mapping them is not totally absurd. It is tempting, for example, to see
as "firms," whether one-man or partnerships, the craftsmen and contractors
who are known from epigraphic accounts to have worked on building or re-
pairing Greek temples, and to use that evidence in order to imagine the utterly undocumented but undoubtedly substantial world of private building
and contracting. Likewise, though "the shipowners from Hippo Diarrhy-
tus," "the agency of the grain merchants of the colony of Curubis," or the
other bodies attested on the Piazzale delle corporazioni at Ostia are guilds
rather than firms (*Corpus Inscriptionum Latinarum* XIV 4549, nos. 12 and 34,
with Meiggs 1973: 283 ff. [Piazzale] and 311–36 [Guilds]), and though the
Roman *negotiatores* ("business men") on late Hellenistic Delos (Rauh 1993)
are visible as cult groups rather than as "firms," it would be perverse not to
see as at least protofirms the Murashû enterprises of Babylonia, or some of
the banking houses of fourth-century Attica, or the tax-farming groups of
Hellenistic Egypt (Préaux 1939: 450–59, especially 457 n. 2) or the late
Roman Republic, or to acknowledge that other such "firms" may have existed. However, the objection to adopting the "firm" as a central model is

two-fold (even apart from the fact that "firm" is not a single species). First is the near-certainty that in the absence of capital markets, of much in the way of "company law," or of the social acceptability of the private employment of one free man by another, few if any "firms" can have emancipated themselves from the organizational model of the household without coming to resemble cult groups.[2] Second is the observable fact that firmlike entities, while not necessarily marginal, shared productive economic space with other entities of very different formats.

As for the "state," though of course for many practical purposes the polities of Mediterranean antiquity can be treated as impersonal collectives comparable to modern states, with theoretically attributable (even if not practically quantifiable) GNPs and GDPs, taxation policies, "governments," and so forth, yet most if not all fell into one of two categories, neither of which can be satisfactorily assimilated to mainstream modern forms. Either they were monarchies (whether through conquest, election, or inheritance), in which case the ideological and administrative model was that of the household, however hugely extended and attenuated it might have to be in practice; or they were communities of *homoioi* ("comparables"), who formed a company of unlimited liability of which the citizens were by definition the shareholders (whether equal or unequal could vary).[3] Each category generated forms of economic behavior that lay outside the boundaries of current mainstream economic analysis. Monarchies generated, on the one hand, confiscation and extortion and, on the other, ostentatious largesse to cities, cults, or individuals; in each case potentially on such a scale as to affect the "economy" of the "polity" significantly. Thus they need to be factored in to any model of its redistributive mechanisms (Bringmann and von Steuben 1995). Communities of *homoioi*, in contrast, typically so defined participation in the *koinon* or *res publica* as to require personal military or political or financial service of its members by virtue of their social or economic standing, a requirement deeply embedded in the language via the semantic fields of such words as *telos*, *munus*, or *leitourgia*.

Such behavior carries implications for any economic model-building activity of antiquity that are so far-reaching as to comprise a third reason for distancing ourselves from mainstream economic discourse. It is not just that the movement of resources involved in discharging such obligations needs to be tracked (and, at least in theory, quantified); the return for such investment of resources also needs to be identified in some way. That need is most pressing in the case of resource movements that contained an element of ostentation, of largesse, or of political investment. That is no marginal requirement, for much recent work has clearly shown that euergetism and ostentatious display on the part of individuals played major roles throughout antiquity as means of legitimating higher social and political status (Veyne 1976). Yet the problem of encapsulating the intended return to the benefactor within any system of representations is acutely intractable (not to mention that of "measuring" it in any one specific context, which is a problem of a different order). To ignore it, by dismissing such "social returns" as lying outside the processes of production and consumption, is to leave out of account a major component of economic interaction.[4] To incorporate it requires jettisoning most of the theoretical assumptions of classical economics. There can be little doubt about which course does more sympathetic justice to the societies whose behavior we are trying to map.

At the risk of laboring the obvious, the above may perform the service of making explicit the instinctive assumptions that underlie much if not most work on the economics of literate Mediterranean antiquity. Insofar as such work is taking place in an isolated environment, it is worth adding a fourth equally obvious reason: namely, neither the drives and psychological profile attributed to *homo oeconomicus*, nor the assumption of the effective operation of price mechanisms, can be applied across the spectrum of ancient societies without creating a gross travesty of reality. However, that is not so much a specific argument against applying classical analysis (of any variety) to antiquity as an aspect of the critique of economic analysis in general, and of the competitive equilibrium model in particular, which is being energetically driven by some scholars from within the discipline of economics (Nelson and Winter 1982; McCloskey 1998 [1985]; Klamer et al. 1988; Ormerod 1994 [elementary survey], 1998; Lawson 1997 [full survey]). Since the various critiques may well converge fruitfully in the next few years, it will be wise for ancient historians to watch the game in progress attentively, and maybe eventually to join in.

The Grounds of Unease

However, the act of jettisoning classical economic analysis leaves not so much a tabula rasa as a congeries of current practices that themselves arouse considerable unease. Some six ingredients of that unease can be identified. The first is *compartmentalization* (see Morris and Manning's introduction). If one moves from the works of economic historians of the Bronze Age Near East through those of the Iron Age Near East, Iron Age Europe, archaic Italy, archaic Greece, classical Greece, Egypt, Hellenistic Greece, Carthage, Republican Rome, or the high Roman Empire to those of the fourth and fifth centuries AD, one has the sense of moving though populations whose inhabitants speak mutually incomprehensible languages. Any reader of the papers in Rowlands et al. (1987), Oates (1993), or even Parkins and Smith (1998) will share that sense. Of course, there are reasons. The notion of "antiquity" itself, if claimed to be a coherent subdivision of scholarly activity, needs to be interrogated. Inherited agendas, or modes of discourse, for the study of each area or century or theme are hard to escape from. The task of mastering the source material and the *problématique* for a new study area or theme is forbidding. Predominant patterns of scholarship, such as concentration on the material for one region, or concentration on the distribution patterns of a specific range of artifacts, induce fragmentation. The inevitable result is that a knowledgeable synoptic view is hideously difficult to create.

A second ingredient is *the incoherence of borrowings*: namely, the tendency to use patterns of interpretation, or ideologies, that are consciously or subconsciously taken over from other disciplines or other areas of systematic study, or from current experience. At one extreme, as noted above, stands neoclassical economics; at the other, perhaps, the current emphasis on peasant autarky and peasant strategies (especially Forbes 1982; Garnsey 1988: 43–68; Gallant 1991), which owes much to Third World economic anthropology. In between lie Marxist notions of class, Weberian notions of status (not least via Finley himself, with Whittaker 1996), Polanyian notions of reciprocity and embeddedness, sub-Marxist notions of center and periphery, derived from Wallerstein's 1974 study *The Modern World System*,[5] and cultural history, not to mention the soggy descriptive mode adopted in Davies 1984. Each of these patterns of analysis has its attractions and its inadequacies. What we lack is a metaframework, within which each can be accorded its due weight and applicability but no more.

A third ingredient is *autonomy uncertainty*. This phrase (clumsy, I admit, but I cannot find a better one) flags the challenge that arises if we resile from the economists' view of economic activity as an autonomous area with its own laws, and see it instead as embedded within social action. The problem is not so much whether Polanyi was right to redirect the discourse in this direction, for he unquestionably was, but rather how far the process should be taken. Two examples must suffice. First, as hinted above, the patterns of economic behavior shown by ancient monarchies (not least those of thesaurization, conspicuous consumption, and investment in infrastructure) need proper comparative analysis. Second, an increased awareness of the range of patterns of behaviors shown throughout antiquity by cults and temples as economic actors, and of their importance, forces us to devise ways of mapping such behaviors that cross conventional interfaces and are compatible with the ways in which the behaviors of monarchs, communities, and individuals are described.[6]

A fourth ingredient is *the difficulty of defining "an" economy*, for the term is notoriously Procrustean. These days it is not wholly nonsensical for financial journalists to talk about "the world economy," but it is still meaningful to talk about "the Manx economy" or "the Californian economy" or even "the southeastern English economy." Mediterranean antiquity presents the same imprecision. At one extreme, and for good reasons, Keith Hopkins (1980) could survey the whole Roman Empire and say useful and penetrating things at that level of generality; Rostovtzeff years ago (1941) did the same for the Hellenistic world. At the other extreme lie not only detailed studies such as that of Gary Reger (1994) on Hellenistic Delos, which emphasize that economies are essentially regional, but also recent emphases, illustrated for Mesopotamia, on "the village economy" (see Fig. 6.1).[7] The need to add such spatial modifiers is understandable in itself but implies, indeed enjoins, that analysis of economies, as of trade networks, has to be done at two levels as an absolute minimum and preferably at three: the "localized," the "regional," and the "long-distance" (thus, for example, Alston 1998: 171). Such a recognition admits the possibility, perhaps the probability, that analysis of the same area at different levels of interaction may have to be carried out in different terms. Whether even three levels are enough is a question explored below.

A fifth ingredient, *the distinction between "economy" and "public economy,"* already discussed in Davies (1998: 242), needs no further exploration here. However, a sixth ingredient, the *assumption that economies are "monocolore,"* needs more attention than I gave it in 1998 (240–41). Here Finley's *The Ancient Economy* has to be confronted head on. Running through that book is the assumption that descriptions of an economy, as of a society or a polity, have to be *"monocolore."*[8] In his words, "It is the pattern, of course, that should occupy the central point of any discussion, not the rare exceptional practice" (Finley 1952: 484), and "We must concentrate on the dominant types, the characteristic modes of behaviour" (1985a: 29). For various reasons this is unacceptable. Not only does it erode the distinctions, discussed above, between "local," "regional," and "long-distance," but it leaves no room in its explanatory framework for the possibility that alternative modes of behaving economically, or alternative modes of evaluating what one is doing, can coexist within the same "society" or the same "economy" without any one mode predominating. Even more crucially, it leaves no conceptual space within which to accommodate the ebb and flow of alternative systems through time, or to map the processes by which new practices, values,

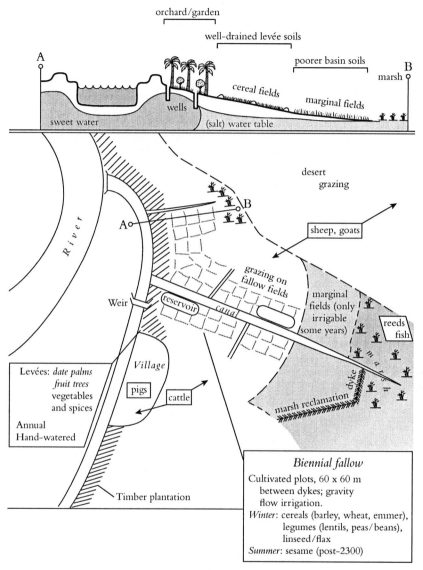

Section A-B
(vertical scale grossly exaggerated)

orchard/garden

well-drained levée soils

poorer basin soils

A

B

marsh

cereal fields

marginal fields

wells

sweet water

(salt) water table

desert
grazing

B

A

sheep, goats

grazing on
fallow fields

marginal
fields (only
irrigable
some years)

reeds
fish

River

Weir

reservoir

canal

Village

marsh

dyke

Levées: *date palms*
fruit trees
vegetables
and spices

pigs

cattle

marsh reclamation

Annual
Hand-watered

Timber plantation

Biennial fallow
Cultivated plots, 60 x 60 m
between dykes; gravity
flow irrigation.
Winter: cereals (barley, wheat, emmer),
legumes (lentils, peas/beans),
linseed/flax
Summer: sesame (post-2300)

Figure 6.1.   A hypothetical sketch of an agricultural cell (after Postgate
1992: 175)

and institutions begin with a marginal or spasmodic existence but may come to be continuous and central.[9] To take one specific and currently contentious area of argument, the post-Homeric period of archaic Greece and its alleged transformation from being a society where "status brings wealth" to being one where "wealth brings status" (van Wees 1992; Tandy 1997), there need be no difficulty with the propositions that both sets of behaviors coexisted, then and later, or that market-based exchange that was independent of the relative status of the contracting parties took place then and later, or in general that Greece as a whole, or even each of its major regions, showed at any one moment an unstable set of different modes of economic behavior, the components of such a set being loosely linked to each other in ways that changed through time. The first step toward sanity for an economic historian of antiquity is to accept that in any landscape at any epoch one should expect such sets of different modes of behavior to coexist, and should therefore expect to be in the business of creating models that show a high degree of intricacy, complexity, instability, and disarticulatedness. The main characteristic of any "unified field theory" that may eventually take root in the study of the economic behavior of antiquity is that it is not unified.

This section, with its implication that what we have at the moment is "a discourse in search of a method," has inevitably been negative. What follows will attempt to be more constructive.

Starting Again: Models of Models

Suppose, then, that we were to start again, with a blank sheet of paper and the remit to devise a set of working models of the economies of Mediterranean antiquity, flexible and polymorphous enough to accommodate the characteristics noted above. The bleak fact is that before that task can even begin, we need to have in front of us, and to be confident in handling and in choosing from, a far greater range of "models of models," or intellectual paradigms, than most of us who come to the subject with linguistic and historical training are used to contemplating. Emphatically, I claim no such expertise, merely a growing awareness that graphs, flow diagrams, equations, and matrices need to be as much in our armory as the verbal formulations of a Finley or a Sahlins, and that the tools of interpretation of reality developed by physicists, mathematicians, and behavioral biologists are likely to be crucial in helping us to understand the economies of antiquity (if only as useful metaphors). All that this chapter can do is to open up the discussion and invite better qualified scholars to take it forward.

If, as hinted above, the likely route forward is away from the idea of a "large unified economic space" as justly criticized by Finley (1985a: 77), and toward a more intricate but disarticulated picture, the way in which we view and map space takes on a new centrality. That is not to make the banal point that all economic activity occurs in a land/seascape, the physical and human geography of which is always relevant if not determinative. Rather, it is to make two much more complex points. The first, fundamental but only briefly to be noted here, concerns *boundaries*. That the boundaries of the economic activities of antiquity did not necessarily correspond in the least with political, cultural, or geographical boundaries should be obvious, though not all current economic historiography of antiquity recognizes the fact. Marfoe's comment is pertinent:

> A further difficulty arises in the terms "Mesopotamia" and "Syro-Anatolia," which imply regional units of analysis with defined boundaries and sharp cultural discontinuities. Neither was true by historic times, and perhaps a more appropriate framework would be a web of overlapping, interlocking but discrete, individual links of enmeshed local systems, forming a highly variegated fabric of connections that range in strength or access and permeability or porosity. (Marfoe 1987: 28)

Less obvious, though currently the focus of much interesting work, is the effect of mental boundaries and isopercepts (Gould and White 1986 [1974]; Mathisen and Sivan 1996). To the best of my knowledge, an assessment of their economic effects in antiquity has barely begun. It is not just (even primarily) a matter of identifying imperialist triumphalism at the public level or Seneca-style economic exploitation at the private level, though no one who reads such reactions to them as Theopompos's view of Athens, or Ammianus's view of Rome, can be unaware of the *economic* (as well as cultural) fallout of thoughtless arrogance or hard-faced landlordism on the part of metropolitan in-groups. It is more a matter of reconstructing the mental processes by which euergetistic activity and conspicuous consumption on the part of the resource-rich are or are not thought to be appropriate investments to be steered toward this or that region or community.

However, it is the second complex point that most needs extended attention: *What sort(s) of space does economic interaction occupy?* Since the problem has both practical and theoretical aspects, discussion may most usefully focus on a sequence of visual representations of such interaction. I begin with two of the four maps in Sherratt and Sherratt (1993), which chart the growth of long-distance Mediterranean trade in the early Iron Age (see Figs. 6.2 and 6.3). They show not just trade but also the inescapable problem of

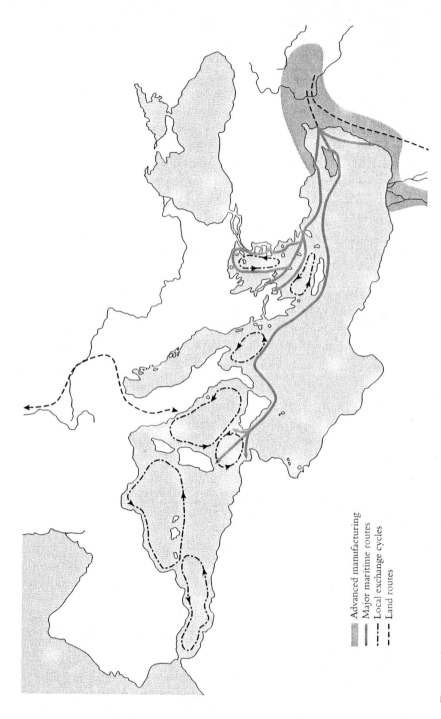

Advanced manufacturing
Major maritime routes
Local exchange cycles
Land routes

Figure 6.2. Maritime routes in the Mediterranean, tenth to fifteenth centuries BC (after Sherratt and Sherratt 1993: Figure A)

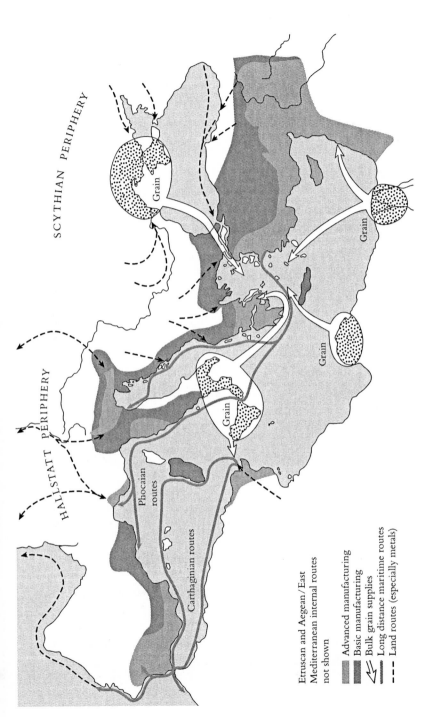

Figure 6.3. Maritime routes in the Mediterranean, sixth century BC (after Sherratt and Sherratt 1993: Figure D)

SCYTHIAN PERIPHERY

HALLSTATT PERIPHERY

Grain

Grain

Grain

Grain

Grain

Phocaean
routes

Carthaginian routes

Etruscan and Aegean/East
Mediterranean internal routes
not shown

Advanced manufacturing
Basic manufacturing
Bulk grain supplies
Long distance maritime routes
Land routes (especially metals)

Figure 6.4.   Settlements in central Greece: The study area (after Rihll and Wilson 1991: Figure 1)

trade-off. The trade routes are set in a simple and familiar representation of a real land/seascape; they are immediately accessible, lucid, and helpful, but at the cost of drastic simplification, achieved by splitting local from long-distance movements, omitting return movements, and omitting inputs in the form of effective demand. A very different type of map is presented by Rihll and Wilson (1991), who represent the regions of classical Attica, the Megarid, Boeotia, the Argolid, and Corinthia as an isotropic surface in order to calculate the consequences of different levels of the friction of distance (see Figs. 6.4 and 6.5). Though the authors' focus was not primarily economic, its relevance to theories of the development of central places and thereby to the understanding of local exchange patterns is immediately

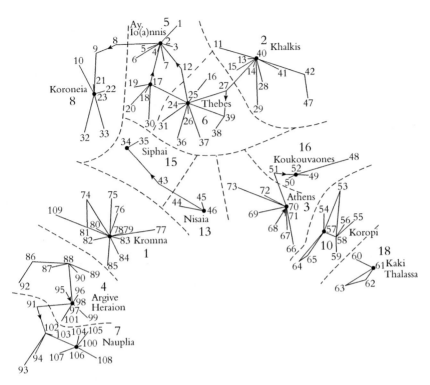

Figure 6.5. Grouping of settlements by friction of distance (after Rihll and Wilson 1991: Figure 4)

obvious. However, their use of a comparatively complex equation indicates a different interpretative model, to which I revert briefly below.

A third, classic example is Keith Hopkins's (1980) model of taxation flows in the Roman Empire (see Fig. 6.6). Though simplified, such a representation has the merit of bringing out a single characteristic very clearly. Its limitations are equally apparent: The "return" (real or symbolic, full or inadequate) from the center and periphery to the middle zone is not expressed, and there is no dimension of time or change.

Finally, a fourth example, Colin Haselgrove's (1987) depiction of the economic mechanisms available to the elite of pre-Roman Belgic Gaul (see Fig. 6.7). Here, much of the activity of the "real economy" is disregarded, and the depiction is again wholly synchronic, but the gains are equally clear: "Returns" are shown, in both real and transmuted forms, a fair degree of social differentiation is incorporated, relations with various out-groups can be separately shown, and the whole ensemble forms a cell that can be applied

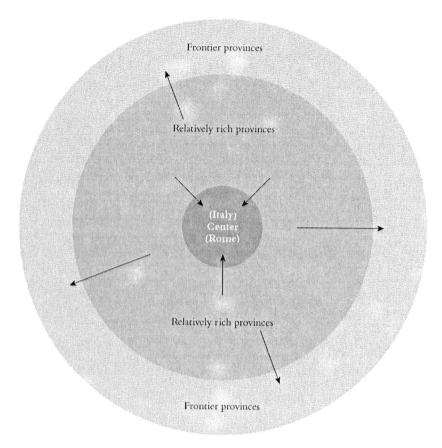

Figure 6.6.   Taxation flow in the Roman Empire (after K. Hopkins 1980)

across a landscape as many times as the relevant social unit is deemed to be replicated in real space-time.

These examples suggest a number of guidelines for comprehending the main economic activities of a society in a single system and of visualizing them in representational terms on a single surface. Five main guidelines suggest themselves. First and foremost, *we are trying to trace flows*. Any and every movement or exchange of goods and services comprises a use of resource, or a change of its (real or symbolic) location, which can be represented as a flow. As noted above, even storage within a household in a near-autarkic system can be usefully represented as such (from person-present to person-future), its counterflow being enhanced security of survival and maybe enhanced social power. Some flows will be unidirectional, such as the well-known examples of the systematic impoverishment of this or that area by

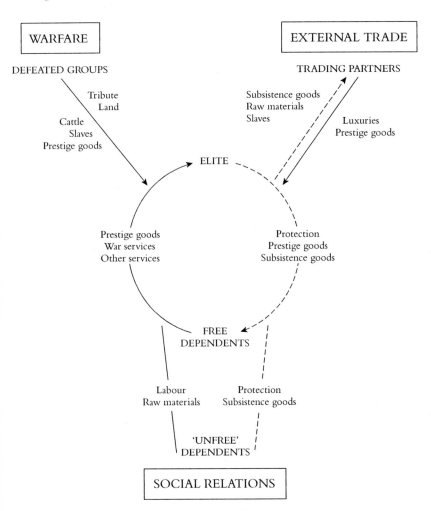

Figure 6.7. Economic mechanisms in pre-Roman Gaul (after Haselgrove 1987: Figure 10.1)

fiscal pressure or ruthless absentee landlordism. Egypt under the Ptolemies or the Romans, or the "middle band" of the Roman Empire in Keith Hopkins's model, may serve to exemplify the former, while Ireland until the Land Purchase Act of 1903, Messenia until the 360s BC, or much of colonial Mesoamerica illustrate the latter all too well. Likewise, it must be possible to plot reciprocal or complex flows such as those that constituted the Athenian grain trade or the Bristol/Liverpool "triangular trade." That "flow" is a metaphor need not mislead; the analogy can be with flows in the natural world (rain–rivers–oceans–condensation–clouds–rain) as much as with fluid mechanics.

A second guideline, already presaged above, is that *the structure within which such flows take place is most easily comprehended visually or diagrammatically.* It can be linked with a third, namely that *complexity in depiction is unavoidable, indeed desirable,* and with a fourth, that *nonphysical flows, especially those generated by euergetism or "social value," have to be represented.* Boulding's paper of 1987, "The Economics of Pride and Shame," and Offer's focus on the "Economics of Regard" (Offer 1997) both valuably suggest ways of marrying theories of social values with economic description, while Boulding's comment (1992: 89) that "it may be a little difficult to include charity in the theory of economic behaviour, but it certainly has to be included in the theory of the economy," provides welcome support for radical approaches. Fifth and last is the caveat, already adumbrated above, that *spatial boundaries apply to public economies but not to real economies.* Such guidelines enjoin a different sort of depiction: not of geographical space but of processual or topological space.

Starting Yet Again: Processual/Topological Space

Here I modify and extend an earlier (Davies 1998) depiction of processual/topological space to illustrate both its possibilities and its limitations. My initial intention had been to try to map on one ordinary Euclidean surface all the main flows predicable of a large and socially complex Greek *Kleinstaat* (microstate). Certain context-specific terminology reveals that the mental model was of Athens, but the basic configuration should be widely applicable. For convenience it was presented in Davies (1998) as a set of stages of development, and the reader is referred there for a more detailed commentary.[10] The first illustration (Fig. 6.8) in the group sketched a first stage of complexity, largely depicting an autarkic agrarian economy but with some recognition of "market"-based exchange within and outside the "region" (however that Procrustean term is to be used). The next image (Fig. 6.9) extended the first in order to encompass the principal flows of resources that were identifiable within a developed *Kleinstaat* economy of the classical period, while a third (Fig. 6.10) attempted to fill it out further by incorporating the main flows of resource and return to and from the "public economy."

Figures 6.8, 6.9, and 6.10 were an experiment, devised in order to establish whether the initial idea would work. Insofar as it does, there are various ways of extending it so as to convey more nuances of information while retaining its location on a single Euclidean surface. Four ways have emerged, which can be labeled as bandwidths, motors, gates, and reservoirs. First are

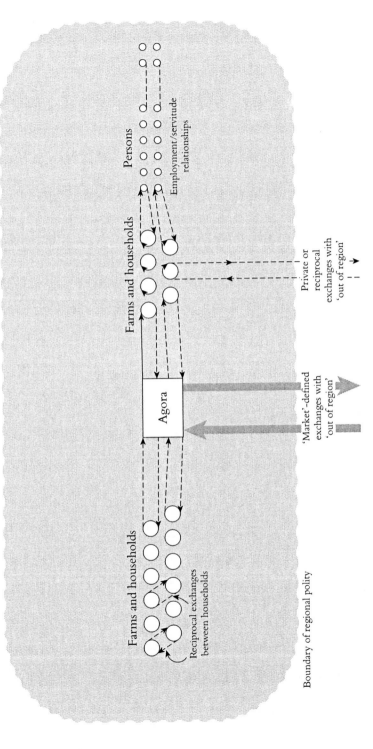

Farms and households

Reciprocal exchanges
between households

Boundary of regional polity

Agora

'Market'-defined
exchanges with
'out of region'

Farms and households

Persons

Employment/servitude
relationships

Private or
reciprocal
exchanges with
'out of region'

Figure 6.8.   Flow chart of resource movement, model 1: Modified household autarky (after Davies 1998: Figure 11.1)

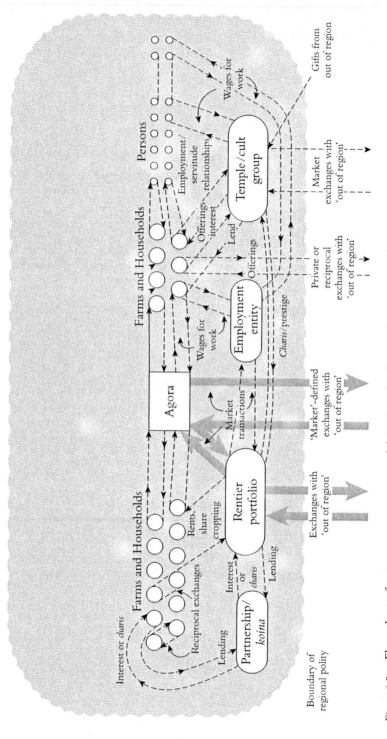

Figure 6.9. Flow chart of resource movement, model 2: Complex flows (after Davies 1998: Figure 11.2)

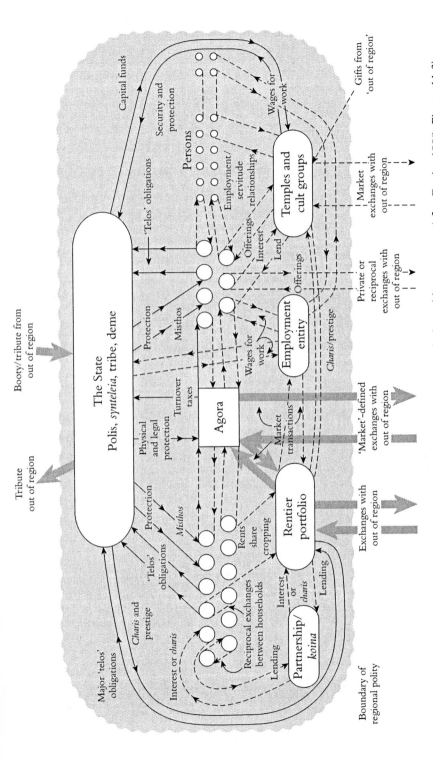

Figure 6.10. Flow chart of resource movement, model 3: Interactions with the public economy (after Davies 1998: Figure 11.3)

bandwidths, a term that I use to describe the trick used in old-fashioned atlases to represent the relative sizes of flows. An image (Fig. 6.11) from a Newnes' atlas of the 1930s illustrates the idea, whereby high-volume sea routes such as those across the North Atlantic generated a thick band, while flows to Mauritius were barely visible. The next two figures show, first, how one could represent a cantonal economy such as Elis or fourth-century Epirus (Fig. 6.12), which was far less market-based than even the most skeptical of Greek historians would claim of Attica; and second, a cantonal or local economy whose economic center was a temple (Fig. 6.13). The prime value of using the bandwidth technique is that it allows us to incorporate into a model such actual indications of quantitative data as it may be possible to excavate and to represent them visually in such a way that the likely earlier and later stages of such flow of resource can be identified. For example, since the sums expended on pay for public office (*misthos*) in a normal year in fourth-century Athens are approximately known (Hansen 1999: 315–16), the lines P^1–P^2 and P^3–P^4 (on Fig. 6.14) can be given something like a "scale" width, which in turn helps us to envisage the (restricted) scale of its impact on the n thousand households symbolically represented by the circles $H_1 \ldots H_n$.

The second category is *motors or "driving forces."* At the risk of forcing the metaphor of "flow," it is worth making the assumption that we are modeling a system of movements that are the product of energy. To identify the impulses that drive resource and exchange around Figures 6.8, 6.9, and 6.10 is partly to resort to answers couched in general terms of human nature, and partly to context-specific attributions of motive. In either case, locating the motors in the "circulation system" of any particular economy helps to determine what kind of economy and society we are trying to model. Thus, for example, if the processual map of Fig. 6.10 were to be used to represent fourth-century Athens, one could construct a case for placing the main motors at points M1, M2, M3, and M4 (as on Fig. 6.14): at M1 to reflect the drive toward the ever more intensive exploitation of land, which has widely been seen as a prominent characteristic of the period; at M2 and M3 to reflect the role of pay for fulfilling active citizenship tasks (*misthos*) as "the glue of the democracy" in Demades' phrase; and at M4 to reflect the scale and social importance of the resources redistributed annually via wealthy men's contributions (part euergetistic, part strong social pressure) to festival liturgies. Of course, reality will have been far more complex, so that debate about the correctness of such localizations is inevitable and utterly proper. A representation such as Figure 6.14 allows us to plot all the possible localizations on a single surface and then to attempt to compare their likely importance and interrelationships.

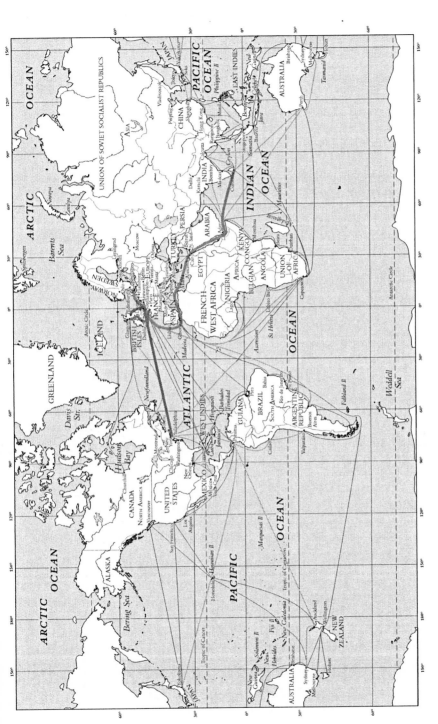

Figure 6.11. World shipping routes of the 1920s (after Bartholomew 1938: viii)

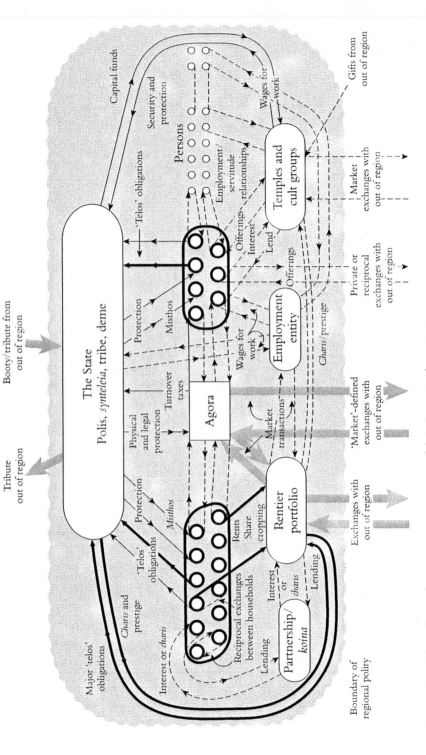

Figure 6.12. Flow chart of resource movement, model 4: A cantonal economy

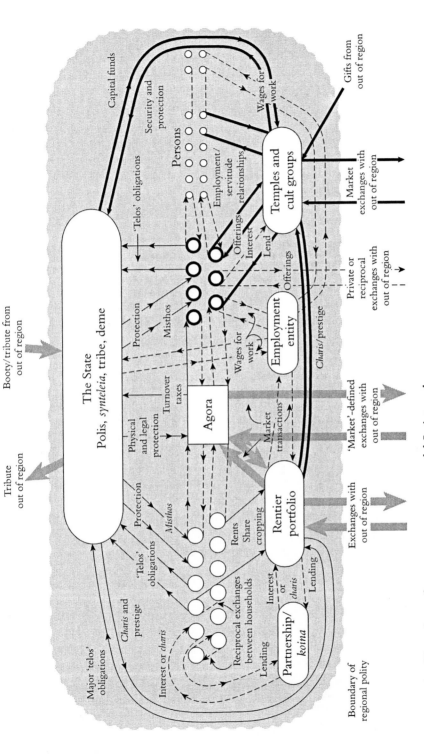

Figure 6.13. Flow chart of resource movement, model 5: A temple economy

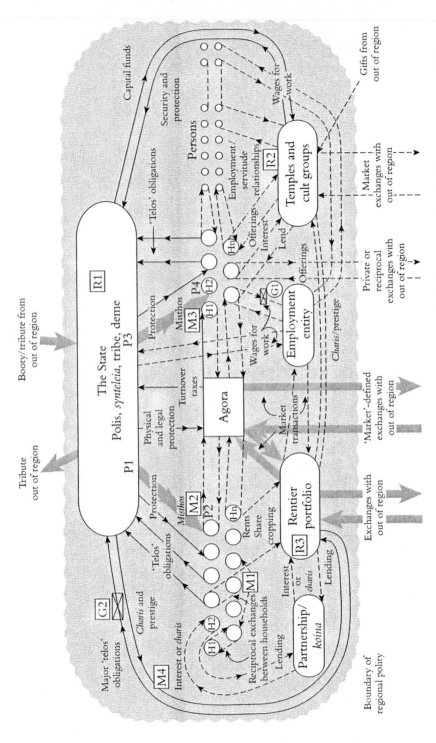

Figure 6.14. Flow chart of resource movement, model 6: Figure 6.10 as modified to incorporate bandwidths, motors, gates, and reservoirs

Third are *gates*, which denote impediments to the rapid flow and exchange of resources, goods, and services. Some will be an intrinsic product
of a given level of technology, such as a stage of transport technology that
yields a very high friction coefficient for distance, or a shortage of bullion
relative to opportunities and needs, which engenders a generally high level
of interest rates. Some may be a matter of social value, such as the Aris-
totelian disapproval of unrestrained money-making (if we can be sure both
that he speaks for a substantial chunk of public opinion and that those who
held the view acted accordingly), or may be imposed by the polity for fiscal
or military reasons (no trading with the enemy; no exporting of this or that
product; a penal level of tax on certain transactions).[11] Again, since every society or "economy" has such gates, the virtue (and the irritation) of Figure
6.14 is that it poses the question of where the principal gate symbols are to
be placed, that is, of deciding just which transactions were impeded by
which gates, and how important or effective they were. As illustrated, G1
is placed across the linkage between household and "employment entity" in
order to reflect the alleged impropriety of one citizen being the private
employee of another (Xenophon, *Memorabilia* 2.8.3–5), while G2 is placed
across the flow of resources deployed for euergetistic and display purposes in
order to reflect the restrictions placed at various times on funerary display
and later on liturgical spending.

Fourth and last come *reservoirs*. I choose this word in order to retain the
metaphor of fluids and flow, but of course it has only to be modified as "reserve" in order to allude to the resource accumulations of the fifth-century
Athenian empire or to the efforts that Androtion, Lycurgus, and others
made to recreate a bullion reserve. The designation R1 on Figure 6.14 indicates publicly held reserves, but since thesaurization took place in private
and cultic contexts as well, the localizations of R2 highlights the existence
of significant resource in the hands of temples and cults, while R3 represents
the well-attested private accumulations of bullion, whether under the floor
as a hoard, or in a bank, or in the *andron* (men's dining room) as a collection
of plate.

The above schemes and representations can only provide synchronic
or "homeostatic" pictures. That criticism, which I owe to Keith Hopkins,
is well taken, but can be met by creating a series of representations predi-
cated at notional chronological intervals, or even better by envisaging an
electronic version of Figure 6.14, so programmed as to be capable of being
scrolled as a representation of the passage of time, to transform itself in
accordance with input data, and thereby to show the changes assumed to
have taken place in real time. Second, as is obvious from the figures, the scale

required to show an economy in the sort of detail sketched above is such that even a *Kleinstaat* no larger than a comparatively homogeneous Greek polis is already straining the limits of practical paper-based representation. For example, to attempt to represent the economy of Hellenistic Egypt in the same way would be impractical, not so much because an economy more obviously driven by fiscal needs, by large estates in royal, temple, or private hands, and by a gigantic royal *oikos* would need to have its "motors" located differently as because the degree of disaggregation of "economies" by region and settlement pattern would generate a picture far too complex to handle.

However, that cannot be the end of the argument. If, as most would now agree, the economy of Hellenistic Egypt (or of any other region of antiquity) *was* complex, we cannot resile from the challenge of representing its complexities in accurate detail. I see three possible ways of meeting the challenge. One is to map such an economy by imagining it as being represented within the orbit of a GIS installation, so that one could zoom in onto any selected part of the picture while retaining the assumption that all activity takes place on a single surface.

The second expedient is to pursue further than I did in 1998 (243 n. 33) the implications of Richard Duncan-Jones's fundamental observation that "the underlying reality [sc. of the Roman Empire] could be a cellular economy in which monetary anomalies were relieved only to a limited extent by fiscal or market mechanisms" (Duncan-Jones 1990: 44). Analogous insights are to be found elsewhere. Drinkwater (1997) has suggested that the regional economies of Roman Gaul could be usefully modeled as a series of ellipses [of internal movement] that intersected at major nodes [for example, Lyon, Bordeaux, and so on]. Kohl (1987: 16) has commented that "the Bronze Age world system of the late third and early second millennia BC was characterized not by a single dominant core region economically linked to less developed peripheral zones, but by a patchwork of overlapping, geographically disparate core regions or foci of cultural development, each of which primarily exploited its own immediate hinterland." Even earlier, for Marfoe (1987: 34; agreed by Moorey 1987: 44) "the system that emerged by the mid-third millennium was a wide but poorly articulated landscape of heterogeneous groups and political units interconnected by fluctuating linkages between mainly elite groups." Given so clear a convergence of ideas from students of different regions and periods, it might be profitable at least to attempt the task of translating them into a usable representation (Fig. 6.15). Its core idea is to break down the unwieldy, and perhaps overpoliticized, format of the final flow diagram (Fig. 6.14) into a structure of nested cells. Level alpha, the household, may be taken for the moment as conceptually

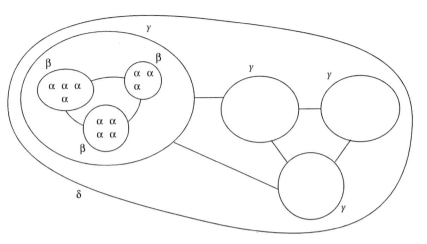

Figure 6.15.   Developed cellular structure for ancient economies

straightforward (though it is not), while the insertion of Level beta serves both to accommodate the agricultural (village) cell (Fig. 6.1, page 133) and to challenge the assumptions inherent in the phrase "the polis [or civitas] economy." Accordingly, if the "cell" labeled "Level gamma" is taken as equivalent to the "boundary of regional polity" of the final flow diagram (Fig. 6.14), then it becomes possible both to envisage an indefinitely extensible set of such gamma-cells and to postulate their encapsulation within a delta-cell. Plainly, that is not necessarily the end of the matter, for if, say, the classical Mediterranean were seen as one delta-cell, India were seen as a second, and Han China as a third, it would be possible to represent the underlying image of the Wallersteinian world-system model as an epsilon-cell.

This may look like playing infantile games. Not so, for at any cellular level the connections between cells (lines, routes, gateways of exchange) can be treated as channels with certain qualities. They can be envisaged as having gates across them in the same way as linkages within the individual cell (for example fiscal impediments, or physical impediments such as pirates); they can be regarded as components of a distance-decay function, comparable to (but probably more adverse than) the inverse square law of transport economics; they can have other transaction costs ascribed to them; and they too can have motors attached, whether in the form of the classical Mediterranean's insatiable demand for spices, or the profits that fed the tax income of Palmyra.

However, there is a third way of meeting the challenge. I broach it with much circumspection, for to do so is to venture into academic areas that are

beyond my present competence. This is to abandon the single-surface assumption and the "flow" metaphor and to adopt instead the intellectual paradigm of most mainstream economics (and of some economic history),
namely to think in terms of equations. If after all "there is a large number of
goods and services and of people and companies even in a small economy,
each with an equation describing their economic behaviour" (Ormerod
1994: 79), a comparable assumption should apply to the components of any
ancient economy. The "absence of data" does not preclude any such approach
from being meaningful; as the equations devised by Rihll and Wilson (1991)
attest, the critical task is accurately identifying the main structural components of relationships and interactions between covariables, not necessarily
quantifying the arithmetic values of the variables. I do not yet know how to
develop the idea. Possibilities are: to retain the notion of a single surface of interaction (though one immeasurably more complex than the Möbius strips
or self-convoluting amoeba shapes that are all that textbooks of topology can
illustrate); to explore the world of self-imitating fractal patterns; to explore
the sorts of dynamic nonlinear models, influenced by chaos theory, which are
being applied to more and more contexts of the natural world; or to conceive
of a multidimensional economic world populated by microentities comparable to the strings of contemporary string theory in physics.

Envoi

I sense that there are four potentially productive ways out of the black hole
of frustration in which many economic historians of antiquity are trapped.
The first is to explore the possibilities, outlined above, of mathematicizing
the language of description. The second, set out in some detail in Davies 2001
and therefore merely alluded to here, is to follow individual substances and
commodities in detail from production to consumption, with the eventual
aim of painting a composite portrait of everything that was made and used.
Some distinguished studies of the "trade" in particular commodities already
exist, but huge gaps remain to be filled, even at the purely descriptive level.
A third is to add further planned installments to the long-established but uncoordinated genre represented by Rostovtzeff (1922) on Zenon or Andreau
(1974) on Jucundus or Reger (1994) on Delos, that is, to study economic life
as revealed by a single archive or class of documents or artifacts.
    A fourth would be to pick up the economists' notion of "transaction
costs" (see Morris and Manning's introduction), but to shift the angle of
view. To use it as a peg for a covertly prescriptivist attitude toward cost cutting is plainly no more helpful than to attempt to trace through time, from

the standpoint of Now, an asymptotically falling curve of reduction in such costs. Rather, it can stimulate us constructively by prompting the following questions: What institutions, practices, and values comprised the environmental framework within which economic activity took place? How did systems evolve that assisted the creation, movement, and delivery of goods and services in a landscape? How did they interact with forms of behavior that had different objectives? It will be obvious that such systems may be "technological" in the broad sense (transportation modes and infrastructure, coinage, and so on) or institutional (polities as providers of security, banks, formal or informal associations), and that their evolution, even in any one landscape or region at any one time, was neither unidirectional nor tidy. Precisely for those reasons, provided that we are prepared to use our imaginations in order to reconstruct the pressures and circumstances that led to their development, to focus on the detailed history of systems and institutions *is* to create a viable and useful form of economic history.[12]

This chapter has not been about ancient texts and artifacts, nor even about modern controversies, but about ways of modeling the salient characteristics of the economic behavior of antiquity when we have no quantitative data worth the name. The main direction of argument has been to advocate modeling in terms of process and of the flow of resources and return on a single surface within topological space (my outreach toward topology, tentatively deployed in Davies [1998], was anticipated in Boulding [1981: 86–87]). Whether that quasi-mathematical model is the most promising option, or whether the metaphor of "cell" should rather be leading us to borrow ideas from the current ferment of study of biological models of complex systems (P. M. Allen 1988; 1997), or whether such ambitious explorations should be held in abeyance until many more studies of individual archives and genres are available, are matters for urgent debate.[13]

Notes

1. It would be rawer still but for discussion and helpful comments offered at its previous outings. For such help I am most grateful to Zosia Archibald, Graham Oliver, and Christopher Tuplin at Liverpool; Richard Duncan-Jones, Peter Garnsey, and Keith Hopkins at Cambridge; and Robert Adams, Mario Liverani, Bruce Hitchner, and Takeshi Amemiya at Stanford; and also to Sir Tony Wrigley (*per ep.*). The paper would not have existed at all but for the Leverhulme Trust's unqualified support, which cannot be adequately recompensed.

2. This is not the place to explore either the extent to which Athenian law accommodated the concept of a juristic person (basic discussion in Harrison

1968: 240–42), or the extent and limitations of Roman public or Imperial permission "*corpus habere*," for which compare *imprimis D.* 3.4.1 pr. and 1 (Gaius III *Ad edictum*) with De Robertis (1971 vol. II: 235–410); still less can the interaction of law and practice be broached.

3. For the basic nexus of ideas, see Walter 1993. Granted, some polities were unquestionably hybrids, showing characteristics of both models. Macedon before Alexander was probably one such, as also almost certainly was the Molossian monarchy of Epirus.

4. It would be tempting to use the phrase "weightless goods" for such "social returns," had that phrase not been currently preempted among economists to denote intangibles such as personal services and computer software.

5. For example, see Rowlands et al. (1987), though there are dissenting voices therein, and Shipley (1993) for an overview.

6. See Postgate 1992: 109–36; and Liverani, Chapter 2. The problem is not confined to antiquity; monasteries as landowners and as productive actors pose the same problem.

7. See Postgate (1992: 175) for the schematic representation of the village as an "agricultural cell" in south Mesopotamia; Eyre (1999), with his statement "Egypt was probably always a village society" and his warning, drawn from N. S. Hopkins (1987: 48 n. 4; with further references), against treating the village as a single model (ibid 35 with n. 12). For "village economies" within "polis economies," see below.

8. I take the word from descriptions of postwar Italian politics, where a *monocolore* government was one comprising members of one party only (invariably the Christian Democrats), as opposed to a coalition.

9. An obvious example: Twenty years ago "green economics" was a mantra of fringe or "alternative" groups but is now both a journalists' cliché and a component of mainstream politics and investment decisions, while not yet being in any real sense the "dominant mode." Unless future economic historians of late-twentieth-century Europe build that mode of thinking and acting into their structures *pari passu* with other modes, their structures—or their models—will simply be wrong. Boulding characteristically hits the relevant note with his section "Ecological Economics" (1992: 239–333).

10. The influence of Plato (*Republic* 2.369[b] ff.) and Aristotle (*Politics* 1.1252[b]) is embarrassingly hard to escape from.

11. Liverani (1987: 67) gives examples from the Late Bronze Age.

12. The theme is explored in more detail in Davies 2001. Since that was drafted, John-Paul Wilson's work on the Iron Age West Mediterranean, which lays a similar emphasis on the importance of the growth of institutions, provides welcome stimulus and support.

13. I am most grateful to Peter Hart for bringing Peter Allen's work to my attention.

Chapter 7

Comment on Davies

TAKESHI AMEMIYA

I find Professor Davies's paper very stimulating. It addresses many interesting problems concerning the analysis and the understanding of the Athenian economy. Here I will take up some of these problems roughly in the order presented in the chapter and comment on them from the viewpoint of an economist and an econometrician.

The first problem addressed, as described in the title of the first section, "The Inapplicability of Classical Economic Analysis." It is concerned with the well-known formalist-substantivist controversy. Davies seems to be on the side of the substantivist, as the title of the section suggests. The substantivist's view is that modern economic analysis presupposes certain behavior patterns for consumers and producers and certain institutions prevalent in modern industrialized economies and therefore is inapplicable to the Athenian economy.

I believe that this view overemphasizes the importance of a theoretical model, or what Finley calls superstructure, in modern economic analysis. Modern economists may give the impression that they believe that every consumer maximizes utility and every producer maximizes profit, but they are actually much more pragmatic. Every applied econometric work does start with the ritual of observing the tenets of utility maximization and profit maximization but quickly moves on to a more realistic statistical model that simply purports to fit the data well.

A purist will try to estimate a so-called structural model that is derived from theoretical behavioral assumptions, but most econometricians are content with estimating statistical models called reduced form. This latter majority of econometricians would be just as comfortable with the Athenian economy as with the modern industrialized economy, aside from the problem of the lack of data in the former. Even the purist, however, cannot completely rely on his or her theoretical assumptions. Take, for example, a demand and supply model, the economist's bread and butter. Utility maximization under the budget constraint tells the economist that the demand will depend on the income and the prices—the prices of all the goods, not just the good in question. Practical necessity will force the economist to select only a few prices as well as to choose a functional form, usually linear, about which economic theory can tell us nothing. To quote Blaug (1992: 144), "In their authoritative survey of empirical research on demand relationships since World War II, Brown and Deaton (1972) noted that much empirical work on demand had been purely 'pragmatic' and carried out with very little reference to any theory of consumer behavior." Similar problems arise on the supply side as well: The economist is well aware that in big firms the assumption of profit maximization is not realistic because of the dichotomy between owners and managers.

The consumer really does not maximize utility, and the producer really does not maximize profit. Nevertheless, the fact that economists—whether they believe in it themselves or not—have kept saying the opposite has had an undesirable effect on society. This is where social sciences differ from physical sciences. The physical world did not start behaving in conformity with Newtonian physics. Thus, Hausman and McPherson write:

> Furthermore, generalizations about what people in fact do, will (unless written in terms of condemnation) influence what people think ought to be done. Even if what ought to be does not follow logically from what is, it often follows psychologically. Saying that human behavior can be modeled as if it were entirely self-interested unavoidably legitimizes and fosters self-interested behavior. Indeed, there is some evidence that learning economics may make people more selfish. (Hausman and McPherson 1996: 219)

One way in which economists achieved this influence, consciously or unconsciously, was by using the word *rationality* in a narrower sense than is ordinarily used. It has been proposed that the ancient Greeks pursued status more than profit. In the ordinary sense of the word, it would be perfectly rational for one to pursue status more than profit if that was what one wanted, but not so for the economist. It would be perfectly rational for common people to marry for the sake of love, companionship, and the enjoyment of having children, but not so for the economist. The rational economist marries in order to maximize the present value of the future income stream. *Irrational* is a loaded word that has been used by whoever wanted to silence the heretics. It was first used by the materialist and then by the economist.

Some substantivists proposed status as an alternative motivation to profit because they overemphasized the importance of the behavioral assumptions for an economic model. Above I have argued the contrary. It is an interesting sociological and psychological problem to ask whether the rich Athenian citizen undertook liturgies for the sake of status. One can specify an economic model involving the total amount of liturgies, however, without knowing the answer to that question, just as the modern economist can specify a supply and demand model without assuming utility maximization and profit maximization. For a student of the Athenian economy it is more important to understand an accounting identity that involves the amount of liturgies. Namely, the amount of liturgies that represents the flow of money from the rich to the poor must match the net revenue of the agricultural and manufacturing products that the rich receive from the poor. Thus I wholeheartedly agree with Davies's emphasis on economic flow charts. The noted economist Thomas C. Shelling, in his commencement address to the Department of Economics at the University of California, Berkeley, on May 20, 1994 (published in *The American Economist* 39 [Spring 1995]: 20−22), said that the only five candidates for things he learned in economics that are simultaneously true, important, and not obvious are all accounting identities.

As Davies notes, when we associate each flow by a number, we obtain a system of equations that represents an economy. Such a system will consist of accounting identities as well as equations representing production technologies. I have mentioned an example of an accounting identity above. The other important equations will be the import-export identity, an identity that equates the need for grain with domestic production plus import. A major problem with such a system of equations is the gross inaccuracy of the numerical values of the variables that are involved. The values can be estimated only within a very wide range. For example, some estimates put the total population in Athens in the late fourth century at two hundred thousand and some at three hundred thousand, and the amount of wheat imported in a given year in the fourth century might have been as large as eight hundred thousand *medimnoi* or as small as four hundred thousand medimnoi. I am currently investigating how much we can narrow these ranges when we make all the variables satisfy the system of equations. For example, let A be the population; B, the per capita consumption of grain; C, the area of cultivated land; D, agricultural productivity; and E, the grain import. Then we must have $A \times B = C \times D + E$, and certain estimates of these five variables will be incompatible with the equation.

Flow charts and mathematics for solving equations will be undoubtedly useful in the study of the ancient economy, as Davies points out. As for the use of more sophisticated mathematics, however, I am not as optimistic as Davies. The more mathematically sophisticated the model becomes, the further it tends to deviate from reality, and yet it becomes more difficult for the mathematically naive to discern just what is wrong with the model. Davies refers to Rihll and Wilson (1991) as an example of the use of sophisticated mathematics in the analysis of the ancient economy (population). Unfortunately, the assumptions of the model are not explicitly stated, and only the mathematically sophisticated reader will understand that theirs is a model for a steady-state equilibrium population. I doubt if such a model would be appropriate for the analysis of population in such an extremely volatile age as Geometric Greece. General equilibrium analysis is the area of economic theory where the most sophisticated mathematics has been used. Concerning this area of study, Blaug (1992: 169) writes as follows: "Enormous intellectual resources have been invested in its endless refinements, none of which has even provided a fruitful starting point from which to approach a substantive explanation of the workings of an economic system."

Finally, I am in full agreement with Davies's criticism of Finley's position that "we must concentrate on the dominant types, the characteristic modes of behaviour" (Finley 1985a: 29). Davies goes on to say that "the first step toward sanity for an economic historian of antiquity is to accept that in any landscape, at any epoch, one should expect such sets of different modes of behavior to coexist, and should therefore expect to be in the business of creating models that show a high degree of intricacy, complexity, instability, and disarticulatedness." I must say that it is the sanity every economist should strive for, not just an economic historian of antiquity, and that, unfortunately, it has seldom been attained.

Part III

Egypt

Chapter 8

The Relationship of Evidence to Models in the Ptolemaic Economy (332 BC–30 BC)

J. G. MANNING

> The health of the overall economic system, overwhelmingly dependent on agriculture, was consequently controlled as much by environment as by human variables. Ultimately, the central government was weak when the national economy was weak, although a weak government could equally lead to a weak economy.
> —Butzer, "Long-Term Nile Flood Variation and Political Discontinuities in Pharaonic Egypt," 1980

> Science progresses step by step and nobody should be afraid of committing mistakes in dealing with new and unexplained material, assuming that his study of this material is thorough, animated by a sincere desire to find the truth, and founded on a well established general conception.
> —Rostovtzeff, *A Large Estate in Egypt in the Third Century BC*, 1922

In this chapter I describe the relationship between the complex documentary evidence from Ptolemaic Egypt and the building of general models of the Ptolemaic economy. The study of Ptolemaic Egypt, and in particular the study of the Ptolemaic economy, has until recently been the exclusive preserve of papyrologists, specialists in the reading and interpretation of papyri. There has been very little in the way of general treatment of the economy in the context of broader issues within economic history.[1] There has been good reason for this. The documentation is written in both Greek, the language of the central government, and in the difficult to read demotic, the late form of cursive writing that came into use in the Saite period (664–525 BC). Greek and demotic papyrology are separate specialties. The disciplines meet separately and have their own journals and, until quite recently, there has been little attempt at synthesizing the Greek and demotic material. We are thus still some distance away from a truly synthetic account of the Ptolemaic economy. Such an account would incorporate data from the Greek and demotic papyri and ostraca as well as archaeological data, coins, inscriptions, other historical evidence, and economic theory. I believe that an economic history of Ptolemaic Egypt can be written, but I am less confident about the possibility of proposing a dynamic, testable model. This is the nature of the ancient economy—we must remain more descriptive than analytic, and less sharp than in studies of later economies, despite what is a considerable amount of documentation for some sectors of the economy. For example, statistical analyses, or simple time-series studies, cannot be done with this evidence. So many data are utterly lacking, including some basic information on the expenditure side of the state's economy. But such fragmentary data should not lead to total despair in writing economic history or in proposing general models; it is indeed problematic in all economic history.[2] In any case I have more modest aims in this chapter. I intend here to give an overview of the field and with a few examples show the relationship of the evidence to model building. I will not be comprehensive in my treatment of the primary or the secondary sources; indeed, I will focus on studies written before Finley's influential work. But I hope that my coverage will give the reader a solid idea of the methodology of the field and how it contrasts with other areas of research on the ancient economy.

The question before us is: How does the type of evidence that has come down to us from the ancient Mediterranean world shape the way in which we build models of the ancient economy? Moses Finley's *The Ancient Economy*, a work that continues to dominate the study of the ancient economy, built a model that intended to cover the whole of the Mediterranean over fifteen hundred years. In fact Finley's treatment covered only classical Greece and Rome. What the work lacked in detail, it made up for in clarity of analysis and the scope of its coverage. Finley worked within a Weberian social science framework and conceived of the issues in terms of "ideal types." A few examples drawn from literary evidence were enough to illustrate his basic points about production, class, private property, and the lack of economic thought in the classical world. In stark contrast, the text-based approach of Near Eastern historians and papyrologists emphasizes the particular details of the sources themselves, usually studied within what are identified as "archives," and most studies do not stress general implications. The result of Finley's work was the contrast it intentionally drew between the ancient Mediterranean and the late medieval European worlds; in particular, the absence of economic growth in the former, and real, sustained economic growth in the latter. Egypt and the Near East were excluded by Finley, despite the fact that these civilizations had important long-term impacts on the "stock of knowledge" of the Mediterranean world, because they were irrelevant to the contrast he wanted to draw.[3]

Finley defended his exclusion of Egypt by claiming that the economies of Egypt and the Near East were organized differently than the classical world. In the former, the economy was centered around "large palace- or temple complexes" that "virtually monopolized anything that can be called 'industrial production' as well as foreign trade . . . and organized the economic, military, political and religious life of the society through a single complicated, bureaucratic, record-keeping operation" (Finley 1985a: 28). For Finley, this type of economic organization, centralized and autocratic, was significantly different from the classical world until the era of Alexander the Great and the Roman Empire. Yet Finley barely touched on Hellenistic or Roman Egypt. Importantly though, the economic organization of Egypt in these later periods relied much less, if at all, on distribution through local temples. Finley's work focused on what he called "dominant types" and "characteristic modes of behaviour," echoing Weber. Private ownership and private production, he wrongly claimed, were hallmarks of classical civilization and not prevalent in the Near East or Egypt. And for the later history of these regions, despite many important changes, Finley did not include much about them because he did not isolate a "Hellenistic" economy. Rather, even for this period, Finley distinguished between "ancient" and "oriental" sectors of the economy, without considering the historical development or the rationalization of the two.[4] Clearly much was ignored in his categorization, and there is good evidence to suggest that Finley was hostile to the use of the papyri, and to papyrological methodology more generally, and uninterested in the Hellenistic world at large (see Bagnall, Chapter 9). In part Finley's dismissal reflected the disciplinary boundaries, still prevalent, between ancient (usually meaning classical) history, Assyriology, Egyptology, papyrology, and epigraphy, with all of these separated by a great distance from social science methodology and economic history. Whether one chooses to emphasize the general or the particular, whether one asks a good question or merely seeks to describe, substantially alters the kind of economic history one produces. The gap between the northern and eastern Mediterranean created by the disciplinary boundaries often appears larger than it really was. There is astonishingly little exchange between mainstream ancient historians and papyrologists. Although Finley was probably right to isolate the classical world from the ancient Near East and from pharaonic Egypt on the basis of the differences in economic organization, the Hellenistic kingdoms that grew out of the Persian empire were more closely connected to the rest of Mediterranean history and are important for understanding the Roman imperial economy.

Ptolemaic Egypt

The Ptolemaic regime in Egypt belongs to a broad historical era known commonly as the Hellenistic period.[5] The term *Hellenistic* has since its inception carried negative connotations of decline (see Green 1990). This period of Egyptian history tends to be treated as a stepchild. For Hellenists, it represents a period of cultural decline. For Egyptologists too, its subject matter is no longer "Egypt" but is cast instead as the "late" period, the *basse époque*, implying low in terms of date *and* culture. The study of Ptolemaic Egypt has been the preserve of specialist papyrologists and epigraphers rather than of ancient historians, who often demur because of the vast amount of material and the now impressively large body of secondary literature. As a result, a separate field of ancient history, papyrological history, has emerged (see Frier 1989; Bagnall 1995). Results, published usually in specialized journals, can take years to get into the mainstream. But the last two decades of scholarship have seen a renewed general interest in the period. One reason for this is the impetus provided by Edward Said's book *Orientalism* (1978), which has engendered postcolonial readings of Hellenistic history. Yet another, stronger, reason for the renewed interest has been papyrological studies that have made more accessible both the sources themselves and their interpretation. Hand-in-hand with this happy trend has been the revival of the study and publication of demotic texts (DePauw 1997). The demotic language was used primarily to record private legal contracts and tax receipts and is crucial for our understanding of Egyptian institutions and the organization of local economies.

By the time Alexander the Great entered Egypt, it had been part of the Persian empire for two centuries. During this period, the use of coinage, market exchange, and more extensive trade contacts were developed. Whatever Persian intentions were, the fact is that Egypt was increasingly integrated into a larger world, continuing the socioeconomic shift toward the Mediterranean begun in the Ramesside period (circa 1200 BC). The Ptolemies further developed trade routes, particularly Ptolemy II, who devoted considerable energy to opening up trade by building roads that connected the Nile to Red Sea ports. Under the Ptolemies, the language of the administration was Greek. Egyptian—both demotic, used on papyri and ostraca (small sherds of pottery or limestone), and hieroglyphic, used on monumental inscriptions—continued to be used at the local level by Egyptian priests and others. While there are some political narrative histories of the period, the papyri and ostraca offer the only opportunity in Hellenistic history to reconstruct economic structures and behavior. But it is the complexity of this evidence that has kept most historical analysis restricted to a small group of specialists. The question, for the papyrological historian, and the real challenge, comes in the interpretation: How widely can the documentary evidence be applied? To what extent does it reflect normative practice? Does it document the aims of the state as well as provide positive proof of the rural realities of the economy of Ptolemaic Egypt? And are models helpful or necessary?

The Evidence

In contrast to Finley's approach to the ancient economy, the study of the Ptolemaic economy has been driven by the study of documents and *explication de textes*. The approach is best seen in the two most influential scholars of the Ptolemaic economy, Claire Préaux and Michael Rostovtzeff. Archaeology and numismatics have only recently, and only partially, been considered within broader discussions of the economy.[6] The rich material from Egypt has placed the Ptolemaic period at the forefront of the study of the Hellenistic world, yet Egypt is often avoided by the ancient historian. The avoidance is caused by three related reasons: (1) the technical training that is required to read Greek (and demotic Egyptian) papyri requires a large investment of time; (2) the Egyptian evidence is considered parochial precisely because it comes from Egypt, which many historians see as unique in terms of ecology and culture, and only valid for a circumscribed time and place; and (3) as a result of the first two reasons, since the papyri are very difficult technically, full of interpretive land mines, and are ephemeral in the data they provide, they are therefore of limited value for the economic history of the period.

Each new archive or group of texts brings additional information and changes the general interpretation of the period. Our working knowledge of the Ptolemaic economy, then, has been built up over the last eighty years by the slow accumulation of facts from the papyri. Publication of first editions of Ptolemaic papyri continues, but the most important collections of Ptolemaic papyri had already been published by the 1950s (Bagnall 1982/83: 13). Yet there is important work to be done even after papyri have been made available. These activities include the republication of older material, the correction of spurious readings, and the reconstruction of private and official archives that have been scattered by the antiquities market (legally or otherwise) or separated in original studies by the language of the document (Pestman 1990; Vandorpe 1994). There are also newly excavated Ptolemaic papyri, which come from what is called cartonnage—papyrus texts reused in the mummification process of humans and animals (for example, the papyri in the Heidelberg collection published by Duttenhöfer [1994]). Each new study brings with it, usually, a vast bibliography in support of this evidence. This is not to diminish recent work in any way. For example, the collection and reediting of previously published papyri, as well as new documentation for the Ptolemaic census, and the important results that this study will produce, will fundamentally improve our understanding of the political organization, tax structure, and demography of the third century BC.[7] The demotic material contains more important new information, particularly about the relationship between villages and the central state and the functioning of Egyptian temples, which were still important institutions under the Ptolemies but much diminished in their economic importance. Here, much work remains to be done, particularly on integrating demotic and Greek material. Until recently, documents written in these two languages were studied and published separately, even if they were part of the same bilingual family archive. The demotic papyri are generally records of the activities of temples and priestly families. As such, they often provide good local records of private economic activity and suggest that we should rethink the model of a highly centralized economy and move toward an analysis that views the state as a federation, and Ptolemaic policy as having a regional strategy.

The skewed survival of documentation (skewed in several ways—in the type of documents that survive, and in the geographical and chronological scatter) makes it extraordinarily difficult to assess regional variation in the land tenure regime on the basis of the texts alone.[8] For example, from Upper (southern) Egypt, there is much more private documentation written in demotic than in Greek. This documentation records in the main private contracts of conveyance of real property, agreements between private parties, marriage contracts, and the like. The Greek administrative layer of texts is far thinner here. But does that mean that the Ptolemaic state was less effective in, or less concerned with, this region? Or can we say that there was a different system of administration, in effect relying on the local temple institutions to run the region on behalf of the kings in Alexandria? Or does the lack of the same kind of Greek administrative material from the Arsinoite (Fayyum) and Herakleopolite nomes (administrative/political units) in the north, which we have relied on to build our picture of the administrative structure of Ptolemaic Egypt, simply mean that this material was not preserved in Upper Egypt? There is some reason to infer this latter possibility, but as yet, little proof. A more likely model of Ptolemaic institutional history would posit a gradual bureaucratization of Upper Egypt, with a social lag in this region (compared to the Fayyum at least) because of the old institutional arrangements that the Ptolemies left in place.

The gulf between the historical methodology of Moses Finley and of most scholars who have worked on Ptolemaic Egypt centers on the use of

the papyri, which has tended to deflect scholars away from general considerations into the particulars of reading and interpreting texts. The key factor, for which Finley criticized work on Ptolemaic Egypt more than once,
comes in the weighing of this evidence (how many attestations are sufficient
to prove that a factor or structure was normative?), and the conversion of
this evidence to show not only government intentions but rural reality as
well. Finley termed this positivist accumulation of evidence from texts the
"tell-all-you-know" technique (1985b: 63). In criticizing papyrological
methodology, he referred to two large and influential works. The first was
Peter Fraser's three-volume study *Ptolemaic Alexandria* (1972), a history of
the city built up in large part by gathering all of the "evidence" from the
documentary sources. The book asked no questions; it merely sought to describe. The second part of Finley's critical remarks was directed at the study
of archives, specifically the large and important group of texts known as the
Zenon archive, a corpus that has been central to discussions of the Ptolemaic
economy of the third century BC.[9] Finley singled out an early study by
Claire Préaux (1947), and made the (not invalid) criticism that despite her
claim to produce a "synthesis of economic history," the work is little more
than a catalogue of facts (Finley 1985b: 34–36). The archive itself, in his
view, was no more than day-to-day records of business activity, with no sign
of more sophisticated planning or organization, and giving only an "illusion" of accounting and of economic planning. The gulf remains wide between building general economic models and interpreting the texts, between economic historians and papyrologists, although Roger Bagnall (1995
and in the next chapter) has suggested a good middle ground in writing
"papyrological history." But the sense persists that theory is in some ways
not as necessary as in other areas of ancient history because of the thickness
of the documentation itself. The texts, as it were, "speak for themselves."
This basic lack of historical methodology arises from the fact that most
papyrologists are trained in philology, paleography, and, in a few cases, law.
The resulting attention to the details of texts, legal clauses and the like, as
opposed to the asking of questions, goes a long way in accounting for the
perceived differences between Moses Finley and Michael Rostovtzeff.

  Papyrologists generally divide the evidence by language into the categories of Greek and demotic, and subdivide each into papyri and ostraca. Often
these groups are studied and published separately, sometimes years apart, by
specialists in these fields, even when "archives" are written in both Greek and
demotic.[10] There are of course other kinds of evidence, such as inscriptions
written in Greek and Egyptian, coins, and, increasingly, archaeology. But it
has been the papyri that drives the models, and in particular the Greek papyri

from the Fayyum region. There are now about forty-eight thousand Greek
papyri and ostraca from the Ptolemaic and Roman periods, the overwhelming majority from the Ptolemaic period coming from the Arsinoite nome (the
Fayyum), and the neighboring Herakleopolite nome, including the important third-century BC papyri from the town of Ankyronpolis (El-Hibeh) (in
general, see Rupprecht 1994). Far less Greek material has come from the Upper Egyptian Nile valley, where the demotic documents outweigh the Greek.
There remain only a handful of datable Greek texts from before 285 BC (see
Fig. 8.1).

   Our basic understanding of the Ptolemaic economy has been built up using Greek administrative papyri from the mid-third and late-second centuries
BC. For the so-called royal economy, a few key papyri stand out. Among
these, papyri from Gurob (P. Petrie) and Ghoran (P. Lille, P. Sorbonne),
P. Rev., P. Tebt. III 703, and the Zenon papyri, all from the third century BC,
and the Menches archive (late second-century BC), have been the main
sources for the structure of the Ptolemaic administration (Thompson 1999:
125–26). But a fundamental problem remains: Can we generalize from the

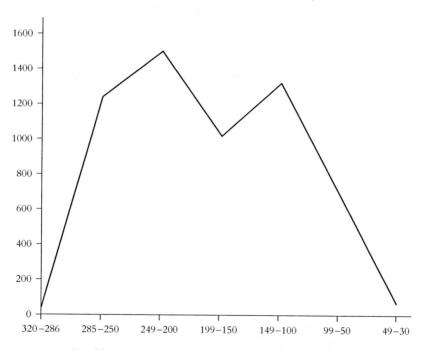

Figure 8.1.   Datable Greek texts by half-century for the Ptolemaic period, 320
to 30 BC (From the *Heidelberger Gesamtverzeichnis der Griechischen
Papyruskunden Ägyptens*)

Fayyum evidence? A large land reclamation project, organized by Ptolemy II and III, and the settlement of new populations (Greeks, and others) in new towns, especially on the edge of the south Fayyum, made the area a particular concern of the state. This is suggested by the higher percentage of "royal land" here than in the Nile valley. One of the contrasts that emerges from an examination of the Greek and demotic papyri together is that the state directly intervened in the economic organization of the third-century Fayyum, whereas in the Nile valley, the state used old institutions (temples, an already established land tenure regime) where possible. It is worth mentioning that much of this Greek documentation comes from villages on the desert outskirts of the Fayyum and derive from animal and human cartonnage. By the very nature of the materials used to embalm sacred animals and in the manufacture of human mummy masks, the texts have been discarded according to rules that are often unclear to us (perhaps sold off by local bureaus as a local fiscal measure mandated by Ptolemy II) and are therefore skewed in their content and date (E. G. Turner 1980: ch. 4). More ephemeral texts tended to get discarded and therefore preserved as cartonnage (Verhoogt 1997: 44). The data in them must be used with extreme care. The archive of the village scribe Menches (in fact not an archive but a selection from an archive, and not that of the village scribe Menches but of one of his successors), for example, provides rich details of the administration of land, from the land survey to the actual accounting of projected and assessed rents from all of the land (about 2,650 acres) around the village of Kerkeosiris in the south Fayyum. On careful examination, the figures of rents collected look suspiciously similar from year to year, giving occasion to suspect that numbers were sometimes simply carried forward from year to year. For example, prescriptions for the details of land to be sown with specified crops and the expected rents at the beginning of the year should have been balanced with recalculations of rent that could be collected on the basis of the survey of standing crops. All of this, however, is in advance of the actual rents that were collected (Crawford 1973: 242–43). Thus assessing the real productivity of the land, even with land registers over a ten-year period, is fraught with interpretive difficulties. Yet the model, or at least the basic understanding, of the Ptolemaic economy has been built up from these texts.

The Models—Theory and Praxis

Two scholars have dominated the study of the Ptolemaic economy, despite the fact that their great works were written more then fifty years ago. These scholars are Claire Préaux, whose work *L'Économie royale des Lagides* appeared in 1939, and Michael Rostovtzeff, who wrote two books that are still widely read today: *A Large Estate in Egypt in the Third Century B.C.* (1922) and *The Social and Economic History of the Hellenistic World* (1941).[11] These works are still monuments in the field because of their scope, and they form the basis for all subsequent work. Both authors produced syntheses, but in their use of large amounts of documentary evidence, they were descriptive rather than model driven. I focus here on Rostovtzeff, whose narrative style makes his work highly readable but difficult to pin down, and who has been more influential in the English-speaking world. Préaux substantially revised her views in 1978, but Rostovtzeff never did so. As a result, his statements are frequently contradictory.[12] To summarize his views, Rostovtzeff argued that the Hellenistic world was characterized by several key factors: as Cartledge (1997: 11–12) puts it, "A single, interdependent economic system characterized by sustained economic growth that was driven above all by long-distance interregional trade conducted by agents of a rising urban bourgeoisie." Another key component in Rostovtzeff's "model" was that the Ptolemies continued Egyptian institutions where possible (Samuel 1989: 53). But this aspect of Ptolemaic Egypt has not been explored. The resulting "social lag" in institutional development should in fact be an essential ingredient in any model of the economy of Ptolemaic Egypt (Manning 2003).

Rostovtzeff, in all of his work on the Hellenistic period, shows that he had a great command of the Greek papyri available in his day (and was aware that the Egyptian material was important). He did not consider the period as a time of collapse of Greek culture but as a new age of experiment, the articulation of new political institutions, and of economic development and growth. His optimistic view of the evidence from the papyri, and his accumulation of facts drawn from them, contrasts with Finley's attitudes and his social science methodology. Rostovtzeff's first study (he called it an "article" although its length, 209 pages of text and indices, certainly qualifies it as a monograph) focused on the Zenon archive.[13] This collection of documents, something on the order of seventeen hundred usable texts, was the records of Zenon of Caria (southwest Turkey) who had immigrated along with thousands of others from the Greek world in search of opportunity in Egypt. He served as the estate manager of Apollonios, the *dioiketes*, or finance minister, of Ptolemy II Philadelphus (282–246 BC). The bulk of the texts comprise official correspondence and other documents used in the management of the estate, ten thousand *arouras* (about sixty-seven hundred acres) around the town of Philadelphia. There are other documents within the archive, however, that are private papers of Zenon acting on his own behalf. One recent attempt to isolate the private papers of Zenon counted 450 texts (Orrieux 1981, 1985).[14]

As Rostovtzeff stressed in his introductory chapter, this archive is among the most important collections of papyri from the early Ptolemaic period, a time when the Fayyum region was put under intensive cultivation. Along with what is known as the "Revenue Laws" papyrus (P. Rev.), the Zenon archive has formed the core documentation for what was believed to be a planned economy. Rostovtzeff keenly felt that the documentation from the large estate offered insights into the "conception of the ancient world in general" (1922: 15). His study of the archive was based only on texts that had been published at the time (350 papyri of the total of about 1,700 usable papyri). But, he added, his "conception" of the papyri had been formed already, and the publication of his ideas would aid publication of subsequent papyri. Here is a crucial distinction between his and Finley's methodology. Rostovtzeff's model, and its underlying assumptions, was implicit. But it is important to note that he did have a working model. Above all, he stressed the close relationship of the king and the finance minister to the estate and its management. But locating the texts within the specific geographical and socioeconomic context of the third-century Fayyum is crucial to their interpretation, and a different understanding of the function of the large estates within the royal economy is possible.

The estate of Apollonios was a revocable gift estate given to him by the king (see Clarysse [1979] on the documentation for these large estates). Several such "owners" of large estates are attested in the third-century Fayyum. In one sense, the estate was simply a larger version of the small plots of land that were apparently given out to Ptolemaic officials. But it was also much more. It was a "model estate" that took advantage of economies of scale to exploit labor and production. It was a place of agricultural experimentation in new crops and new livestock, and it was particularly dedicated to commercial operations in vineyards and in oil crops. Apollonios kept a close watch on the operations, although the land was leased out and even turned over to others to manage.[15] Each year, for example, Apollonios sent memoranda to his manager telling him what type of seed was available and in what amounts (P. Cairo Zenon 59292, 420–30, cited by Crawford [1973: 236]). Judging from the records of some accounts at least, these memoranda were not followed particularly closely.[16] The king clearly also showed an interest in such large estates. But here royal interest intersected with the private interests of Apollonios; a part of the land was under his direct management and even more directly under those on the ground, including Zenon and the principal farmer on the estate, Herakleides. The estate seems also to have been a place where experiments could be tried. Many appear to have failed. The short-lived success at poppy cultivation on Zenon's estate, for example, grown largely on marginal land on the estate, can be attributed to the decline in the experiment in the gift estates of the third century BC (Crawford 1973: 248). Ptolemaic policy had important long-term effects, among the most important of which was the introduction of durum wheat and more intensive viticulture (Thompson 1999).

Rostovtzeff's second study, a magisterial work in three volumes (planned originally as a "short survey"), was a historical synthesis of the extensive and complex evidence from inscriptions and papyri for the entire Hellenistic world. Here one sees another clear contrast with Finley's conception, showing that Rostovtzeff was rather more on the "modernist" (Meyer) end of the Bücher-Meyer debate. It is true that the debate drew sharper lines of distinction between the academic camps than actually existed (Saller, Chapter 11). But the differences that did exist were surely caused by the evidence, which fostered a different historical methodology. Finley stressed general patterns; Rostovtzeff gave detailed descriptions. In the preface to this great work, he emphasized the limitations of the study, and he stressed description rather than posing a model of economic behavior because of what he thought was the complexity of the documentary evidence. While Finley used two key literary texts that he thought provided good evidence for the social attitudes of the structure of the ancient economy, Rostovtzeff used every text available to him, a fact not lost on the reader who manages to plow through the 1,295 footnotes (not including the addenda and corrigenda) of the third volume. Underlying his treatment was a belief in the unity of the Hellenistic world and in the efficiency and rationality of the Ptolemaic system, run by a large and professional bureaucracy. All of this, of course, may be read into the Ptolemaic correspondence. But there are other ways to read the evidence, and we are more prone these days to distinguish Ptolemaic aims from the rural Egyptian reality. Rostovtzeff, to be sure, stressed the reign of Ptolemy II, well-documented by the Greek papyri. As I have already suggested, however, this leads to static assumptions rather than explanations for the considerable change between the third and first centuries BC.

Most scholars today work below the level of large-scale narrative, studying single archives and other groups of related texts. Rostovtzeff was only casually acquainted with the large numbers of demotic papyri, and the number of published papyri and ostraca in both languages has expanded considerably. No one person at the moment can command the entire range of documentary evidence like Rostovtzeff did in his day. In essence Rostovtzeff used the papyri to suggest that a fundamental shift occurred in the Hellenistic period, a shift from the classical Greek world to a more modern kind of economy planned by the government, which above all was interested in economic growth (a view countered by Samuel [1983]). The papyrological evidence, particularly the Zenon archive, is indeed radically different from the kinds of evidence available from other parts of the ancient world. Rostovtzeff took the Zenon papyri as proxy data for an "Egypt in miniature . . . typically representative of the newly created centers of economic and social life" (Rostovtzeff 1922: 129, 126), because the evidence for the Ptolemaic period (at the time) was at its thickest here. But the Fayyum was a special place, and the archive hardly represents trends in the whole of Egypt, let alone in the whole Hellenistic world. It was a showcase for Ptolemaic wealth and power, visited by foreign dignitaries later in the Ptolemaic period.[17] His understanding of the economic operations in the large estate were constantly reinforced by other evidence from the third century, in particular the "Revenue Laws" papyrus (P. Rev.),[18] and P. Tebt. III 703,[19] a text that Rostovtzeff himself edited with detailed commentary in 1933.

Both of these texts have been central to our understanding of Ptolemaic administrative organization and economic policy in the third century BC. They both provide a detailed description of the operation of the monopoly industries and the close supervision of the nome officials over agriculture, irrigation, and animals. It is important to note, however, that both texts are written from the central government's point of view. P. Tebt. III 703, written by the *dioikêtês* to the official in charge of royal revenues in the nome, known as the *oikonomos*, is not a comprehensive guide to the office, and it contains no specific references to time or place (Bagnall and Derow 1981: 134). The Tebtunis papyrus is part of a long pharaonic tradition of instruction, while P. Rev. is part of the Greek economic thought on tax farming, although adapted to the very different conditions of Egypt. It is now considered, after Bingen's important work (1978), to be not a single treatise on taxation policy but a composite text. Both texts are in a sense treatises on government intentions, practical and adaptive to the conditions of Egypt. But, like so much of the correspondence, they tend to show the administrative structure of the state, as opposed to what actually happened in the countryside. It is that gap between intentions, about which we know much, and the changing rural realities of three centuries of Ptolemaic rule that is so very hard to close. The demotic papyri, in contrast to the official nature of much of the Greek papyri, document individual and household economic activity. They are especially valuable for the light they shed on the landtenure regime in the Thebaid and the significant deviations from the economic organization of the Fayyum.

Both Rostovtzeff's and Préaux's influential works were synthetic accounts of Ptolemaic Egypt, and both scholars saw few differences between the documents of administrative intention and the actual "reach" of the state. Because both scholars emphasized the Greek papyri from the Fayyum, they built their descriptions of the Ptolemaic economy from the point of view of the state and from one special region of the country in which direct, unmediated royal intervention is most in evidence. A real difficulty with these large-scale syntheses is that we only see the organization and the performance of the economy at a local level and at certain times in certain places. This fact is particularly relevant for the study of the Ptolemaic land-tenure regime, which has been based until recently almost exclusively on the documents from one village, Kerkeosiris in the Fayyum, over the course of a single decade, 120–110 BC. The key issue from the point of view of evidence and model building is the ability of the state to impose rents and commands on tenant farmers and to collect these rents over the long term. Most scholars have followed Rostovtzeff and Préaux in believing that the Ptolemaic state was effective in imposing orders from above throughout Egypt (see Rathbone 1994).

The Underlying Thesis of a Strong State

This dominance, or "reach," of the state in the economy is the principal distinction usually made between all ancient economies and later ones. There was no "check" on state power, no "theoretical limits" (Finley 1985a: 154). Ptolemaic Egypt was for Rostovtzeff (1922: 3–4) a "strong and well organized state," dominated by a minority Greek population. The hypothesis of a strong state—meaning not only the state's presence in the economy but also the state's ability through its institutions to maintain a sustainable taxation regime through a highly centralized bureaucracy—was a key assumption in Rostovtzeff's and Préaux's work. I call this the Greek domination model.[20] Both scholars moderated their views on state strength later, and the reevaluation of the Ptolemaic state is one of the most important paradigm shifts in the last twenty years.[21] But despite this growing sense of the state's limits, driven by the work of Bingen and others, the idea of centralization, and the administrative success that this implies, persists in historical circles, though much less so in papyrological ones. The Ptolemaic economy, so the old model goes, was rationally organized and centrally planned, while at the same time it maintained ancient Egyptian institutions (local economic organization around temple estates controlled by priesthoods coordinated by an autocratic ruler) centered on the ancient administrative structure of the nomes.[22] The Ptolemies followed pharaonic theology by claiming owner-ship of all the land, and thus all sources of production in Egypt, and state in-come was coordinated through the large bureaucracy. This was certainly the ideology of the Egyptian state, and the strongly centralized, autocratic (or hydraulic) model of Ptolemaic Egypt had at its origins this reading of the an-cient Egyptian state. And of course the circumscription of the narrow Nile valley by desert on both sides did make Egypt the strongest social cage in world history (Mann 1986: 80–92).

But the Ptolemies' claims to resources had to be coordinated by the bu-reaucracy and backed up with coercive force or at least the threat of its use. And coercion there certainly was, as we know from specific incidents of tax collection and in general from the size of the rural police force.[23] The mas-sive revolt in the Thebaid (the southern Nile valley), which effectively ex-pelled Greek presence there for twenty years (207–186 BC), is enough to suggest that there were problems of enforcement. However well organized and efficient its economic structure appears, however theoretically unlim-ited its power was, the Ptolemaic state was constrained in holding its hin-terland, in coercing local officials, and was subject to the same shocks as ear-lier Egyptian states: invasion, revolts, and ecological disaster (that is, low or high Niles). The royal "monopoly" of key industries (oil, salt, linen) that regulated production and fixed prices of raw materials was a new manifes-tation of this old conception. The key productive factor, land, was either di-rectly managed by the crown ("royal land"), the rent and tax on which added up to 50 percent of the annual yield, or conceded to others (officials, soldiers, and temples) at lower tax rates. While Rostovtzeff believed that land in Upper Egypt may still have been dominated by temples, and thus re-moved from direct state control at least in the early phases of Ptolemaic administration, the Ptolemaic kings managed all land within the same state structure. In the case of temple land, this was accomplished through agents.[24] This has been the general picture of the land-tenure regime in Ptolemaic Egypt: "The majority of the population, Egyptian tenant farm-ers, were inconsequential: The spirit of the nation was one of indifference — the dull obedience of serfs who possessed no initiative, no animation, and had no patriotism, whose thoughts were wholly concentrated on the prob-lems of their daily bread and economic interests" (Rostovtzeff 1922: 170). Rostovtzeff's naive reading of the Egyptian state as a unitary "nation," and the implied dominance of the tenant farmers by the regime, has become embedded in much subsequent work. The revolts throughout the period have often been characterized, incorrectly, as "nationalist" rebellions. Yet to be explored in any detail is the social organization of Egyptians around the

family, village, and profession—the usual condition of premodern states—
and its relationship to the Ptolemaic state economy. The legacy of Rostovtzeff's work is this "statist," "dirigiste," or command economy model, in
which orders were issued from the king down the chain of administrative
command. Throughout his work, Rostovtzeff stressed the ideals of the
Ptolemaic "administrative machine" as against the realities, and his "model"
of the Ptolemaic economy was static rather than dynamic. The king, as the
pharaohs before him, was the embodiment of the state and controlled the
population absolutely.[25] Royal farmers were firmly bound to the land by an
oath taken at the time of the state loan of seed at the beginning of the agricultural year. The state had become disembedded from other parts of
society, an autonomous actor, able to organize production and labor, control prices and tax efficiently, all with an enormous (yet efficient) bureaucracy. This is where Rostovtzeff's "general conception" of Ptolemaic Egypt,
influenced by his own experience in Russia just before the revolution,
shaped his reading of the papyri. But nineteenth-century nation-state rationality (and power) did not exist in the third century BC (Austin 1986:
451). Once this is stripped from the interpretive model, the papyri appear in
a new light. Rostovtzeff, for example, argued that the Greek term "without
contract" meant that farmers were forced by the state to lease land, leaving
the royal farmer without means of protection from predation. But a new
analysis of the term places it within a more pragmatic context. The term in
fact described the usual form of lease of royal land, which was transacted
"without written contract." There was no need for a written lease agreement on such land, and the farmers were booked on the basis of the annual
survey of the fields (see Shelton 1976; Rowlandson 1985: 342 n. 42).

Another key institution for Rostovtzeff was the annual sowing schedule,
which he thought was imposed from the top down onto each village. We
now know that in fact the annual report was composed on the basis of the
annual inspection of standing crops gathered at the local scribal bureaus, discussed in a meeting in the nome capital before being sent to Alexandria
(Verhoogt 1997). The process was used in order to predict revenues for the
coming year, not to impose a crop schedule on the villages (Vidal-Naquet
1967). The reality, probably, was much less efficient, with power being dif-
fused through local control of water resources, a standard dynamic in Egyptian history. N. S. Hopkins's conclusion about modern Egypt that "the state
pretends to regulate everything and in fact regulates nothing" (1987: 98) applies equally well here. There are clear indications of state intervention in
the countryside in the early Ptolemaic period. But the key factors in the
organization of Ptolemaic economic power were coercion and monitoring

(land survey and crop reports at the local level, placing new layers of control over old institutions like temples) by means of a hierarchical bureaucracy. The state is indeed well documented at the local level in the Greek papyrological record, in the guise of local officials who negotiated leases, regulated a complex and regionally diverse land-tenure regime, registered plots of land every year, and enforced agreements. All of these factors, however, imply high transaction costs and thus inefficient rather than efficient institutions (North 1981, 1985). The coercive use of force came as the result of a generally weak property-rights regime. In good years, the Ptolemaic system probably ran effectively. But in times of bad floods, the natural tension between the state and farmers led to coercion.

The Ptolemaic reclamation of the Fayyum was in the main due to the new canal work in the area, not entirely the result of drainage, as Herodotus reported (Crawford 1971: 41 n. 1). The project led to new settlement by cleruchs (reservist soldiers given rights to land in exchange for a promise to serve in the army when needed) and others.[26] The organization of labor for the project shows the capacity of the Ptolemies to muster and control rural labor and, like the building of the Red Sea canal by Darius I some two hundred years before, was both a manifestation of the king's ability to control nature and a statement of royal power. The direct government involvement in the project and the influx of cleruchs to the region combined in making the region a more homogeneous zone of Ptolemaic dominance. By the end of the reign of Ptolemy II, the region was renamed in honor of his sister/wife Arsinoe, with its capital at Crocodilopolis. Why was the Fayyum reclaimed under the early Ptolemies? The answer lies in three areas.

The first two of these are ecology and location. The Fayyum depression was capable of large-scale reclamation, while the Nile river valley was not. The Fayyum was also close to Memphis, whose port provided a good supply line to Alexandria. No doubt much of the produce that sustained Alexandria was grown within a short radius of the city, as in later antiquity (Haas 1997: 36). The third consideration was politics. Reclaiming land, rather than seizing it from temples or individuals with preexisting claims, was the path of least resistance. Giving new claims in the Fayyum to the cleruchs streaming in from the Mediterranean was politically far better than seizing old land from Egyptians and risking dislocation and political disturbance. All of this royal activity in and around the Fayyum led to more direct management and a larger amount of royal land under direct authority of the king and leased by the "royal farmers." The tenure on royal land, and the rents collected on this category of land, formed the entire basis of the royal economy, and it was the status of the royal farmers that formed the cornerstone for Rostovtzeff's views on the nature of the Ptolemaic economy.

Royal farmers were the principal means of the exploitation of royal land, and they are most in evidence in the Fayyum. These farmers were the primary producers of royal revenue, but their numbers cannot be determined (Rowlandson 1985: 329). Rostovtzeff (1922: 87) believed that they were in a weak position ("a mass of cattle") relative to the machinery of government and were bound to the land on long-term leases with harsh terms. Tenure was at the same time precarious, and the king could give the land over to a higher bidder or maintain it at a fixed level until conditions made farming the land untenable. Most scholars who have commented on agricultural production in Ptolemaic Egypt have followed Rostovtzeff (for example, Ste. Croix 1983 [1981]: 153). Yet the frequent strikes and litigation suggest the tensions and the necessary negotiations between government and farmer.[27] Furthermore, the picture developed by Rostovtzeff did not fit the general agrarian conditions of Egypt, which were always subject to fluctuations because productivity was so closely tied to the annual flood of the river. A more flexible response was required.

More recent assessments of Egyptian farmers under the Ptolemies have tended to show that they rather more resembled farmers elsewhere in the ancient world, having a status between slave and free. The basis for the claim of the fixity of tenure on royal land was based on the concept of what is termed the *diamisthosis*, the large-scale leasing of crown land at fixed rents over a long period of time that could be changed by another long-term lease by the king when conditions made the terms impossible. The concept was based on a difficult passage in one papyrus concerning one plot of land (210 1/8 *arouras*; roughly 139 acres) that was to be assigned to a special category of land "to be inspected by the scribes."[28] Recently published documents from the Fayyum show that terms of the lease could be changed frequently, and that the Ptolemaic system was probably much more flexible and ad hoc than Rostovtzeff's theory admits.[29] Rowlandson's careful analysis (1985) of all of the evidence for royal farmers has suggested a radically different interpretation than Rostovtzeff's. Many different people carried the title "royal farmer," cleruchs as well as Egyptian priests and others. This was clearly a technical administrative term. The general consensus is that in fact the status of royal carried certain benefits, including royal protection from certain obligations, so much so in fact that groups of people got together to take on the lease of royal land, even of small plots of royal land that were too small to sustain several persons. And indeed, the rent on royal land was fixed at a higher rate than other classes of land.

There have been no successors to Préaux and Rostovtzeff. Rather, most recent work on the Ptolemaic economy has been devoted, as I have tried to show, to refining these large-scale works and filling in important gaps. Papyrological scholarship today is highly specialized and still has little taste for more theoretical approaches. But more critical readings of the papyri, new material, better archaeological information, and the study of the Greek and Egyptian material together are beginning to suggest a very different picture of Ptolemaic Egypt from Rostovtzeff's or Préaux's.[30] Austin (1986) has called Eric Turner's chapter in the second edition of the *Cambridge Ancient History* a "flat rejection of Rostovtzeff." Many of Rostovtzeff's general statements have been called into question. While Rostovtzeff viewed Ptolemy II as the innovator of the new Ptolemaic system of command and control, Turner (1984; compare to Austin 1986: 452) has also added that Ptolemy II was the destroyer of Ptolemaic Egypt as well. Neither one of these views may hold up if new evidence from the reign of Ptolemy I comes to light.[31] My own view is that a plan to manage Egypt was already beginning to be executed by Ptolemy I, but the implementation of this plan and the concomitant process of what I have called the "Ptolemaicizing" of economic institutions took the better part of a century.[32] War as a mode of production was absent in Rostovtzeff's analysis yet in the third-century war provided a significant part of the royal revenues and may indeed account for the early economic success of the regime (see Austin 1986).[33]

Conclusions

What distinguishes the study of the Ptolemaic economy from most other ancient Mediterranean economies (first-millennium BC Babylonia and Roman Egypt are exceptions) is the quantity of documentation. This has led scholars to emphasize the study of the papyri and ostraca themselves. Some new trends include the integration of the local evidence (the tax receipts, the registration of demotic legal instruments) of the Ptolemaic bureaucracy with the central state institutions and new, perhaps more realistic, views of the power and effectiveness of the central state. In this light, the same documentary evidence so well deployed by Rostovtzeff and Préaux tends to look more reflective of bureaucratic structures than the rural realities. The Fayyum region has loomed large in the general picture of the Ptolemaic economy because of the role played there by early Ptolemaic kings. The state was very much involved in the Ptolemaic economy, especially in the Fayyum, although its success at collecting rents and controlling the countryside was more limited, and economic power more ad hoc than earlier studies have assumed.[34] Given the differences in land-tenure conditions throughout Egypt, a uniform system of control would not have been practicable. And indeed, as more evidence is brought to bear, the Fayyum looks more like an exceptional place of innovation and direct management then the Nile valley, which, although part of Ptolemaic state, was more difficult to control. Politically, from the point of view of longer-term history, most recent assessments of the Ptolemaic economy have stressed social and institutional continuities with the Saite and Persian periods. But the institutional change under the Ptolemies must also be considered (tax farming, banks, coinage, royal granaries displacing the tradition of local temple management).

Before a general model of the Ptolemaic economy can be articulated, a framework must be built that will integrate all of the local evidence of economic activity and organization into a framework of the state. It is the manner in which local village economies and ancient social structures were integrated into the new state structures of the Ptolemaic period that should form an important part of any future work. Social theory and new institutional economic analysis will, I believe, be helpful (see Morris and Manning's introduction). The relationship, for example, of old and new institutional structures, which surely generated friction and inefficiencies and created a social lag between new economic and older political and social institutions, must be brought to bear on the documents. And of course, most important of all, a model must be built that weighs the documentary evidence that has survived with those that have not survived and indeed against transactions that were never recorded.[35] As I have tried to show here, historians always work within a preconceived framework, a model if you will, and are products of their own times. It is preferable, therefore, to make this framework explicit in the analysis, as Finley always urged. The papyri by themselves, ungrounded in theory and unarticulated within a general framework of the state, become less important than they should be. The ad hoc, flexible nature of the Ptolemaic regime (one of its strengths), and the social lag caused by the presence of old institutional arrangements in the south, may provide the basis of a far richer, more dynamic understanding of this important period of ancient Mediterranean history.

Notes

I would like to thank Ian Morris, Erich Gruen, and Roger Bagnall, who read drafts of this paper and offered suggestions and criticisms for its improvement.

1. An exception is the early essay by Weber (1909).

2. Rawski 1996: 29. I will lay out my own views on models of the Ptolemaic economy in two articles, to be published in *The Cambridge Economic History of the Graeco-Roman world*, ed. Ian Morris, Richard Saller, and Walter Scheidel; and *The Oxford Encyclopedia of Economic History*, ed. Joel Mokyr.

3. I take the term *stock of knowledge* from the "new institutional" economic analysis of North (1990).

4. Finley 1985a: 183. The "oriental" sector, predominantly in the economies of Ptolemaic Egypt and Seleucid Syria, was in Finley's opinion unchanged by the new political regimes, which were merely extensions of the older system of exploitation, with large state sectors and little private enterprise or private production.

5. The term, only roughly translated from the German "Hellenismus," derives from a famous passage in Droysen's study (1836), where he used the word to describe the state of mixed culture in the East that gave rise to Christianity in the period from Alexander's campaigns at the end of the fourth century BC to the Roman conquest of the East. See the remarks of Bowersock 1990: xi; Cartledge 1997: 2–3.

6. The archaeology of Ptolemaic Egypt has until recently been dominated by the search for papyri. It is invaluable for documenting the expansion of trade routes in the eastern desert out to the Red Sea and the increased use of coinage. See the overview by McClellan (1997). On the process of monetization, see von Reden 1997b. Survey work in the Fayyum has yielded important historical information. See briefly Rathbone 1996.

7. Willy Clarysse and Dorothy Thompson, P. Count., forthcoming.

8. Greek administrative records come, in the main, from two nomes, or districts, in Egypt: the Fayyum, an area extensively reclaimed under Ptolemy II and III and therefore having a higher percentage of "royal land" under the direct management of the crown; and the Herakleopolite nome, just to the east. On the atypicality of the Fayyum, see Thompson 1999. On the "discontinuities" in the history of Ptolemaic Egypt caused by the skewed evidence, see Bingen 1984.

9. Finley overstated his case for not considering the Zenon material as an archive. For a papyrologist, the use of the term *archive* describes texts that were kept together in antiquity. See E. G. Turner 1980: 47; Pestman 1995. There are good reasons to think that the Zenon archive did in fact have a filing system, now lost by the scattering of the papyri after their discovery.

10. For the careful distinction between archives and dossiers made by papyrologists, see Bagnall 1995: 40–48. The publication gap between Greek and demotic papyri from the same archive was shown by Grunert (1980) in his study of the Totoes archive from the site of Deir el-Medina, western Thebes. The papyri were excavated by Ernesto Schiaperelli in 1905. The nine Greek papyri were published by G. Vitelli in 1929, while the demotic papyri were published in 1967, with extensive and important corrections by Karl-Theodor Zauzich in 1971–73.

11. For the University of Wisconsin and the background of the first book, see Bowersock 1986: esp. p. 396. The latter book was written during Rostovtzeff's tenure at Yale University, which began in 1925. I do not consider here Rostovtzeff's chapter on Ptolemaic Egypt for the *Cambridge Ancient History*, vol. 7 (1928), which is a more general discussion of the period.

12. Austin 1986: 451: "The reader [of Rostovtzeff] has the uneasy feeling of hearing voices, not just one single voice."

13. The literature on this estate is massive. For an orientation, see Pestman 1981; and the surveys of Orrieux 1983, 1985; Clarysse and Vandorpe 1995.

14. For the criticism of isolating documents based on an assumption of two systems of accounts, see Franko 1988.

15. In the latter case, it seems that cleruchs (reservist soldiers) were given land from the estate itself. See further Crawford 1973: 240–41.

16. This is especially true in the case of overproduction and with important crops like poppy, one of the oil monopoly crops. See Crawford 1973: 245.

17. P. Tebt. 33 (112 BC; republished in *Select Papyri* II: 416). This is a letter from the *dioiketes* to the royal scribe and other local officials responsible for making preparations for the visit of a Roman senator to the Fayyum. On the details of the letter, and the chain of command involved, see Verhoogt 1997: 103–5.

18. Text edition by Grenfell and Mahaffy (1896); extensive comments by Préaux (1939). Bingen (1952) published an important new text edition and has reinterpreted the whole document (Bingen 1978).

19. Published in the third volume of the Tebtunis Papyri. See the comments by Samuel (1971).

20. See, for example, Tarn and Griffith (1952: 189–209), a very generous account of the efficacy of the Ptolemaic economy and its bureaucratic structure, at least for the third century BC; the strong state hypothesis had its most fervent believer in Heichelheim (1970). See the comments of Rathbone (1994) and Manning (2003).

21. Rostovtzeff (1941: 282), in speaking about Ptolemaic policy of maintaining temple administration over land, suggested that they "were not strong enough to encroach in this way on the rights of the temples." Préaux

(1978: 376 n. 1) confessed that she, along with Rostovtzeff, had emphasized too strongly the dirigiste model.

22. Rostovtzeff (1922: 126) also stressed continuity with pharaonic Egypt, creating something of a contradiction between the rationality of organization stressed by the Greek papyri and the fact that the Ptolemies added a new layer of control on top of old institutions.

23. On the rural police force, see Thompson 1997.

24. Rostovtzeff 1941: 283. Rostovtzeff argued, rightly, that temples were part of the state and as such organized the tenure of their donated estates through tenant farmers attached to these estates and who held land in virtual private ownership. I believe, for reasons I cannot go into here, that while the Ptolemies did not change this old pattern of local land management, the process of "Ptolemaicizing" the bureaucracy eventually displaced the old temple structures of managing the local land economies and thus fundamentally altered rural economic (and religious) institutions.

25. Rostovtzeff 1922: 126. He offered as specific parallels the kings of Dynasty 4, 11, and 18, that is, the height of centralized power in pharaonic Egypt, for some reason leaving out Dynasty 19, a much more effective period of coerced labor.

26. Butzer 1976: 36–38.

27. Rostovtzeff 1922: 86.

28. P. Tebt. 72, 440–72. See the important comments in Shelton 1976: 120–21; Verhoogt 1997: 27.

29. The new papyri discussed by Shelton were crucial in demonstrating, for example, that the rate of cessions of royal land from one farmer to another was as high as one-third of royal land from year to year. This contrasts sharply with Rostovtzeff's rigidity. See the remarks in Rowlandson 1985: 337.

30. A good example of the results of the combined study of the evidence may be found in Thompson (1988: ch. 2), a description of economic life in Ptolemaic Memphis.

31. An important new study of a demotic family archive from the reign of Ptolemy I has appeared in Depauw (2000).

32. I develop this "dynamic" model of the history of Ptolemaic institutions in Manning 2003.

33. If we can believe the ancient figures, war booty certainly was a significant source of revenue in the early Ptolemaic period. Austin (1986: 465) compares the total annual revenue of Ptolemy II Philadelphus cited by St. Jerome (fourteen thousand, eight hundred talents of silver), with the revenue brought in by the Third Syrian War of Ptolemy III Euergetes (forty thousand talents of "booty"; fifteen hundred talents alone captured from a chest in Cilicia during one skirmish of this war). On war as a mode production in the Hellenistic economies in general, see also Préaux 1978: I: 366–70.

34. Samuel 1989: 59–60. The intervention of ancient states into the economy was also an important element of Finley's analysis (1985a: ch. 6).

35. For example, the near-total absence of animal sales from the Ptolemaic period has been explained as good evidence for state domination of the private economy. But the absence of animal sales is more likely the result of the accidents of preservation. Animal sales are preserved in large numbers in the Roman period (well over one hundred donkey sales alone), because we tend to get papyri from the towns in the Roman period, and thus perhaps a more "normal" spread of document types surviving, and cartonnage from village record offices from the Ptolemaic period. It is also likely that many private transactions, particularly those involving parties who knew each other, were completed without written contract (Manning, forthcoming).

Chapter 9

Evidence and Models for the
Economy of Roman Egypt

ROGER S. BAGNALL

One of the most striking aspects of the colloquium to which this volume owes its genesis was the diversity of reactions expressed by contributors to the role played by a retrospective view of the work of Moses Finley. For Egypt, Finley certainly represents at best an ambiguous inheritance. Most readers of Finley's works on the ancient economy and on historical method are likely to develop a negative view of the contribution that the study of Hellenistic and Roman Egypt might make to any larger historical horizon— if, that is, the land of the Nile does not escape their notice entirely in reading Finley, for it does not play a prominent role in his discussions. Even the knowledge that Finley's hostility to papyrological documentation comes at least in part from his experiences with an uninspiring introduction to the field at the hands of William Linn Westermann during his time at Columbia is insufficient to justify what to a papyrological historian can only seem exceptional wrongheadedness.[1] Finley's aversion to documentary studies extended also to epigraphy.[2] And yet the reality is somewhat more ambiguous than pure negativism, as we shall see.

Certainly the negative remarks are easily found. The uniqueness of Egypt is stressed repeatedly: "In the long history of the Graeco-Roman world, massive documentation characterized only the peculiar society of Egypt and to a limited extent the imperial courts of the later Roman Empire" (Finley 1985b: 15). Similarly: "Only Graeco-Roman Egypt, conceivably the Seleucid empire (about which we know next to nothing on this aspect) and in a

rudimentary way Rome under the emperors were sufficiently bureaucratic."
The documentation of the papyri is called "a paperasserie on a breath-
taking scale and an equally stupendous illusion" (Finley 1985b: 33–34).
The papyri are not only an illusion but too miscellaneous to be very useful
(Finley 1985b: 30, quoting A. H. M. Jones). They do not provide data
(Finley 1985b: 32), and they have no analytic character.[3]

But two passages suggest a different approach. Finley acknowledges
(1985b: 45) that groups of related documents can in fact provide real information about the ancient world. And at one point he uses a papyrus (a lease
of pottery works) to provide the explanatory model for archaeological data—
thus contradicting his own claim that evidence cannot yield models, not to
speak of undermining the notion of the uniqueness of Egypt (Finley 1985b:
24). Finley's criticisms of the papyri, I shall argue, are ill founded. From these
more positive approaches, however, there is something to be learned, and it
may be suggested that Finley's partial recognition of the uses of papyri had
been blotted from view by his frustration with the quality of most historical
writing using the papyri.[4] Indeed, even his attempts to describe abstractly
just what he means by the term *model* sound mostly like the anguished cries
of someone who has read one too many books consisting of an amassing of
facts without any attempt at explanation; for "model" in these passages comes
remarkably close to meaning "explanation" (Finley 1985b: 60, 66). In his
own practice, however, "model" seems sometimes to mean Weberian ideal
type, sometimes middle-level theory (Finley 1985b: 60, 106).[5] It is largely in
the latter sense that I shall pursue the issue of models.[6]

Whether the problem of the distinctiveness of Egypt still needs belabor-
ing at this point is hard to say. Among those who know anything about the
subject, the viewpoint that Finley expressed is long dead. But there are
plenty of signs that his attitudes are still commonplace in the larger world of
ancient history. The uniqueness argument has collapsed under two burdens.
The first is the discovery of Egyptian-style documentation in other places.
The second is the successful demonstration that the evidence even of Egyptian papyri can be brought to bear on major issues in the study of the Roman economy.[7] The second will occupy most of the rest of this chapter, but
the first deserves a few words before we pass on to that task.

We now have a considerable body of written material on papyrus, parch-
ment, wood, and clay from non-Egyptian sources. A recent survey of the
Near East yielded some 609 inventory numbers, including both the older
finds from Dura and Nessana and postwar discoveries, like the various archives from around the Dead Sea, the recently found and still largely unpublished papyri from the Euphrates valley from the mid-third century, and

the sixth-century rolls from Petra still in the course of preparation for publication (Cotton et al. 1995). Hardly any part of Palestine, Syria, and northern Mesopotamia is now entirely lacking in papyrological finds. Not less important is the fact that the range of document types is similar to that in Egypt: family documents concerned with property, letters, legal matters, the census, military business, and the like all appear. Written documents, letters, and accounts have an air of overwhelming ordinariness, in exactly the manner we are accustomed to with the Egyptian papyri. Documentary formulas are similar: the handwriting could come from Egypt, the language is familiar but sometimes with Semitic flavoring. In short, the conclusion that written documentation functioned in the Near East as it did in Egypt is inescapable.

Problems of preservation make it unlikely that the West will ever be quite so generous. But two important recent finds have shown what earlier discoveries of tablets in Dacia and at Herculaneum had suggested: Writing was used in the western provinces with much the same degree of ordinariness. These are the ostraca from the fort at Bu Njem in Libya and still more the writing tablets from Vindolanda on the northern frontier in Britain.[8] Particularly in the case of Vindolanda, detailed analysis has shown that the use of writing was not the preserve of some few individuals but was, even in the early years of Roman rule of Britain, widely spread and deeply ingrained; once again, absolutely normal and unremarkable. As Alan Bowman has observed, "It is enough that several hundred individuals could [perform the act of writing] within a framework of convention and expectation which would have rendered their texts easily comprehensible at the other end of the Roman Empire" (Bowman 1994: 125).

Nor is that the only lesson to be derived from these far-flung discoveries. Added to Egyptian documentation and archaeology, the discoveries highlight important aspects of the ancient economy. An example is water management. Anyone acquainted with the Mediterranean soon notices that ancient settlement and cultivation extended well beyond the limits of habitation and farming in subsequent centuries, sometimes even beyond present-day limits. As consensus develops that world climate has not changed dramatically from the Roman period to the present—or at least the very recent past—the task of explaining the cultivation patterns of the Roman period becomes more acute. The papyri from Petra, combined with archaeological observation in the vicinity, show that a sophisticated combination of use of spring water and control of water from irregular rainfall allowed extensive agriculture and arboriculture in its area (see provisionally Koenen 1996: 183–85). They thus join such disparate evidence as the tablets and ostraca from the Kharga and Dakhleh Oases (see Bagnall 1997b) and survey work in Libya (Mattingly 1994, especially ch. 7) in illuminating the wide range of tools available to landowners in the Roman east who tried to support themselves, and ultimately the whole structure of urban life, on marginal lands. The Egyptian documentation, in this light, seems no more particular than any other; it reveals a specific ecosystem, or rather several specific ecosystems, but so would evidence for any other region. There is no basis for any assumption that one region is normal.

At this point it might seem tempting to give a cheerful shout of triumph and claim that Egypt's evidence is thus fully ready for the mainstream of historical study of Roman antiquity. But this is not the case. Finley and those who, like him, have denigrated the use of papyrological evidence or simply ignored its existence have to a considerable degree produced a self-fulfilling prophecy.[9] Although much work in papyrology has always been driven by no questions at all, but simply by the accumulation of data on some point, there have always been exceptions.[10] Interestingly, however, the impact of larger ideas was for the first three-quarters of this century considerably greater in studies of the Ptolemaic and so-called Byzantine periods than in those of the Roman period. There has never been an equivalent for the Roman period of the great interwar syntheses of Ptolemaic Egypt by Claire Préaux and Michael Rostovtzeff, dominated by a general theory of Egypt as a centrally planned, dirigiste economy with a dominant role in production in the hands of the state (Préaux 1939; Rostovtzeff 1922, 1941). Nor has there been any equivalent to the pre-1960s consensus that Egypt after Diocletian was essentially a protofeudal state, in which spatial, occupational, and economic mobility had been suppressed for most of the population and great magnates dominated the scene.[11] These broad conceptions were certainly large-scale models of particular ancient societies; neither has much credibility among specialists today, although they will still be found in derivative works. The impetus for the demolition of the Ptolemaic model came to a large degree from inside papyrology, in considerable part by Préaux herself and by her student Jean Bingen, but Finley's writing on the ancient economy has certainly affected the discussion considerably. In the case of late antiquity, the revisionist impetus of A. H. M. Jones's magnum opus (1964) took time to percolate into papyrology, and when it did the discussion was also strongly affected by the movement in late antique studies led by Peter Brown.[12]

Nothing like this, as far as I can see, happened with Roman Egypt. James Keenan (1982: 23–24) has suggested that the reason for the lack of grand syntheses of Egypt from Augustus to Constantine (or Theodosius, for that matter) is in part that the pace of publication of papyri from the Roman period has hardly slackened from the earliest days of papyrology to the present. For the period from the fifth century on, there was a substantial lull after 1924, when relatively few substantial new volumes appeared; and after the early 1930s, the amount of new material of Ptolemaic date also dropped off substantially. In effect, the pauses created the space for synthesis, for taking stock and for the creation of major research tools. No such pause occurred for papyri of the Roman era.

This hesitation was in fact expressed by the most important single exception to this generalization, the Princeton historian Allan Chester Johnson, who remarked in 1936 that "it may be premature to attempt an economic survey of Roman Egypt while the ancient sites continue to yield their treasures of papyri and ostraca," but who proceeded immediately to say, "yet the main lines of Roman exploitation may now be traced with some accuracy" (A. C. Johnson 1936: vii). His 1936 survey was in fact mainly descriptive, but it contained substantial analytic passages as well. With his students and colleagues, Johnson continued to produce the only substantial body of synthetic work on economic issues, including Wallace's study of taxation (1938), West and Johnson (1944) on currency, and Johnson and West (1949) on the Byzantine economy. This series culminated in 1951 with Johnson's book on Roman Egypt, based on his Jerome Lectures of 1947–48, *Egypt and the Roman Empire*.

This book, however, was not a general synthesis but a series of six interconnected studies, discussing fiduciary currency, inflation, land tenure, "serfdom" and taxation in Byzantine Egypt (this in the usual papyrological manner referring to everything from Diocletian on), and the administration of Egypt. Nowhere does it offer an overall model of the economy of Roman Egypt. We can, nonetheless, sketch Johnson's view of the subject from remarks scattered throughout the book. Egypt, for him, was largely self-sufficient, needing to import little but iron. The peasantry and urban "proletariat" lived barely above a subsistence level and were largely absent from any other economic transactions. They produced the large wheat surplus that gave Egypt a generally favorable balance of trade and paid its taxes but did little else. The urban population consumed some imported luxuries, but these were of marginal significance and highly regulated by a strongly centralized government. The currency was fiduciary until Diocletian, and the "creeping" inflation visible at least until 269–76 is largely to be attributed to rising external demand for Egypt's wheat as production elsewhere fell. The more dramatic rise in price levels around 275 was also the product of external circumstances rather than changes in Egypt itself. Fourth-century inflation, by contrast (and Johnson is very tentative about this period), seems to reflect changes in the denomination of billon coinage and in their metal content compared to the denominations.[13]

The Roman land-tenure system, Johnson thought, was essentially a continuation of the Ptolemaic one, with the overwhelming bulk of the land in imperial ownership and farmed under hereditary lease; private land was scanty. In this situation, large estates did not grow up. Not until the fourth century was much land turned over to private ownership, and even then really large estates did not become a feature of the Egyptian landscape (see A. C. Johnson 1951: 67–86). In Johnson's view, the period from Diocletian on was a big improvement, with the removal of many inequities, so that "the peasant enjoyed greater liberty and greater prosperity than ever before" (1951: 156).[14]

Johnson's contemporary Westermann also did some writing on Roman Egypt, but his great preoccupation in the 1920s and 1930s was the Zenon papyri and Ptolemaic Egypt. He therefore never produced a work on Roman Egypt with the broad scope of Johnson's.[15] Nor did Michael Rostovtzeff, whose major contribution to the study of Egypt was on the Zenon archive from the Ptolemaic period, and who when engaged with the Roman period was largely taken up with the material from the excavations at Dura-Europos in Syria.[16] Arthur Boak, working throughout this period on papyri of the third and fourth centuries, especially from Karanis, produced a number of articles setting forth a view indebted to the pessimistic school of thought represented by Bell.[17] And it is difficult to point to any British or continental scholar of their period who was engaged to the same degree with the Roman period and attempted broad-gauged synthesis. Rather, the questions asked by most papyrologists working on Roman Egypt continued to be driven not by the larger field of ancient history but by the internal dynamics of papyrology, a field largely shaped by philology and law. It is perhaps not surprising in these circumstances that Johnson's relatively optimistic view of the society and economy of late Roman Egypt drew little support; as we have seen, he had in any case no coherent overall model for the earlier Roman centuries to match the powerful descriptions of Ptolemaic and Byzantine Egypt that were prevalent in the field, and both Westermann and Bell had low opinions of Johnson and his work.[18]

Nor in the intellectual climate of the period up to the 1960s could one ignore what was said about the Ptolemaic and Byzantine periods in forming an opinion about the Roman era. For papyrology was dominated by the view that a high degree of continuity affected Egypt throughout the centuries, and above all that Augustus largely took over a going concern in 30 BC and changed it as little as possible. Once that premise is accepted, it is evident that

Roman Egypt also should have been a period with a high degree of state control over the productive apparatus and an oppressive bureaucratic and taxation regime. Although detailed studies began to challenge this continuity by the early 1950s, it was a paper of Naphtali Lewis's at the 1968 Congress of Papyrology that demolished it with a head-on and widely accepted attack.[19] At least for the last thirty years, then, the intellectual climate has been such as to allow for the need of models to explain the economy of Roman Egypt as a distinct phenomenon.

Lewis's own general book on Roman Egypt, published in 1983, does not attempt to do this. It is a largely descriptive work, aimed at a general reader, and argues no general thesis. Once again, however, one can elicit from it some broad conceptions. These include a largely subsistence economy in the rural villages, except for a handful of the more affluent; geographical mobility mainly as the result of unbearable fiscal pressure; a high incidence of flight and manpower loss as the result of heavy and inflexible taxation; a slave population mainly engaged in domestic service or wage-earning occupations; and a mainly private water-transport fleet.[20]

It would, alas, be idle to suppose that recent progress has now given us a model for the Roman period of an attractiveness comparable to that of the older ones for the Ptolemaic and Byzantine periods, not to speak of greater explanatory power. Many questions essential to understanding the economy of Roman Egypt still lack any serious discussion. If one asks about studies that take on matters of class or markets, for example, it is hard to give much of an answer. But some subjects have fared better, typically those where the usability of the evidence of the papyri is more obvious. In what follows, I shall describe some of the areas where real progress has been made, then try—very tentatively—to summarize the overall view of the economy emerging from them, and finally turn to assess the potential for further work, particularly of a quantitative nature.[21]

It is not surprising that land and agriculture have been the largest beneficiaries of inquiries based on the conscious use of models. Of course such models were present even from the earliest times, but in the earlier literature they come largely from the late Roman legal sources. The heavy reliance on the Theodosian and Justinianic codes, and on older concepts of medieval feudalism, to explain the status of land ownership and of agricultural labor, not only in late antiquity but throughout the Roman period (and sometimes even earlier), has come under strong attack in the last two decades (especially by Carrié [1982, 1983]). But replacing the models of the colonate and feudalism has still required coming to terms with the legal sources, and even though more recent literature on feudalism has not figured much in discussions of late Roman Egypt, the development of a view of the Great Houses as carriers of burdens on behalf of the state surely owes something to changing views of later periods (see especially the classic treatment of Gascou [1985]).

The very notion that land ownership was highly concentrated, and ever increasing, throughout Byzantine Egypt has been shown to require considerable modification. In part this shift in thinking has come from the application of statistical techniques borrowed from modern economic history and development economics to the data provided by land and tax registers from Egypt (Bowman 1985; Bagnall 1992). In part, it has come from a revisionist understanding of the relationship between city and country, in which there are no one-way streets and in which villagers are seen as actors in their own interest and not only as acted upon (see Keenan [1980, 1981] for examples). Although this latter strand has not been self-consciously presented as part of a larger intellectual current, it is hard not to see it, at least in retrospect, as one aspect of the attempt, as it were, to empower ordinary people of the past, to see them as autonomous individuals negotiating their fates in the context of the available choices. Microhistory has been particularly devoted to this approach, which has also influenced much feminist work.[22]

Earlier Roman Egypt has been affected by models in quite different directions. Two major works address the use of tenancy in agriculture: Kehoe (1992) consciously applies to a limited number of archival groups a model based originally on study of Pliny the Younger and the inscriptions concerning imperial estates in North Africa to the use of leasing by larger landowners; Rowlandson (1996) surveys synoptically the scattered documentation from Roman Oxyrhynchos. The two complement one another well, with Kehoe's driven primarily by economic questions, Rowlandson's by social interests.

If operation through leasing has become much clearer from these works, so too has direct operation of large estates through Dominic Rathbone's book (1991) on the Appianus estate in the Fayyum, where the center of attention is a centrally managed but geographically dispersed array of holdings devoted to producing a marketable surplus of wine but also meeting expenses in part through growing other crops. Rathbone explicitly sets his book in a context of bringing major questions about the Roman economy, including the sophistication of accounting and the role of economic rationalism, to bear on the Egyptian evidence and in turn testing hypotheses about them with that evidence.

Rathbone's book is the bridge to another major area of the economy—urban production and redistribution—because his description of the

Appianus estate demands a means of turning its wine surplus into cash; it implies, that is, an extensive city-based trade in wine, even if only within Egypt (we have no reason to think that the quality of Egyptian wine would have attracted any external market). For example, the Fayyum may well have shipped most of its produce to Alexandria. It could well, however, have sold part to upper Egyptian cities where vineyards were less extensive.

Other studies have begun the task of understanding urban production (see van Minnen [1986] for a general treatment). As Finley recognized, it was above all the involvement of government in certain economic activities that led to their being documented in great detail, and the relative lack of information about craft, or even small-scale industrial, production in the cities of Roman Egypt is not evidence for the unimportance of this work. That is, one cannot both regard documentation as the product of government and at the same time use the lack of documentation as evidence for a consumer city that had little productive capacity. Against Finley's assertions to the contrary (1985a: 135–37), it has been shown beyond reasonable doubt (van Minnen 1986) that Oxyrhynchos had an extensive textile industry, producing cloth somewhere on the scale of an early modern European city.[23] All of this work on the urban economy has been rooted in attempts to bring the papyri into the larger discussion about the character of the ancient city, particularly a wish to break out of the producer/consumer dichotomy that has so dominated the subject.

In the domain of status, studies have focused in two areas. One is the *coloni adscripticii* of the late period, who form part of the investigation of large estates already described. The other is of course slavery. The centrality of discussion of slavery in ancient historical studies has been such that the papyri have never stood outside the debate as they have in other areas, and it requires only a brief description for it to be obvious that the questions debated are derivatives of the models of ancient slavery contested for many decades. There has long been a consensus that Egyptian slavery was largely domestic in character and thus mainly a matter of consumption rather than production.[24] In the urban economy this view still holds, and slavery is above all an urban phenomenon in Egypt. But although the number of rural slaves engaged in agricultural work was not very large, it may nonetheless have made a significant difference to some types of households (Bagnall 1993a: 123–27). And I have argued recently that Egyptian villages were significantly involved in the activity of collecting exposed city babies, bringing them up as slaves, and selling them back to the cities (Bagnall 1997c). The supposed decline of slavery in late antiquity, another staple question on a larger canvas, has been posited for Egypt as well. This has been both called into question and defended during the last decade.[25] The issue is partly structural (Did the Egyptian economy change in ways that would have made slaves less useful?) and partly evidentiary (Does the decline in attestations of slaves point to a decline in the actual number of slaves, or is it, as I have argued, an artifact of the character of the papyrological evidence for late antiquity?).

Another critical area of the ancient economy is transportation. Egypt has long stood outside the raging debates about the feasibility and economy of overland transportation, because almost all parts of it were reached by the Nile and the connected network of waterways, surely the most cost-efficient transportation system of any sizable part of the Roman Empire. Although the existence of land transport by donkey and camel, and even to a limited extent by wagon, has long been recognized, it has been assumed to be a marginal element in a water-dominated system.[26] No doubt that is basically right, but the last couple of decades have seen an enormous amount of exploration of the Egyptian deserts and oases, which can only have depended on transportation by pack animal, and these studies have opened new perspectives. The Eastern Desert was the land of two important economic phenomena: in its southern sector, of the Red Sea trade via Myos Hormos and Berenike; and in its northern sector, of the work of mining and quarrying centered on Mons Claudianus and Mons Porphyrites.[27] These are both exceptional cases, to be sure, driven by luxury import and export goods in the one case and by high-value products, of which the government was the principal consumer, in the other. In both cases the government was directly involved. But it was not simply a matter of a few bags of spices or of gold crossing the desert on camel. Just the supplying of the Red Sea outposts and of the extensive network of small desert forts and quarrying operations was a gigantic business, and the goods the Romans exported to India and East Africa included such relatively bulky items as wine.[28] Obviously cost was not a determinative factor in some of these desert operations—one had no choice but to pay the going cost to transport a porphyry column to the Nile—but it is unlikely that cost was irrelevant in getting Italian wine to Berenike for shipment to India, even if the market at the other end was a royal court.

The Western Desert offers an entirely different perspective on this problem. The first four centuries of Roman rule saw a vast expansion of settlement in the Kharga and Dakhleh Oases, both of which ultimately became independent nomes (the Hibite and Mothite) with their own metropoleis and civic elites. There was evidently a sizable increase in wealth to support this governing class. At the same time, we find units of the Roman army being stationed in the region. There is now a strong hint from the Kellis Agricultural

Account Book (Bagnall 1997b) that the foundation of the wealth that allowed
the full participation of the oases in the Roman economic and social system
was olives and olive oil, as was the case in Tripolitania (Mattingly 1994), another region where marginal land came under cultivation in this period. Only
the ability to export this produce to the Nile valley can have generated wealth
on this scale. The private letters from Kellis show that the Dakhleh Oasis had
close ties to the part of the Nile around Lykopolis and Antaiopolis, directly
across three hundred kilometers of desert rather than via the longer but easier route through the Kharga Oasis.[29] It seems increasingly clear that it was
possible to transport high-value but not luxurious goods, like olive oil, by
land across vast stretches of desert and still have them competitive in Egyptian
markets—where, to be sure, olive oil was always in somewhat short supply.

Even from a cursory look of the sort we have given to recent work, it
becomes obvious that quantitative arguments play a key role in many of
these subjects.[30] Some of these are questions of scale, which are important
in the works of Rathbone and van Minnen, for example. Some are applica-
tions of specific quantitative techniques, which are present in the studies of
the distribution of land (Bowman 1985; Bagnall 1992). In my work with
Bruce Frier on demography, standard demographic modeling is central to
many of our main positions (Bagnall and Frier 1994).

Most of the quantitative investigations have been based on one of three
types of evidence. First come synthetic compilations of data carried out by
ancient authorities, usually to provide a basis for taxation or to demonstrate
that taxation had been properly carried out; the Hermopolite land registers
are a preeminent specimen of this genre. Second there are assemblages of
similar texts that can be treated as a sample, even though in no case do we
really have anything like a representative sample; the census declarations are
a good example of this type of data. Third come the large archives, where we
can get complete enough information about an individual family or enterprise to assess key economic aspects of its life, even if comparability remains
a perennial problem; the Heroninos archive may represent this group fairly.

Even where these types of data are not available, all is not lost. Smaller
archives also can yield less complete but still useful information, and having
enough of them allows comparison; Kehoe (1992) shows something of what
can be done with such bodies of material. And even nonarchival material,
if collected in enough quantity and carefully analyzed, yields insights
complementary to those provided by the archives, as Rowlandson (1996)
demonstrates.

The remarks above have probably given the impression that a lot of
progress has been made in the last decade or so in the deployment of the

papyri for purposes of economic history, both through the application of questions and techniques from the mainstream of ancient economic history and through detailed analysis of bodies of papyrological evidence. That impression seems to me correct. A new model for the economy of Roman Egypt has in fact emerged in specialist circles, even if it has not yet been set forth in comprehensive fashion; it underlies many of the detailed studies I have cited. The next few years should see at least two attempts to offer an overall synthesis or a generalized model for the whole period in question.[31] One of these is van Minnen's forthcoming book on the economy of Roman Egypt, announced but not yet published. Rathbone has also now undertaken to produce a large-scale synthesis, with a quantitative bent, on the subject. With these coming, it is impossible and inadvisable to do more in the present chapter than to sketch some of the main outlines of what recent scholarship would suggest a synthetic view of the economy of Roman Egypt might contain.

First, the Roman government set out to dismantle the remains of the Ptolemaic state and its more interventionist approach (Rathbone 1994). The professional bureaucracy was largely replaced by liturgical service over the period from Augustus to Hadrian. To make this possible, land was turned over to private ownership on a large scale, particularly from the old Ptolemaic military allotments. A landowning elite quickly grew up in the nome capitals, which were given gradually increasing powers of self-management and responsibility for the surrounding countryside. In this way Egypt was assimilated to the patterns prevalent in the rest of the eastern Roman Empire. The process was certainly not instantaneous, but its completion—not beginning—in the third century with the grant of city councils reflects how far the change had gone. Although some landowners had substantial holdings, there was a much more substantial group of middle-range owners, and very large, consolidated estates never developed in Egypt. These elites managed their dispersed estates in a variety of ways. As elsewhere in the Roman world, tenancy played a central role, particularly for arable land; but capital-intensive fruit crops tended to draw more direct management, with the larger operations run for efficiency and profit. The rural economy was highly monetized and closely tied to that of the cities through leasing, credit, and marketing. The villages, too, had a substantial stratum of midrange landowners, well above the subsistence level and often very closely linked to the operations of the urban economy. The productivity of the agricultural sector was very high and seems to have risen during the Roman period.

The cities, in their turn, were far from being merely the residence of these landowners and their dependants. At least the larger of them were also scenes of substantial and specialized craft production, with export in mind. This too is probably the work of two centuries of development. It is harder to pinpoint the extent to which this trade was internal to Egypt and to what degree it was directed at foreign markets, but certainly some of the goods sold abroad, like linen and papyrus, were produced in the nomes and not in Alexandria. In any case, the efficiency of the Nile as a transportation route made it possible for the entire valley to operate as a single unit to an extent rarely found elsewhere in the ancient world. The desert extremities were tied into this Nilotic backbone—to the east because the mines, quarries, and trade routes were imperially managed and dealing in high-value goods, to the west because the oasitic ecosystem was able to produce olive oil worth transporting by land to the valley.

It is now widely considered that the Egyptian economy became extensively monetized already in the Ptolemaic period. The Roman government did not change that fact, despite its continuation of the Ptolemaic habit of maintaining a distinctive system of coinage in Egypt. It is becoming clearer that inflation was a far more limited aspect of the economy than historians—haunted by the specter of interwar inflation in Europe—were prepared to believe. In the third century it was (as Johnson already seems to have grasped) missing until about 275, and then again absent until Diocletian; even in the fourth century, when it seems to have been massive if one simply judges by the changes in prices, it was a monetary phenomenon—the combined product of debasements and retariffings of coins—with limited impact on other economic activity.[32]

Within these broad outlines there are plenty of questions on which syntheses are likely to differ. From all indications, van Minnen's book will take a position at the "optimistic" end of the spectrum of opinion, arguing for a large population and a highly productive urban economy. That is, it will offer a near-total revision of the model of the economy summarized above from Johnson and other works of the past sixty years. If these positions are likely to be controversial, it will (I expect) be more because of the extreme lengths to which they are pushed rather than because the basic views expressed are different from those of most specialists today.

There are also plenty of aspects of the economy missing from the brief summary above, mainly because they have not yet received the same kind of attention. It is therefore natural to ask if this kind of progress can be sustained. I shall suggest several directions in which I believe that it can. First, of course, the great attraction of documentary and archaeological disciplines is that they keep bringing new material to light. Although the pace of papyrological publication is irregular, over the course of a decade or two quite a bit of relevant new material is published. Almost the entirety of the material mentioned above concerning the role of the desert economy and its relevance to the analysis of transportation economics in Egypt was found since the mid-1980s, to offer just one example. It is true that established Western collections have fewer dramatic novelties to offer now than was once the case, but even they are by no means exhausted; and excavations continue to shed light on regions of Egypt hitherto poorly known, showing that we assume uniformity at our peril.

Second, there is a lot of published material that has never been subjected to serious analysis. Sometimes this is a matter of the scattering of connected items through many separate publications, sometimes a matter of the limited questions with which editors approach their texts. Many of the archives treated by Kehoe (1992) would individually repay more detailed studies, and the recent resurgence of studies of the Apion papers of the sixth century shows that even the best-known of archives often have scarcely been touched.

Third, any number of topics concerned with the economy have never had an intelligent study. Perhaps the single most important for Roman Egypt is taxation. There is, of course, a voluminous bibliography about taxation, but it is almost all concerned with identifying the existence of taxes, under-standing the ways and means of collection, and establishing rates. And much even of this bibliography is now out of date. But no one has ever made a se-rious attempt to understand what the overall burden of taxation was like for different actors in the economy and what kinds of incentives and disincen-tives were created by this particular system of taxation. The details of litur-gical service, too, have been studied in great detail, but there has been no real attempt to ask similar questions about the impact of the system.[33] Still less has anyone correlated these systems and tracked their development over time. This is a daunting project but an important one. Egypt's imports, so readily dismissed by Johnson, demand reexamination. Egypt certainly needed to import wood and charcoal as well as iron. Our evidence is very poor, but one might begin by pondering the essential resources that were not indigenous to Egypt and formulating estimates of their quantitative importance.

This leads me to pose the question of the feasibility of creating a model in a more explicitly quantitative sense: Could we build a working model of the economy of Roman Egypt, of a particular Roman province, that is, with both its universal and its particular dimensions? I do not, of course, mean a set of spreadsheets in which most of the cells are filled in with hard data, which might not really be a model anyway, but one that embodied a set of hypotheses. There are sufficient data, I think, to test enough of these hy-potheses to assure some rigor in the model. Egypt may be the only part of the ancient world for which there is enough evidence to test a reasonable number of the assumptions.[34] Constructing it would be a large-scale collaborative venture involving a lot of groundwork as well as the model-building itself.

Notes

I am grateful to James Keenan, Naphtali Lewis, and the editors for comments on earlier drafts of this paper.

1. I am grateful to Naphtali Lewis for his recollections of Finley's time at Columbia. He writes (letter of 9 February 1998), "He was for a few years in the '30s WLW's favorite, prize student, before the relationship soured. Moe, Meyer Reinhold and I were the [total] student body in WLW's 1932 papyrology seminar on the Zenon papyri. We taught ourselves to decipher, which is easy enough in that script where the writing is intact; but what we did with our deciphered texts was rudimentary and uninspiring—little more than *explication de textes* and search for parallels. Much given [all his life] to snap judgments, Moe must have decided then and there, I suspect, that this stuff was unimportant—out of the mainstream and therefore negligible."

2. See *Proceedings of the British Academy* 94 (1996): 587, on Finley's role in the election of George Forrest rather than David Lewis as Wykeham Professor at Oxford. For a more general account of the origins of Finley's aversion to emphasizing evidence, see 466–70.

3. Finley 1985b: 36: "However, all the evidence satisfies me that such notions [synthetic accounts] were alien to him [Zenon] and his society, that his mass of paper consisted of day-to-day documents intended for day-to-day purposes and little more." He sees the Roman picture as more of the same.

4. Much of Finley (1985b) is in fact a polemic (see 63 ff.) against Peter Fraser's *Ptolemaic Alexandria* (1972), with its (as Finley saw matters, and not unjustly) positivistic and unreflective approach to not merely the papyri but other evidence.

5. Somewhere in between is Keith Hopkins's definition (1995/96: 41): "A model is, roughly speaking, a simplification of a complex reality, designed to show up the logical relationships between its constituent parts." Hopkins (64 n. 2) misrepresents me as "explicitly den[ying] the utility of models" (citing Bagnall 1993a: 310), but there I say only that "the complex reality of the agricultural economy of Egypt is not readily represented by broad generalizations or simple models," which is not the same thing.

6. One case of the use of models in the study of Ptolemaic Egypt deserves mention here, as I shall not discuss it below because it is neither concerned with Roman Egypt nor mainly economic in character. This is the proposal by E. Will to adopt modern colonialism as a model for approaching Hellenistic

kingdoms and particularly the Ptolemies. The results of attempts to put
Will's proposal into practice have been rather mixed, consisting partly of
careless handling of the facts and partly of careful analysis of a traditional sort
in which the colonial theory is applied like a veneer. For a discussion with
bibliography, see Bagnall (1997a), where it is argued that a use of colonialism
as an ideal type is of little use, but a sensitivity to mid-level explanations of
specific phenomena is helpful.

7. See esp. Rathbone 1989. He focuses there on "the economic position
of the rural population, the character of ancient economic behaviour, and the
nature and scale of Roman taxation" (161). Recognizing the individuality of
all provinces, he shows the usability of Egyptian data for key questions concerning the Roman economy.

8. *O. Bu Njem*; Bowman and Thomas 1994.

9. Examples appear constantly; the most recent to cross my desk is Alcock
(1997), which manages not a single contribution on Egypt (no doubt one of
those "inevitable and unfortunate gaps in coverage" mentioned on p. vi).

10. See Jördens 1995: 37 n.; despite her disclaimer, however, her article
is by no means an example of the type.

11. For discussion, see Keenan 1993; Hardy (1931), especially, embodies
this view, but Keenan cites abundant literature supporting it, especially many
works of H. I. Bell.

12. Keenan (1993: 141) refers to articles by Rémondon and Keenan himself in the mid-1970s as marking a shift.

13. Currency occupies pp. 1–36, with many of Johnson's general views
on pp. 18–29; inflation, pp. 37–66; see esp. p. 39 on monetary velocity.

14. See also pp. 88–99 on the status of the peasants and p. 118 for
Diocletian's removal of inequities in the tax system.

15. It may be noted that E. R. Hardy, whose dissertation on Byzantine
Egypt has been mentioned in note 12, was Westermann's pupil. As Keenan
(1993: 141) has pointed out, however, the dominant influence is that of Bell,
and it may be doubted that Westermann had any original contribution to
make to the study of the sixth century.

16. That is not to say that Rostovtzeff was uninterested in the Roman
papyri, which he uses throughout his *Social and Economic History of the Roman
Empire* (1926).

17. See Boak and Youtie (1957), the title of which is by itself sufficient.
In Boak's Roman history textbook (many editions, see, for example, *History
of Rome*, 3rd ed. [1943]), Egypt gets no more than passing mention. The same
is true (naturally enough, given the title) of his *Manpower Shortage and the
Fall of the Roman Empire in the West* (1955).

18. "Relatively" is to be emphasized. The preface to A. C. Johnson (1936)
is full of the decline of agriculture and of villages, the "anarchy of the third
century," and the "flight of the peasant from the soil." Westermann's views,

which can be found in his correspondence with Bell about the operations of
the papyrus cartel, are confirmed for me by Lewis: Westermann "never missed
an opportunity to denigrate Johnson." For Bell on Johnson, see Keenan 1993.

19. N. Lewis 1970; see also N. Lewis (1984) for further development of
the theme, surveying work in the intervening years. Braunert (1964) offered
the first major detailed and nuanced study of a major question of social history
of Roman Egypt in quite some time, and the wider historical context is important to his framing of questions; he also treated the Ptolemaic and Byzantine periods. But in his examination of migration and population movement
he explicitly rejected the possibility of using statistical methods.

20. N. Lewis 1983: 57 (slavery), 67–71 (villages), 142 (transport), 159–65
(taxation and flight), 203 (mobility). His account of agriculture (107–33)
and trades (134–55) is essentially enumerative.

21. It should need no special emphasis—but it is a matter of some pleasure
to observe—that in a chapter like this it is impossible to mention many
valuable contributions in which models from the larger world of ancient
studies are brought to bear on the papyri. Some of these are discussed
throughout Bagnall 1993a; on the general question of the sources of the
questions discussed in papyrology see Bagnall 1995: 90–108.

22. On the roots of this approach in microhistory, see G. Levi, "On
microhistory," in Burke 1991: 97–117.

23. See Bagnall (1993a: 82–83) for a discussion accepting the main lines
of van Minnen's argument but suggesting that his numbers may be too high.

24. Bieżuńska-Małowist (1977) is the classic statement of this position,
with full description of the evidence as it stood then.

25. Bagnall (1993b) argues that the supposed quantitative evidence for
decline is worthless; Fikhman (1997) remains in favor of a decline.

26. See Bagnall (1985a) for a general assessment and Jördens (1995) for a
detailed examination of the trade in transport animals.

27. For a brief survey with bibliography, see Maxfield 1996. On Berenike,
see most recently Sidebotham and Wendrich 1996.

28. On the supply of goods like wine and oil to Mons Claudianus, see
Tomber 1996. The ostraca from Berenike (published by R. S. Bagnall,
Christina Helms, and Arthur Verhoogt in *Papyrologica Bruxellensia*) show
extensive export of fine wines just as described in the *Periplus Maris Erythraei*.

29. See *P. Kell.* I (ed. K. A. Worp) for Greek letters; *P. Kell.* V (ed.
A. Alcock, I. Gardner, and W.-P. Funk 1999) has numerous Coptic letters
showing the ties to this part of the valley (not least that the dialect of the in-
coming letters is characteristic of that region).

30. For a general discussion of quantification in history written from
papyri, see Bagnall 1995: 73–89.

31. In Bagnall (1993a), I have developed a general view of the post-
Diocletianic situation.

32. See Rathbone (1996) for the third century (his title is slightly mislead-ing, for he does not in fact claim that there was no price inflation, only that it was absent until 274/75); see Bagnall (1985b) for the fourth.

33. Drecoll (1997) deals only with the third and fourth centuries, and without any serious economic analysis.

34. One may ask if the discovery of papyrological documents outside Egypt will make it possible to construct comparable economic models for those regions as well. This seems improbable unless substantial new discoveries are made. The Dead Sea archives from the early second century provide information on private landowning, but the volume of material is still rela-tively small. When the Petra papyri are published, they may contribute significantly to our assessment of the operation of the agricultural economy of that area. From preliminary reports there do not seem to be any texts ca-pable of contributing to a quantitative appreciation of the Petra economy, but at least some important qualitative information will offer a new basis for interrogating the archaeological record, including the remains of water-control systems and paleobotanical materials.

Part IV

The Roman Mediterranean

Chapter 10

"The Advantages of Wealth and Luxury"

The Case for Economic Growth in the Roman Empire

R. BRUCE HITCHNER

In the second century of the Christian Era, the empire of Rome comprehended the fairest part of the earth, and the most civilized part of mankind. The frontiers of the extensive monarchy were guarded by ancient renown and disciplined valour. The gentle but powerful influence of laws and manners had gradually cemented the union of the provinces. Their peaceful inhabitants enjoyed and abused the advantages of wealth and luxury.

—Edward Gibbon

Introduction

Edward Gibbon's verdict on the second-century Roman Empire may now seem overstated, but it still reflects, I believe, an essential truth: The Empire was the most stable, resource-rich, culturally integrated, and economically developed state of antiquity.[1] In this chapter, I shall focus specifically on the issue of economic development, and argue that most, if not all, of the conditions were in place for real economic growth to have occurred in the Roman Empire between the later first century BC and the early third century AD.

Defining Economic Growth

What do I mean by economic growth? Put simply, economic growth refers to a rise in the average real income per head and a corresponding rise in population. But how do we determine whether growth occurred in historical societies where statistical information on income and population is lacking? The answer does not lie, in my view, in the creation of proxy statistics, but in the application of what Eric Jones (2000 [1988]: 31) calls "cliometric methods of debate."[2] This means identifying instances where the signs of positive economic growth are significant. For Jones the most persuasive cases "are where large fractions of the population are reported to have been using new methods and consuming more than ever before, where change continued for more than a century, and where it altered the structure of the economy so that a noticeable proportion of the workforce moved out of agriculture into more productive occupations" (Jones 2000: 31).

Economists are in general agreement that economic growth in history is a product of a variety of factors, some of which I have already argued were present in the early empire. These include an advantageous physical environment, a stable political, legal, and institutional climate, investment in agriculture, manufacturing outside the household, trade, capital accumulation, technological progress, and investments in human capital and the stock of knowledge. To these I would add two caveats. The first is that capitalism is not an essential prerequisite for growth in history. Even in the modern period, for example, the noncapitalist economies of Communist Eastern Europe were capable of growth. And second, elite rhetoric in premodern societies does not necessarily reflect universal conduct.

The Case for Growth in the Roman Empire

ENVIRONMENT AND INFRASTRUCTURE

From both environmental and institutional perspectives, the Roman Empire held considerable promise for its inhabitants. Edward Gibbon had it about right when he wrote: "The empire of Rome comprehended the fairest part of the earth." Situated at the extreme western edge of Eurasia, the Roman Empire remained, until the later part of its history, largely free from invasion and the turbulent population movements that buffeted the Near East and central Asian steppe. Its location around the long-indented coastline of the Mediterranean was a boon to communication and the movement of goods in comparison with the great land-locked empires of central and southwest Asia. Even more importantly, the empire fell within two distinct but complimentary environments in terms of resources: the Mediterranean and the cool temperate climate of Europe.

The merits of the Mediterranean were well-recognized by Moses Finley:

It is a region of relatively easy habitation and much outdoor living, producing on its best soils, the coastal plains and the large inland plateaus, a good supply of the staple cereal grasses, vegetables and fruits, in particular grapes and olives, with suitable pasture for small animals, sheep, pits and goats, but not on the whole for cattle. (Finley 1985a: 31)

Nevertheless, the Mediterranean environment required innovation and creativity to be productive. This was manifested agriculturally in a combination of intensification and diversification to produce surpluses for storage and redistribution. The Mediterranean long served as an effective mechanism for redistribution, but under the peaceful conditions of the empire, this process was enhanced significantly (Horden and Purcell: 370–72).[3]

The European parts of the empire were likewise blessed with great navigable rivers, heavier soils of high arable potential, and relatively evenly distributed resources. The merits of Europe's environment from a productive perspective are best captured by E. L. Jones:[4]

Europe was not, by Asian standards, a lush habitat . . . in warm regions man was subject to endoparasitic infestation which caused each society there to reach a plateau of attainment and then stagnate. Northern winters, in contrast, prune deleterious organisms as they lie in the soil and water. Ploughing also exerted control over soil parasites, while it was the Iron Age plough that first brought up enough soil nutrients to produce a good yield in northern areas where rain occurs throughout the year and there is little evaporation. (Jones 1987)

The empire's good fortune in geography and environment was matched by the vast human, material, and institutional assets that came with conquest and integration (W. V. Harris 1979). These assets included well-established agricultural economies, cities, trade and communication networks, and institutionally strong states particularly in the eastern Mediterranean. Indeed, the Roman unification of the Mediterranean and Europe into a single political entity represented nothing less than the most significant compression of space, resources, and human capital in antiquity and not repeated again until the rise of the European trans-Atlantic empires in the seventeenth and eighteenth centuries.

But all of this would have mattered little had the empire wasted its wealth on the relentless warfare so common to antiquity. The empire was protected and secured by a professional military whose primary purpose was to preserve the peace. Indeed, the empire was fortunate in having an army that protected it but for the most part stayed in the barracks when it came to politics. The secret of the empire may have been that emperors were chosen by the legions, but the very fact that Tacitus characterized this reality as a secret exposes a fundamental truth—the army was not a dominant or negative force in the daily life of the empire. This is astonishing when we contemplate the profound importance of martial values and warfare in early Roman history. Yet Augustus and subsequent emperors managed to subordinate the army to the best interests of the empire. All of this was nothing short of a revolution in the way in which militaries functioned in antiquity and it gave birth to an era, known fittingly as the pax Romana.

The Romans, much like Britain in the nineteenth century and the United States in the late twentieth, attached great responsibility to the task of providing stability and security. Tacitus articulates this in a speech he puts in the mouth of the Roman general Cerialis, addressing the Gallic tribes, the Treviri and Longones, during the civil wars of AD 69:

> You cannot secure tranquility among nations without armies, nor maintain armies without pay, nor provide pay without taxes. . . . For, if the Romans are driven out—which Heaven forbid—what will follow except universal war among all peoples? The good fortune and order of eight hundred years have built up this mighty fabric which cannot be destroyed without overwhelming its destroyers. . . . Therefore love and cherish peace and the city wherein we, conquerors and conquered alike enjoy an equal right: be warned by the lessons of fortune both good and bad not to prefer defiance and ruin to obedience and security. (Hist. 4. 74)

The profound transformation in the ancient world brought about by the new security order brought into being a civilian society. "The empire had become a world in which most people lived in peace for most of the time."[5] Moreover, when conflict did occur, its intensity and duration was rarely shaped, as it is today, by intense nationalism and ethnic conflict.[6] The long peace of the empire meant that the investment of taxes in the maintenance of a standing army was put to some positive infrastructural benefit, in particular through the construction of roads, aqueducts, and even new towns in the regions where troops were stationed, as opposed to the negative costs of conflict in manpower and damaged landscapes.[7]

The relatively low cost of maintaining peace, at least until the early third century, contributed in turn to a relatively benign government that invested a sufficient portion of its wealth in roads, bridges, harbors, warehouses, drainage projects, rivers and canal navigation, and marketing facilities—investments that reduce transportation costs and promote trade.[8] Moses Finley overstated, I believe, the level of misappropriation of state resources when he asserted that "ancient states were capable of mobilizing extensive resources for amenities and for military purposes, and the trend was upward in a kind of megalomania, from the Golden House of Nero to Diocletian's nine-acre palace in Dalmatia in the private sphere" (1985a: 148). Roman rulers funded smaller military budgets than the early modern French monarchs who controlled a landmass less than a tenth the size of the empire, and their conspicuous consumption did not compare in volume or scale to that of some later Asian monarchs. In fact, from Julius Caesar onward Roman rulers were alive to the importance of regarding the population of the empire, not as subjects to be exploited, but as a vast clientage to be served. As Tiberius, Augustus's successor, is reported to have said, "Other men's decisions may be based on their own interests, but rulers are situated differently, since in many important matters they need to consider public opinion" (Tacitus, *Annals* 4.39).[9] At the very least this suggests that the Roman state was inclined toward actions that promoted the public good.

The Roman Empire was also distinguished by its insistence on the rule of law and its encouragement of secure institutions that unified the world. These institutions existed in both material form in milestones, imperial portraits, military standards, holidays, "but also in securing the good will of local, commercial, political, and religious institutions."[10]

Despite its overwhelming military power—the empire both out of necessity and a desire to promote unity—depended on local elites and local governing structures to maintain and promote its political power throughout the empire. Where local power structures were found to be inadequate, the empire did not hesitate to introduce the structures of administration necessary to ensure stability. This policy can only have encouraged the creation of a society that proved capable of maximizing the economic benefits of peace and stability.

The investment in infrastructure was sustained by an innovative monetary and fiscal policy that was breathtaking in both its scale and achievement. Its main elements were the establishment of a currency and a complete reorganization of the tax structure under Augustus (31 BC–AD 14), which together laid the foundations for a truly global economy.

Coins in three metals (gold, silver, and bronze) were minted, eventually in very large quantities, and intended for circulation in all the provinces except Egypt. Bronze coins circulated locally, interacting with the natural economy and the silver coinage for purposes of rents and taxation. Silver coinage was largely used for taxes as well as everyday purchases. However, it was gold that dominated the monetary economy of the empire. The new currency undoubtedly lowered the transaction costs involved in the exchanges of goods, increased opportunities for credit, and enhanced the economic integration of the empire. The gold coinage also helped the movement of high volume/high value trade in luxuries (Hopkins 1995/96).

The tax reforms introduced by Augustus were no less revolutionary in

212

R. BRUCE HITCHNER

their uniform criteria for counting people and establishing equally uniform standards for measuring and assessing the value of agricultural land. These measures fostered production and promoted a more marked market orientation of it for three reasons. First, the land tax was linked to the monetary value of estates, and thus not arbitrarily fixed. Second, the value of estates was expressed in monetary terms and the land tax largely collected in coin, thus promoting monetization throughout the empire. And third, the ending of the practice of employing of tax-farmers and tax-farming companies must have lowered the burden of the land tax.[11]

The new tax system probably also exercised a positive influence on production because of its low rate in relation to GNP, its share being less than 5 to 7 percent of the public sector.[12] And a low land tax paid in coin will have likely promoted productivity.[13]

In sum, the unity, stability, remarkable resources and institutional stability of the early empire created an environment that must be considered favorable to economic growth.

THE EVIDENCE FOR GROWTH

The existence of conditions favorable to economic growth in the Roman Empire is not in itself proof of growth.[14] As Finley observed in his critique of Keith Hopkins's model of growth in the Roman Empire (1985a: 182–83), there is a distinct "possibility of exploitation without any increase in productivity." Nevertheless, the evidence for growth in population and production seems sufficient to question Finley's assumption.[15]

We shall never have precise information on the population of the Roman Empire, but there is reason to think that population rose at a pace adequate to offset a high mortality rate, but not so rapidly as to outpace its resources (Frier 1999; Thompson and Hawthorn 1995; W. V. Harris 1994). As Bruce Frier notes: "To a considerable extent the wealth of the empire was in the last analysis, simply the high size of its population, which even if still widely lived in poverty, could fairly provide the resources that the state required for governance and protection" (Frier 1999: 104). Add to this the evidence for the clearance, cultivation (see below) and peopling of new land (for Africa in particular, see Lassère 1977), and urban growth and expansion and it seems reasonable to assume that population was rising under the empire and perhaps at a slightly faster pass than at any previous time in the history of Europe and the Mediterranean (Frier 1999).

The Roman Empire's incorporation of most of Europe, the entire North African littoral, and the Levant was nothing less than an unprecedented accumulation of capital in so far as it greatly increased the available land and resources per individual. To the immediate advantage of the empire, a significant part of this new acreage was already under cultivation and thus immediately capable of generating income and revenue. At the very least, this new mass of land served to hold population below its maximum while increasing levels of consumption. Yet it was the conquest and absorption of large amounts of underdeveloped land, particularly in the west, that set the stage for growth in the imperial period. This was land to be developed, and as Philippe Leveau (1993) has convincingly shown, the Roman aristocracy was completely alive to the opportunity. No European state accrued such an addition to its resource base until the discovery and settlement of the New World in the fifteenth and sixteenth centuries, precisely the period when modern European growth began.

Large tracts of this newly acquired land in Africa, Gaul, Spain, the Danubian provinces, and other parts of the empire were subjected to centuriation and arable development on an unprecedented scale by both the state and private individuals (Mattingly 1997b; Keay 1988; Choquer and Favory 1992; B. Campbell 1996; Leveau 1996; D. L. Stone 1997; *CIL* 14.3608 = *ILS* 986). This investment was not restricted to regions of high arable potential, but also to more marginal landscapes such as wetlands in Europe and the predesert steppes in Africa (Leveau 1993, 1996; Van Bellamy and Hitchner 1996; Van Ossel and Ouzoulias 2000; Potter 1981; Hitchner 1988, 1990, 1991, 1995; Barker et al. 1996; Salviat 1986) and was achieved by a combination of owner-occupied farms and secure low-rent tenancies, tenure systems generally acknowledged to be favorable to growth (Kehoe 1984; Mattingly 1997b; Kolendo 1992; Vera 1987, 1988; Whittaker 1978, 1995). This investment was driven by three factors: first, the interests of the Roman state in securing and increasing food production above the minimum; second, the *avaritia*, or desire for profit, on the part of the Roman aristocracy through the investment and development of land to supply the state or for purely speculative interests (Leveau 1993: 12–13);[16] and third, the dissemination of knowledge of lands, agricultural techniques, and other processes by geographers, encyclopedists, and technical writers (Greene 1994: 30).[17]

TECHNICAL CHANGE AND INNOVATION

The vast investment in agriculture was complimented by more technical change, innovation, and serialization than is often acknowledged (Wilson 2002). Moses Finley, in particular, did not see much evidence of technology in service of production in the ancient world, nor did he imagine that archaeology would change the picture.[18] But his focus tended to be on the failure of the ancients, in particular the elites, to put to productive use the grander innovations and inventions, reflecting Finley's particular concern with status and its impact on the organization of labor. It is not, however, the more spectacular technical innovations and inventions in history that seem to play the greatest role in bringing about economic growth, but the inconspicuous ones that manage to find their way through economic systems. On this count, the Roman Empire fares quite well. It is now clear, for example, that water power was put to greater use for productive purposes, and at an earlier date, than imagined; the most spectacular evidence of this being the recent discovery of second-century AD turban-driven water mills at Chemtou and Testour in Tunisia, and new evidence from Barbegal that the mill there also belongs to the early second century (Wilson 1995; Leveau 1996). Similarly, the control of water—either for irrigation, as in North Africa; or to recover arable for cultivation and pasturage, as in Italy, southern Gaul, and the Fens in southeastern Britain—constitutes a massive geographical extension of a modest technology designed to increase agricultural productivity (Hitchner 1995b; Barker et al. 1996; Potter 1989). Roman awareness of different soils also led to the deployment of different agricultural strategies, including double cropping, the employment of liming and compost, and greater manuring (Favory et al. 1994). The spread of iron tools, much like water mills, allowed for greater exploitation of natural resources and more effective cultivation of the heavier and deeper loams.[19]

There was also innovation in harvesting and food processing. Recent evidence from North Africa, in particular, shows some modifications in the design of lever presses for the purpose of increasing the volume of olive oil production. Likewise the movement from single small presses to batteries of more powerful olive- and winepresses in both Provence and Africa reflects a technological change to meet the needs of regional markets (Brun 2003; Brun 1986; Mattingly and Hitchner 1993; Hitchner 1993; Mattingly 1997b).

These changes in agricultural technology were the result of investment by small and large landholders alike. As M. Millet (1990) points out in the case of Roman Britain, "All these arable changes represent increased investment in rural production and, when taken with the development of rural industry, they appear consistent with diversification." He associates these changes with the "rich landowners who were more willing to invest and experiment with new methods than their less wealthy neighbors." The situation was the same for large-scale olive oil producers in North Africa. But to assume that such investment was entirely derived from those of means is to deny the real desire of smallholders to improve their lot. Indeed, the archaeological evidence from around the Mediterranean such as it is suggests that small and large properties alike were outfitted with the necessary farm equipment, facilities, waterworks, and other essentials for increasing production, a pattern of activity positively associated with growth.

Survey evidence from the Mediterranean and Europe shows that the vast surpluses of land acquired by the Roman state were inexorably being filled up with farms and villas down to the third century AD, when the land frontier was more or less closed out (Barker and Lloyd 1991; Greene 1993; Dietz et al. 1996; Van Ossel and Ouzoulias 2000). The general absence of evidence for a sharp rise in food prices in the early imperial period suggests that production was meeting food demand, and the devotion of large areas of Spain, Gaul, and Africa to food production for export would seem unequivocal evidence of growth in agricultural output.[20] The spread of olive cultivation in the back country of Provence and to areas inhospitable to other crops such as the Iberian plateau, African steppe, and predesert is perhaps the best example from archaeology of this phenomenon, representing nothing less than an overall increase in both food and income per hectare (Brun 1986, 1989; Mattingly 1988, 1997b; Hitchner 1993). The surpluses generated from the increase in the production and export are also reflected in the wealth reinvested in both the ostentatious character of rural estates and the remarkable array of monuments and houses throughout the African and European provinces.

The development of speculative viticulture belongs to the same trend and is dramatically illustrated in southern Gaul by the recent excavations of huge storehouses of treading vats, presses, and cellars containing more than a hundred dolia. The capacity of some storehouses in the Var is estimated to be as high as three thousand *hl* (Brun and Conges 1994). While this does not necessarily correspond to production capacity, as several vintages may have been stored, they imply large surface areas devoted to vines, perhaps in excess of three hundred hectares. Viticulture, moreover, extended well beyond the Mediterranean basin into the Loire, Lyon, and Burgundy regions (Laubenheimer 1989; 1990: 77–104).

Stock-raising constituted one of the principal forms of elite investment for commercial purposes in late republican Italy (Leveau 1992: 36; Kehoe 1990), but under the empire, its expansion as an industry is evident. Recent survey and excavation in the Crau plain near Arles shows a massive development of sheep breeding, estimated at more than one hundred thousand

animals, probably for the purpose of supplying clothing and textiles to the
army (Badan et al. 1996: 305–6; Hitchner 1994). The same may be true for
central Tunisia, where a complimentary system of estate-centered and mon-
tagnardic stock-raising emerged in the imperial period (Hitchner 1994).[21]

Marine resource production is yet another manifestation of the expansion as well as diversification of agriculture (Trousset 1992; Wilson 1999;
Curtis 1991; Reese 1979–80). Recent work on salt fish, garum, and murex
production along the Africa littoral reveals an industry that involved both
towns and villas (Wilson 1999; Ben Lazreg et al. 1995), and although the full
scale and extent of the market has yet to be determined, African amphorae
recovered in excavations in southern France and from shipwrecks suggest
that the export of processed marine products was substantial.

Finally, there can be little doubt that cereal cultivation increased dramatically under the empire, chiefly to meet the demands of the *annona* at *Rome*
and the expanding number of urban centers. One possible indirect indicator
of increased cereal production is the push to create new arable land through
the drainage of lakes and marshes as the heavy humid soils that result were
not well suited to olives and vines and were therefore probably intended for
the production of cereals and stock-raising (through the production of hay)
(Leveau 1995). It is precisely this development that is likely to account for
the construction of the Barbegal Mill overlooking the Vallée des Baux, a
wetland drained and cultivated in the early imperial period.[22] The recently
discovered water mills along the Bagradas River in North Africa should also
probably be read as a technological response to increases in cereal production in an area already under cultivation in the pre-Roman period (Leveau
1996; Bellamy and Hitchner 1996; Hitchner 1990; Wilson 1995).

THE DEVELOPMENT OF A NONAGRICULTURAL
PRODUCTION SECTOR

Despite the difficulties of estimating the population of the Roman Empire,
the archaeological evidence of settlement suggests that population was probably on the rise in the imperial period. More people required more jobs, and
while agriculture undoubtedly continued to supply the bulk of them, increased employment outside of agriculture increased to meet the demand.[23]
One possible indication of a significant shift in employment out of the agricultural sector and into manufacturing may be found in the gradual filling
out and expansion of towns in many parts of the empire during the first and
second centuries. To be sure, there may be a variety of explanations for this
trend, but one of them must surely be that Roman cities with their ambi-

tious building programs and public amenities were seen by expanding rural populations as providing easier and more profitable opportunities for employment than agriculture. Over time, manufacturing of pottery, glass, mosaic, metal, and other goods make their appearance in the towns, villas, and farms of the countryside (Dunbabin 1978; W. V. Harris 1993; Stern 1999; Wilson 1999). Of particular interest is the growth of local manufacturing designed to replicate high-demand imports from Italy or other core production areas, but which eventually replace these imports altogether, a phenomenon referred to by development economists as "import substitution" and an important proxy indicator of local economic growth.

But does all this manufacturing constitute a genuine industrial sector? Although the term *industry* carries heavy baggage when dealing with the ancient world, development economists define it to include household and handicraft production as well as hierarchical production with full-time working employees at a central place.[24] There can be no doubt, then, that the Roman economy had a recognizable industrial sector. This is most apparent in the rise of provincial pottery production. It is less important in my view whether the legal, social, and productive organization of manufacturing was underdeveloped and less than febrile by modern industrial standards. What counts is responsiveness to demand. As Gunnar Fulle (1997: 146) has shown in his recent analysis of the Arretine pottery industry, the growth of the workshops "suggests—at least for the sector of mass pottery production—a notable flexibility of the Roman economy," involving an "optimization of known structures with minimum qualitative innovation." Ultimately, however, it is the sheer volume of manufactured goods recovered on sites all over the empire that attests to the scale of industrial production in the Roman world, a situation not seen again until the eighteenth century. This fact was recognized by Finley (1985a: 59), but as was often the case, he could not accept the possibility of growth in a world bound by status. For him, manufacturers and traders were of low status and hence exploited, rather than indicative of growth in the Roman economy.

INCREASED TRADE

Max Weber contended that "agriculture is an involuntary transport industry." Under the Roman Empire, this truth was acted out on an unparalleled scale involving the massive shift of food and associated goods from certain core provinces to Rome, other major centers, and the armies on the frontiers (K. Hopkins 2002). It need not matter from the perspective of growth whether much of this commerce was state driven. What counts is

that it occurred for an extended period of time and in the process stimulated
and complimented smaller-scale local distance and local trading activity.[25]
A good example of the growth of regional trade under the empire may
be found in the case of the oyster industry in Roman Provence (Hitchner
1999; Brien-Poitevin 1996).[26] Recent excavations of sites around the
series of *étangs*, or small shallow lakes, between Marseille and the Rhône
delta indicate that prior to the Roman period, the local inhabitants consumed large quantities of shellfish, chiefly mussels, harvested from the *étangs*.
Following the Roman conquest, a shift from mussels to oysters occurred,
possibly in emulation of Roman tastes. In the imperial period oyster consumption is found as far north as Orange and the Alps of northern Provence
(Digne), among every social group, to judge from the presence of oysters at
urban sites, villas, and modest rural settlements.[27] The increased demand for
oysters was evidently met by farms established for this purpose around the
shores of the *étangs*. The integration of Provence into the empire and the
subsequent development of an infrastructure of roads and canals thus contributed not only to a subtle shift in culinary tastes but more importantly to
the emergence of a heretofore nonexistent market for oysters.[28]

   The development of the oyster industry also reflects another economic
phenomenon at work in the early imperial period: an increase in consumption. Again, drawing on the evidence from Gaul, Greg Woolf (1998: 174)
has noted that "the sheer quantity of small objects increased enormously
[from the pre-Roman period], to the extent that archaeologists are forced to
approach Roman sites in ways very different from those applied to prehistoric settlements." This development, which is repeated at sites all over the
empire, constitutes something of a "consumer revolution" not seen again in
Europe until the early modern period.

THE PATTERN OF GROWTH: FROM
CENTER TO PERIPHERY

An argument for growth in Roman Europe and the Mediterranean need not
assume that growth was universal throughout the period under discussion.
Some regions expanded economically while others undoubtedly stagnated
or even declined. There are also indications that regions experienced cycles
of growth and stagnation. First-century BC Italy was the first to experience
genuine economic expansion, though it was mainly concentrated in central
and northern Italy (Barker and Lloyd 1991). However, by the mid-first
century AD the pace of Italian growth slowed considerably, judging by
the dropoff in exports of wine and ceramics. This cooling off was a direct

result of the growth in the production of these products in Spain and Gaul, formerly the main markets for Italian goods.[29]

The emergence of the Spanish and Gallic provincial economies also illustrates a deeper pattern in the economic history of the empire: an evolution of growth from center to periphery, or more precisely to the limits of the arable frontier. This evolution was uneven in as much as some areas grew faster than other, especially those that served the needs of the state or army such as southeastern Spain, southern and central Gaul (Leveau et al. 1993; Woolf 1999), and northern Africa Proconsularis (Dietz et al. 1996; Mattingly 1997b, 1988). But by the second century, these early performers were joined by other regions such as northern Spain (Keay 1988; Leveau et al. 1993), northern Gaul and southern Britain (Van Ossel and Ouzoulias 2000; M. Millet 1990; Wightman 1988), the African steppes and Tripolitania (Barker et al. 1996; Mattingly and Hitchner 1995; Hitchner 1993), and these are only the most obvious examples. Where we can observe this process closely, the picture is of wilderness or new lands being colonized and developed agriculturally, a process of expansion that undoubtedly increased the average area available per capita in the empire. The cultivation of these lands provided the empire's population with an unparalleled share of the biological resources of Europe and the Mediterranean.

Conclusion

The Roman Empire may not have been precisely as Edward Gibbon imagined it, but it was a fortunate state in terms of its resources and inheritance and, generally speaking, it managed them well both politically and administratively. This remarkable set of circumstances produced in turn a society that was relatively free to exploit the economic, social, and cultural opportunities afforded by the empire. In essence, more people were able to do more with more than ever before, and they acted on that freedom. The result was economic growth in the early empire. It does not matter, and is in any case irrelevant, that this growth was not the same as that achieved in the modern age or that it did not last.[30] What matters is that it occurred and on a scale sufficient to sustain "the advantages of wealth and luxury" for more than two centuries.

Notes

Although there is much in this chapter which Sir Moses Finley might have disagreed with, it could not have been written without the benefit of *The Ancient Economy*. However diverse our perspectives may be on the nature of the economy of the ancient world, we are all, in many ways, the beneficiaries of the groundbreaking work of Moses Finley.

1. As I shall argue more fully in a forthcoming book, the Roman Empire was an early and successful example of globalization.

2. By "proxy statistics" I am referring to the attempts of historians to calculate such things as population and tax figures on the basis of fragmentary and anecdotal information.

3. This chapter was largely written without the benefit of Horden and Purcell (2000) which had not yet been published.

4. Jones 1987: 6. There are also indications that the empire flourished in a slightly warmer climatic phase. See Greene 1986: 82–8; Gilbertson 1996: 293–99; and Randsborg 1991: 23–29.

5. Cornell 1983: 139–70, esp. 167–68.

6. Warfare also, in contrast to the present, rarely interrupted and sometimes benefited trade.

7. Taxes were collected mainly for the purpose of paying for the army. See Mattern 1999: Chapter 4.

8. Although prices in the Roman Empire appear to have doubled or even tripled between the first and third centuries AD, the period of steepest increases appears to have been after the first quarter of the third century. A rise in prices may, nevertheless, reflect a growing economy.

9. Whether Tiberius actually held to this view is irrelevant; what is important here is that there was some sensitivity to issues of public accountability on the part of the central government.

10. Ando 2000: 41.

11. LoCascio 1994: 77–85.

12. Hopkins 2002: 201; Goldsmith 1984: 263–88 and 1987: 48; Duncan-Jones 1994.

13. LoCascio 1994: 82–84. Indirect taxes and portoria on interprovincial trade were also low.

14. For negative assessments of the Roman economy's performance, see Finley 1985a; Garnsey and Saller 1987; Woolf 1990; Whittaker 1990; and Kehoe 1992. Keith Hopkins (1980, 1982, 1995/96) is ambivalent on the subject. For cautiously favorable assessments, see Hitchner 1993; Mattingly 1988, 1994, 1997; Mattingly and Hitchner 1995.

15. I draw, in what follows, on evidence mainly from the western provinces with which I am most familiar. Nevertheless, I am confident that the pattern of economic activity found in the west was valid for the whole of the empire.

16. A frequent refrain of Finley (1985a) and other historians doubtful of the performance of the Roman economy is that the legal and banking framework for doing business in the empire was utterly restrictive to growth. It cannot be disputed that there was serious legal underdevelopment by modern

standards in contractual arrangements involving corporate organization and trade, and a genuine primitiveness, again by current standards, in financing, credit, and banking mechanisms. (But see Rathbone [1991], who argues on the basis of papyri for the use of credit arrangements.) Still, if these constraints were so debilitating, why do they not seem to have impeded, as we shall see below, vast investment in agriculture and manufacturing and a very visible increase in trade at all levels throughout the empire? The answer, I suspect, is that Roman law provided that which was essential for investment and engagement in productive activities: contract enforcement and relative security of assets. Note Howgego (1992: 29) in this regard: "The organization of Roman businesses cut across boundaries of rank and status and thus may have gone some way to make such facilities [banks] available further down the social scale." There are very few societies even in the modern world whose legal and banking systems do not restrict economic freedom in some fashion. But as anyone who has participated in a business venture in the high risk rough and tumble of a developing country knows, only the absence of secure rights at property and the rule of law will truly stop investment and participation in production.

17. Kevin Greene (1994: 32) observes that "large centralized empires may provide encouragement to technology-transfer through the extensive use of written documents."

18. "The beauty of fine temples should not distract us from the fact that most public works—roads, walls, streets, aqueducts, sewers—required more muscle than skill. But at that point our sources, with their disinterest in such matters, desert us, and archaeology cannot help" (Finley 1985a: 75).

19. The introduction of the metal plow led to greater control of parasites and exposure of nutrients, thereby producing better yields particularly in the northern provinces, where rain occurs throughout the year with little evaporation.

20. K. Hopkins (1980: 104) claims that "the economy of the Roman empire, in spite of its sophistication in some respects, was predominantly a subsistence economy." But note in this regard the remarks of Lloyd Reynolds (1986: 16): "[The] term . . . 'subsistence economy' . . . has a dual connotation: people consume what they produce, and they live in some sense at a minimum or conventional level of 'subsistence.' Both statements contain an element of truth, but both are also treacherous. The ratio of home production to home consumption rarely approaches 100 percent. . . . The conventional level of 'subsistence' is also flexible. In adverse periods, it can be depressed further than one might have thought possible in advance, and it is quite flexible upward when conditions are improving."

21. Drained landscapes were particularly well suited to stock raising. See Leveau 1995.

22. The Fens in Britain were probably developed as imperially owned land

under Hadrian and became the site of numerous peasant-level settlements for similar purposes. On the Hadrianic development of marginal lands, see Potter 1981.

23. Andrew Wilson (2002: 30) has now developed this theme more fully. He asserts that "the Roman period was unique among all pre-industrial socie- ties in its ability to sustain unparalleled urban development, a standing army, and, probably, a larger sector of the population engaged in non-agricultural production than any other society up until the 18th century. Agriculture re- mains fundamental, but the Roman Empire saw both aggregate and per capita economic growth." He attributes this growth "to significant technological progress, both in agricultural technology to sustain a higher number of non- agricultural workers, and in non-agricultural technologies, such as mining.

24. Manufacturing on farms is a form of household production and is gen- erally recognized as evidence of structural change.

25. Note in this regard the rise of local fairs and markets. On the rise of local fairs and markets, see Shaw 1981; Andreau 1987; Frayn 1993; and De Ligt 1993.

26. These lakes or *étangs* were also devoted to salt-manufacture. The drained Fens were put to similar use, see Potter (1989).

27. That this change was not the result of a decline in mussel populations, but a culturally driven phenomenon—that is, a systematic choice on the part of the fisher to recover oysters—is clear from the fact that mussels and oysters share the same biotope. This stands in marked contrast to Rome and Italy, where both the literary sources and Diocletian's Price Edict indicate that oys- ters were an expensive and rare commodity.

28. Both the shellfish and fish sauce industries reinforce the argument that "economic activity is more plausibly regional" (E. L. Jones 1987: xv), a frame- work of analysis that has not been sufficiently explored in discussions of the Roman economy as a whole.

29. This should not, however, be taken to mean that the Italian economy stopped growing in the imperial period.

30. The growth that I have argued for here bears some of the characteris- tics of "Smithian growth," as opposed to the modern "Promethian growth." This occurs in pre-industrial empires whose economies are largely agrarian (in contrast to modern economies which depend on the more elastic mineral energy resources). The establishment of the empire, it is argued, brings for- merly autarkic regions with differing resources into a single integrated space which leads to increases in trade and specialization as emphasized by Adam Smith. However, Smithian growth assumes that because the primary basis of such economies was ultimately rooted in land which was fixed, diminishing returns would inevitably set in. There is no evidence that this occurred under the empire as a significant drop-off in agricultural producution only sets in with the breakup of the Empire in the 5th century, and even then only in the northwestern provinces. See Kelly 1997.

Chapter 11

Framing the Debate Over Growth
in the Ancient Economy

RICHARD SALLER

Ancient economic history has been the arena for what must be the most voluminous debate in ancient history over the past thirty years. Much valuable
research has been published, yet, in my view, the debate is in something of
a conceptual rut. Moses Finley's *The Ancient Economy* has been at the center
of the controversy. Since its publication in 1973, a series of scholars have attacked it and pronounced the central thesis "demolished." And yet it has recently been republished in a third edition (2003), edited by Ian Morris, and
continues to be the target of attack for new work.

Indeed, Finley's name has become a kind of glib shorthand used to summarize one side of the debate, in opposition to Michael Rostovtzeff and his
Social and Economic History of the Roman Empire (1957)—the so-called primitivist versus modernist debate (despite Andreau 1995). This discourse has
taken on a life of its own, sometimes far removed from anything Rostovtzeff
or Finley wrote. This becomes obvious when one reads characterizations of
Finley's position, with no page reference to *The Ancient Economy* but, rather,
with a reference to one of the hostile critiques. As a first step toward getting
out of the rut, I want to go back to original texts to clarify what Rostovtzeff
and Finley really wrote and point out the considerable common ground.
Next, I offer a bit of speculation about why the debate has become distorted
by exaggerated or false polarities. Then, I want to suggest some possibilities
for ways in which recent economic theory of development and modern

223

economic history can frame the ancient debate for the purposes of intellectual progress.

The contrast between Finley and Rostovtzeff is commonly summed up in the following polarities: primitivist versus modernist, no-trade versus long-distance trade, autarky versus integrated markets, technological stagnation versus technological progress; no economic growth versus growth, non-rationalist traditionalist versus rational individualists. These polarities are grossly misleading for two related reasons: first, they seriously misrepresent the views of both Rostovtzeff and Finley; and second, the polarities are very far from representing the full spectrum of possibilities, as both Rostovtzeff and Finley knew. By the latter, I mean that it is as if historians have framed the possible views as black and white and then proceeded with ferocious arguments against either white or black, all the while tacitly conceding that the most probable truth is somewhere in between, in the gray. The futility of such posturing need hardly be stressed. This is not to say that there are not substantive disagreements; rather, those disagreements are narrower than sometimes thought and may in many cases be beyond decisive resolution, as both sides agree on closer reading.

Before going to the text of *The Ancient Economy*, let me sketch what I take to be the current characterization of Finley's position, starting with brief phrases drawn from two very distinguished Roman historians. One describes Finley's view as that of "a primitive Roman economy" (W. V. Harris 1993: 15). The other describes Finley as a "static minimalist," who stressed the "cellular self-sufficiency" of local town–country units (K. Hopkins 1995/96: 56). Notice two aspects of these characterizations: "primitive," meaning household self-sufficiency at subsistence; and "static," meaning no growth. Most recently, Horden and Purcell (2000: 106–7) have repeated the association of Finley with the descriptors "primitivist," "minimalist," and a "stagnant" economy.

I begin with the characterization of Finley as a "primitivist" in his interpretation of the ancient economy. It is true that he asserted that modern concepts of economic analysis designed for capitalist industrial economies are inappropriate for antiquity, which is only to say that there is an incomparability in economic organization between economies before the eighteenth century and those modern European economies of the nineteenth and twentieth centuries analyzed by Adam Smith, Ricardo, Marx, and the neoclassical economists. It is not to say that Finley believed that the classical ancient economy was so primitive as to have consisted of autarkic households producing only for themselves without relation to markets. Indeed, the irony here is that in the early 1950s Finley broke with Karl Polanyi, who denied the significance of commercial markets in antiquity precisely because, in Finley's view, the ancient economy was *not* primitive. Contrary to Polanyi's thesis, Finley wrote in 1975, "The intrusion of genuine market (commercial) trade, on a *very considerable scale and over very great distances*, into the Graeco-Roman world had a feedback effect on peasant markets and the rest to such degree as to render the primitive models [of Polanyi] all but useless" (1975: 117, my emphasis).

Finley's very definition of peasant—in his view the predominant type of laborer in the empire—included linkage to wider markets and taxation systems. This characteristic distinguishes "the peasant on the one hand from the primitive agriculturist or pastoralist, who is not involved in a 'wider economic system,' and also differentiates the peasant from the modern family farm, in which the family is an 'entrepreneurial unit' rather than a 'productive unit'" (1985a: 105). Finley placed the labor system of antiquity in an intermediate position between primitive and modern and cited for comparisons a number of studies of peasants in early modern European and modern colonial economies.[1] To burden Finley with the label "primitivist" is to ignore what he wrote or to use the word *primitive* so broadly as to be meaningless.

Clearly, Finley acknowledged the existence of markets in antiquity, and, further, noted that peasants specialized in cash crops for markets if they lived close enough to urban areas or sites of religious festivals (1985a: 106). What he denied was the integration of markets to a point that they can be analyzed as a single unit of supply and demand. There were markets, even linked markets, but not integrated markets. Had the markets been fully integrated, there should not have been desperate grain shortages in individual cities while at the same time other cities were well supplied (1985a: 33–34). In such cases, hungry urban dwellers did not depend solely on higher prices to draw larger supplies from elsewhere in the empire; they resorted to imperial intervention.[2]

Related to markets is trade. By now, the number of scholarly papers demonstrating that Finley was wrong because of the large-scale material remains of trade is legion. Yet, Finley himself noted the amphorae "manufactured in the millions" (1985a: 190), "the important foreign trade in famed regional wines" (133), and the significant group of commercial "cities which by their location were clearing houses and transfer points, deriving *substantial* income from tolls, harbor-dues and dock charges" (130, my emphasis). The major limiting factor in the expansion of trade was the cost of land transport. Yet noting the great grain mill at Arles, Finley wrote that for the towns on the rivers and sea, "water transport . . . created radical new possibilities. . . . In the first place, imports of food and other bulk commodities permitted a substantial increase in the size of the population . . . and improvement in the quality of life, through a greater variety of goods, a greater abundance of slave labor for domestic as well as productive work." This in turn opened possibilities for "specialized production" in the countryside. But "the tempo of development [was] slow and sometimes abortive" (128).

Why was the tempo slow? Because technological progress was slow—not nonexistent, but slow. Finley underlined the fact of "some technological progress precisely where slavery showed its most brutal and oppressive face, in the Spanish mines and on the Roman latifundia" (1985a: 83). Overall, however, comparative evidence suggests that rentier systems of peasant agriculture are not conducive to innovation (109).

According to Finley, we should not expect the kind of fast-paced innovation that in the history of mankind is peculiar to the nineteenth and twentieth centuries, with their capitalist economic rationality (1985a: 144). It is essential to stress here that Finley was not denying the rationality of the ancients but was asserting that their rationality was framed by a different set of values and did not include some of the basic modern concepts such as amortization and double-column bookkeeping. Finley acknowledged that Romans kept accounts, even detailed accounts, but these were aimed at tracking production, sales, and expenditures—the sort of policing function so crucial to, and typical of, the absentee landlord. Policing is of course a rational strategy for the absentee landlord, but it is not the same as an analysis to identify profit rates in various parts of the business operation with the aim of directing investments to the points of highest profitability. Overall, Finley did not deny growth or assert that the ancient economy was "static." In fact, "the level of consumption increased in the course of ancient history, at times to fabulous proportions" (139). More particularly, "the expanded commercial activity of the first two centuries of the Empire was not [solely] a Roman phenomenon. It was shared by many peoples within the Empire" (158). As a result, Rome enjoyed some growth, but not "significant growth in *productivity*," to be distinguished from aggregate production (175, my emphasis, also 140)—a point to which I will return.

Curiously, some of Finley's prominent critics have heroized Rostovtzeff as the anti-Finley. And yet on certain fundamental points, the two agree. Above all, Rostovtzeff believed that the peasants constituted "an enormous majority of the population of the Roman Empire" who "lived in *very primitive* conditions" (1957: 346, my emphasis)—a stronger assertion of primitivism than I can discover in Finley. Furthermore, Rostovtzeff was far from arguing for integrated markets, allowing for the fact that "every inland city tried to become self-sufficient and to produce on the spot the goods needed by the population" (177). The reason was the expense of overland transport (146). And even sea transport was costly enough to prompt decentralization of manufacturing to the provinces in order to save those costs. In addition, Rostovtzeff believed that the *annona* was the largest consumer of imperial trade (158–59), stressing the command aspect of the economy—the very thesis for which Finley has been taken to task.

Where Rostovtzeff and Finley did part company was in Rostovtzeff's statements about the emergence of "big men, capitalists on a large scale" (1957: 153). Even here, however, Rostovtzeff clearly limited his assertion. He wrote that the numbers and associations of such merchants "may seem to indicate that the commerce of the first and second centuries began . . . to assume the form of modern capitalistic commerce, based on large and wealthy trade-companies. The facts, however, do not support this view. Business life throughout the history of the Greco-Roman world remained wholly individualistic" (170).

Though Rostovtzeff and Finley did disagree on the "scientific" approach to villa production, they agreed on the ultimate domination of the wealthy rentier class of absentee landlords who looked for "safe investment"— Rostovtzeff's phrase (1957: 197, 203)—in land and loans, rather than trying to maximize profits.

For Rostovtzeff, industry did not develop in the empire due to a fundamental lack of demand for goods in a population whose great majority was impoverished peasants. The cities enjoyed greater wealth, but "we must not exaggerate the wealth of the cities," many of whose residents were also poor: the cities' "external aspect is misleading" (191).

Overall, I confess that I was surprised at the fundamental points of agreement between Rostovtzeff and Finley, after years of reading about the "dichotomy" between their interpretations, to quote a recent important publication (W. V. Harris 1993: 15). I have quoted in some detail, because after years of tendentious representations it is important to understand what these two great historians wrote in order to stop the fruitless jousting at straw men. Why the persistent misrepresentation of Rostovtzeff's modernism versus Finley's primitivism? A number of reasons come to mind, ranging from the individual to the late-twentieth-century cultural. First, soon after the publication of *The Ancient Economy*, a polemical tone encouraged the polarization of issues along the lines of growth/no-growth, trade/no-trade, and so on, in a way that quickly lost sight of the texts. Finley himself contributed to the polemic, for instance in the 1985 postscript to the second edition. Second, on some issues of real disagreement, there may simply be insufficient evidence to bring the debate to a conclusion. In *The Ancient Economy*, Finley actually points to areas where further research needs to be done, but these points get lost in the polemic. Third, the polemic has been transformed into a controversy over the value of new archaeological finds. Finley was skeptical about some of the claims of archaeologists and demanded that they address more precise issues than whether there was trade, which he clearly conceded. In retrospect, I wish that he had addressed his challenge to archaeologists in a more constructive and precise way. Fourth, the debate over the ancient economy has taken on a strident, political edge as it has been caught up in the larger politics of the later twentieth century. In the first years after publication, *The Ancient Economy* was tossed around in the Marxist/anti-Marxist controversies, attacked by both sides. I recently noticed an Internet publication by a young Danish scholar, Peter Fibiger Bang (1998), who argues that in the late twentieth century the primitivist-modernist debate about classical antiquity went well beyond the economy to religion and other areas, and should be situated in the politics of the postcolonial era. That is, classicists are covertly arguing about whether their own European heritage is like or unlike the colonial Third World. Bang's idea is at least suggestive.

I am certainly not the only historian to feel that the Finley/anti-Finley debate has become increasingly sterile, but it is less easy to figure out how to break out of it. A first step would be to dispense with the misleading polarities. The next step, to my mind, is to try to specify the areas of contention more precisely, both through models and through more conceptual sophistication.[3] To argue endlessly over whether there was "significant" growth or not is futile, unless we specify what we mean by "significant." It is quite possible that the answer is both yes and no, depending on the implicit frame of reference. By making explicit the frame of reference, by insisting on certain critical conceptual distinctions, and by drawing on a recent economic theory of development, I naively hope for some progress.

Let me begin with a few brief assertions about development economics. Given the vast research in the field, they will necessarily be simple and crude. Yet, for all that economists disagree among themselves, certain basic points have gained broad adherence and have stood up to repeated empirical tests. In thinking about economic growth, it is absolutely essential to distinguish conceptually between per capita growth in production and aggregate growth. Keith Hopkins (1980) has made this point, but it has been ignored in the debates. Total economic production can grow either because the productivity of each worker grows or because the number of workers grows or both. The two extremes would be, on the one hand, the recent experience in the United States when productivity per worker has jumped

and, on the other hand, some densely populated Third World countries today where total population and production have increased exponentially in
the last century but much of the population hovers around subsistence income, not noticeably more productive or better off than ancient rural populations. Even Finley at times conflated those two types of growth (1985a:
146–47), and that has muddled the argument. It seems beyond doubt to me
that some regions of the Roman Empire increased aggregate production as
the population increased (as Finley and Rostovtzeff recognized), but it does
not follow that the per capita productivity noticeably increased. It is in the
latter type of growth that development economists are interested, because it
is the only type of growth that raises living standards in the long run. But if
the issue in question is the tax base of the empire, then aggregate production is the relevant measure. In the end, to assert only an increase in aggregate production based on an increase in population is a fairly weak claim in
as much as it is to assert no more than that the Roman Empire fits into a very
much longer progression of humans more densely populating the earth over
the millennia.

A second fundamental point is that scale is critical, and in particular, scale
over time. To have much meaning, the phrase "significant growth" should
be pegged to some notion of rate of growth. To say, for instance, that productivity and standard of living increased by 50 percent sounds "significant"
but takes on a different meaning if one adds "over a thousand years." It may
well be that time span is the element in the estimation of growth rate that
can be guessed at most confidently. Some comparative figures for economic
growth can offer a sense of perspective. The fastest growing economies in
per capita GDP through the modern era have been the Netherlands during
the seventeenth and eighteenth centuries, followed in the nineteenth century by the United Kingdom, and in the twentieth century by the United
States (see Table 11.1).

Clearly, the great threshold here is between the Netherlands and Britain
and comes around 1800. Before 1800, growth in per capita production was

TABLE 11.1
Fastest growing economies in per capita GDP

Netherlands	1580–1820	+0.2%/year
United Kingdom	1820–1890	+1.2%/year
United States	1890–1970	+2.2%/year
Total Growth OECD countries	1870–1978:	× 6.7[1]

SOURCE: Ray 1998: 48
[1] I'm not sure how to interpret this information.

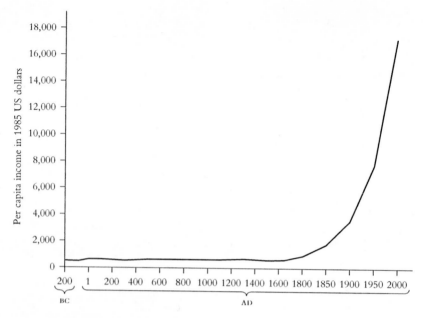

Figure 11.1. GDP per capita income in leading economies, 200 BC to AD 2000 (after Lucas 1998)

almost imperceptible, and the classical economists writing around 1800 simply did not dream of the possibility of dramatic increases (Lucas 2002; D. G. Johnson 2000).[4] At the early modern growth rate of the Netherlands, productivity would have improved only 6 percent over a generation of thirty years. By contrast, in nineteenth-century Britain from one generation to the next productivity improved by 50 percent; and in the twentieth-century United States, productivity and living standards have doubled with each generation.

Perspective is essential to ground the claims about growth. The economist Robert Lucas presented a graph of long-term growth showing dramatic acceleration from 1800 (Fig. 11.1). Within Lucas's graph, one can accommodate some growth in the imperial economy, as depicted in Figure 11.2. This graph postulates economic growth in the first centuries of Roman rule of the Mediterranean. Let me stress that it is a heuristic device to clarify the debate, designed to illustrate that it is possible to specify a growth curve consistent with both sides. In particular, it is consistent with the arguments of Keith Hopkins, who has put forward a sophisticated case for some economic growth stimulated by imperial taxes (K. Hopkins 1980, 1995/96, and personal correspondence). In total, the growth amounts to perhaps as much as

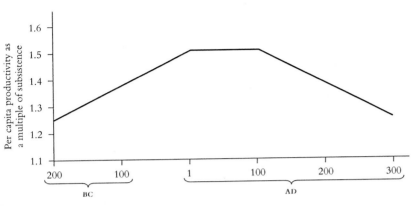

Figure 11.2. GDP per capita growth in productivity, 200 BC to AD 300 (after K. Hopkins 1995–96)

25 percent. The peak of production allows room for urbanization and for four billion sesterces (HS) per year in nonagricultural production, and hence for plenty of trade to generate those millions of amphorae and hundreds of shipwrecks that Finley, Hopkins, and the many critics of Finley point to. And yet, in comparison with the nineteenth century—the comparison of interest to Finley and Lucas—it is still correct to stress the limits of the growth. After all, total growth of 25 percent over three centuries would amount to less than 0.1 percent per year, and even that rate was not sustained.

Was there "significant" growth? From the perspective of a near-subsistence economy in parts of the western empire in 100 BC, the answer could be yes. But from the perspective of Robert Lucas at the end of the twentieth century, the answer is no (1998). I see no point whatever in arguing about which perspective is the right one: that would be tantamount to arguing about whether the glass is half empty or half full. The critics of Finley might well say: "Of course, Rome did not have a modern, industrial economy; that is so obvious, why make the claim?" To which the ghost of Finley, or at least his student, might respond: "Earlier in the twentieth century some prominent historians argued that there was no serious gap between imperial Rome and modern Europe; and even today, it is useful to place Rome in that top graph in order to understand some broad features of Rome's predominantly agrarian economy."[5] On the other side, this is not to minimize the value of the perspective of 100 BC and Hopkins's suggestion of "modest, though significant, economic growth" (1995/96: 57).

Some basic theory of economic development can, I believe, help us to understand why the growth was no more than modest and why, ultimately, it was limited. One might start with four or five basic causes for growth in per capita production identified by economists (Mokyr 1990). The first was emphasized by Adam Smith: trade, which in turn allows for specialization. The most obvious aspect of specialization was the fundamental split between rural and urban production. A second cause of growth is intensification of capital investment. That is, the more a society saves in order to invest in tools of production, the more productive each worker can be. But nearly fifty years ago, Robert Solow (1956) made the fundamental observation that additional capital investment will have diminishing returns, unless the technology of the capital also improves. The logic is clear: Give a farmer an ox and iron plow in place of hand tools, and his productivity will increase; but a second or third plow for the same farmer will not double or triple the production. Hence, the emphasis of Joseph Schumpeter (1934) on improved technology as the engine of sustained growth: this is a third basic cause of growth and the one of central concern in much contemporary research. Over the past fifteen years, Chicago economists and others have refocused their theories on a more fundamental cause than technology, and that is the human capital that invents and uses the technology (Becker et al. 1990; Lucas 2002; D. G. Johnson 2000). That is to say, sustained technological improvements should not be treated as random strokes of good luck but as an outcome of the education and training of people. It is a striking fact that in the late twentieth century the total value of human capital in the U.S. economy—the investment in education and training—is now larger than the value of physical capital. These economists make the theoretical argument that human capital investment is the only basis for indefinite *sustained* economic growth in productivity per worker (Ehrlich 1990), and that increased education of ordinary workers explains a large part of the economic growth of the twentieth century (Lucas 1998).

There is an important corollary of the human capital argument, and that is its tie to the demographic transition. Increased investment in education makes sense against a background of longer life expectancy and fewer children per family, each of whom receives more attention and education, which is then employed through a longer working life (Becker et al. 1990).

One other dimension of economic growth has been emphasized by Douglass North (North and Thomas 1973; North 1990): the institutional framework for economic activities. In particular, North argues that some societies have frameworks that do more to encourage productive innovation and to reduce the difficulties and costs of economic activity than others.

Let me offer a few reflections about how we might think about each of these factors in regard to the Roman Empire. First, consider trade. Clearly, as both Rostovtzeff and Finley wrote, the empire benefited from trade in volume, and long-distance trade probably increased under Roman rule. Keith Hopkins (1980; 1995/96) has further argued that the increase was stimulated by taxation that required the provincials to earn back at least some of their denarii taken as taxes—in other words, to reach a balance of payments. Even with all of the caveats of the critics (for example, Duncan-Jones 1994), Hopkins's argument is likely to be right, in my view. But we should understand the limits of his claim about the importance of long-distance trade in the economy by comparison with agriculture (and, in fact, Hopkins himself is careful to circumscribe it). For Hopkins (1995/96: 59) Rome was the grain consumption center of the empire. He estimates the number of ships needed to supply the grain and suggests that the capital investment in these ships must have been of the order of one hundred million HS—a large number that underlines the significance of this trade. But how far does this modify the stress on land as the overwhelming investment of Rome's wealthy? One hundred million HS is less than some individual fortunes of a few senators and imperial freedmen, and less than 1 percent of the total capital assets of senators (if we take Pliny's fortune as the rough average for senators).

Now, it is reasonable to suppose, with Hopkins, that Roman taxation demanded more surplus from rural labor, forcing peasants to intensify their labor, and that the surplus supported larger urban populations who manufactured goods for trade. Hopkins's evidence, though indirect, does point to an increment in trade in the last two centuries BC (1980; revised numbers in 1995/96: n. 48). It is also true that Hopkins's graph of dated shipwrecks, used as a proxy for trade and growth, does *not* show a rise in the first two centuries AD. If we accept the logic of his argument, we should ask for an economic model that explains not only the growth in wrecks through the first century BC, *but also the absence of growth thereafter, before the decline of the third century*. It would be wrong to read this graph to show that the Roman economy displayed a consistent capacity for sustained growth through the principate before the political shocks of the third century.

My second cause of growth is the intensification of capital investment. Here the fundamental starting point, agreed by all sides, is that production was predominantly agricultural—probably of the order of at least 75 or 80 percent. In some regions of the empire, there was agricultural investment in the sense of extending cultivation, including specialized crops for market. This would have increased aggregate production, and to a lesser extent per capita production. But limits were reached in the absence of major improvements. The willingness of Roman landowners to invest more intensively was limited. As Dennis Kehoe (1992, 1997) has argued, the best description of the dominant attitude toward investment was "satisficing"—that is, the strategy of a safe return for a minimum investment in land. It is plausible to think that there were narrow limits to increases in productivity to be had by pressing peasants and slaves to work more intensively with more or less the same capital (the Hopkins scenario). And such pressure in the longer run may have turned out to be counterproductive in some areas, as capital was sucked out of the countryside, depriving peasants of, for example, their plow animals and even their capacity to raise children (the scenario in Pliny, *Letters* 3.19). Kehoe's research on rural investment, especially in Roman Egypt (1992), suggests that economic decline in some areas in the principate is consistent with the evidence and with comparative studies in development economics.[6]

Of course, there were exceptions to the rentier mentality—emphasized by Finley's critics, but on a closer look some of them actually support Finley's view of land acquisition as a matter of windfall rather than efficient markets and calculated capitalist investment. The elder Pliny (*Natural History*, 14.49–51) reports the exceptional example of Remmius Palaemon, who in the mid-first century AD bought a run-down vineyard outside Rome, invested in it heavily with traditional technology, and increased annual production so much that he sold one year's crop for two-thirds the original cost of the land just a few years after purchase. One could stop at that point and take the story as an instance of a capitalist investment, but the end of the story also bears emphasis. Pliny does not say that Palaemon's example inspired similar capital investment by other Romans, but rather that Seneca moved in to buy the vineyard at four times its original price because he was captivated by a desire (*amore*) to possess this model estate, not to make his own profit by similar investments elsewhere.

Another example recently held up to exemplify capitalist investment is Claudius's draining of Lake Fucinus, studied by Philippe Leveau as an illustration of entrepreneurship. The elder Pliny (*Natural History* 36.124), Tacitus (*Annals* 12.56–57), and Suetonius (*Claudius* 20) all noted this massive project, and Suetonius claimed that Claudius did it as much for profit as for glory. According to the biographer, the project required the labor of thirty thousand men over eleven years. Archaeologists estimate that five thousand hectares were recovered. The land was distributed to those private individuals who offered to help finance the project. If we take Suetonius and his numbers at face value, we can do a simple calculation: At a cost of 36.3 million HS (30,000 men × 11 years × 110 HS in bare subsistence/man-year), Claudius recovered twenty thousand *iugera* of land, worth something less than twenty million HS—that is, the project cost nearly twice the value of the land.[7] Leveau, who did not do the arithmetic as far as I can see, concluded that "this is a rare example for Antiquity of agricultural investment, i.e., of an expense made in the hope of a profit in return" (1993: 12). Well, no wonder it was rare. What is more, the drainage was allowed to fall into disrepair soon after, suggesting that it cannot have been profitable to maintain and that some of the colossal investment must have been at least partially wasted.

To epitomize my point about capital investment, let me briefly comment on Columella's famous illustration of a model investment in a vineyard—a comment unrelated to the ongoing debate about Columella's accounting. My point is more basic: Columella exhorts his readers to invest in a productive vineyard: seven thousand HS for the land, about as much again for a slave vinedresser, and fourteen thousand HS for stakes and slips (3.3.8). This kind of investment no doubt had the capacity to increase productivity above subsistence production, but it had no capacity to generate sustained growth, only one-time growth.

Sustained growth per capita requires sustained technological improvement. There were certainly some technological innovations through the principate—to assert this as if it were an attack on Finley seems pointless, since he acknowledged as much. The important questions are how much did productive technology improve over what time frame, and for what proportion of the workforce. Scale is essential, as one example may illustrate. Örjan Wikander has written about the invention and diffusion of animal- and water-powered mills. On Wikander's account (1984), the mills could save labor and improve production of basic food processing by as much as 10 percent; the use of these mills required three to five centuries to spread around the empire. On the assumption that this improvement was exploited to the very fullest (clearly it was not), it would have contributed to growth at a rate of less than 0.025 percent per year. I say this not to trivialize the water mill but to suggest that it would have required a whole series of such inventions that increased the productivity of the mass of rural workers to reach growth levels comparable to the early modern Netherlands. Perhaps the argument can be made, but Rostovtzeff (1957) and White (1970: 450), like Finley, saw little evidence for dramatic innovation in peasant agriculture.

In the urban sector, technical progress—much of it in the public domain in the form of building techniques, aqueducts, and other amenities—certainly did improve living standards, and that fact should be taken into account in assessing economic growth. At the same time, the limitations of improved technology should also be acknowledged, as Rostovtzeff and

Hopkins have been careful to do. It is generally agreed that the urban population constituted no more than 20 percent of the population. It follows that if the productivity and living standard of the urban minority increased as much as 50 percent over several centuries (say, 100 BC to AD 200), that would constitute growth of only 10 percent for the empire as a whole, spread over three centuries—that is, much less than 0.1 percent per year. And there are reasons to think that such a rate is too generous, because, as Rostovtzeff noted, much of the urban population remained underemployed and at bare subsistence (as in Third World economies today).

Perhaps most fundamentally, those urban amenities did not have the effect of changing the basic demographic regime of the population in a way to tip the balance of decisions about human capital investments, as happened in the nineteenth century. That is to say, recent research has reaffirmed the sense that, despite the aqueducts and sewers, mortality in Rome and other cities of the empire remained appallingly high and life expectancies very low (Shaw 1996; Scheidel 1996: ch. 4, 1999, 2001a, 2001b, 2001c). In that environment, there was no shift toward smaller family size, more investment in the education of each child, and a longer average work life to utilize that human capital. Education and training outside the household were the privilege of the elite few for the most part, and the standard elite education in literature and rhetoric would have had little benefit in increased productivity. To state this is only to state the obvious about differences in cultural values, recognized by Finley and his critics (for example, Wikander 1984: 40).

The question of the institutional framework for economic growth—the last on my list of causes of growth—is quite interesting and complex—too complex for a satisfactory discussion here. Suffice it to say that the Roman Empire provides a test case for Douglass North's claim about the importance of institutions. In many respects, Roman imperial institutions should have encouraged growth on North's theory: the large potential market of the empire, the long periods of peace across much of the empire, the relatively low average taxes, and the legal system protecting property rights. And yet, the area of the empire in which these characteristics were most strongly felt, tribute-exempt Italy, did not lead the empire in sustained growth. Historians argue about whether and when the Italian economy declined, but no one to my knowledge argues that Italy led consistent growth through the principate, as would be predicted by North's neo-institutionalism.

To conclude, the framing of the debate over growth in the Roman imperial economy in the polar terms of primitive versus modern seems pointless to me: It misrepresents the positions of the supposed protagonists, and it obscures areas of both agreement and disagreement. I have suggested that rather than arguing about whether or not there was "significant" growth, without defining the adjective, we might imagine a gentle growth curve for the Roman Empire that is consonant with the observations of Finley and Rostovtzeff, and with the propositions of Hopkins and Lucas. It can accommodate a rise in the level of urbanization in the western empire to a point commensurate with the eastern provinces, and also an accompanying increase in trade. From the perspective of the period of Roman annexation of the East Mediterranean, the aggregate growth could be defined as "significant"; from the perspective of the industrial age, the growth as represented in Figure 11.1 is imperceptible and not sustained. Recent work in the economic theory of development would lead us to expect nothing else.

My hope is that this broad framing will lead either to some consensus about the parameters of the debate or to more clarity in the challenges to Finley (and Rostovtzeff). Are the critics prepared to argue that the growth was so "significant" as to exceed that depicted in Figure 11.2? That would be a claim of major importance, of interest not only to ancient historians but also to economists. If that claim is advanced, what evidence would be required in corroboration? "Millions of amphorae" and monumental urban architecture will not be enough; despite the very modest growth postulated (modest not only by late modern standards, but also by early modern standards), Figure 11.2 can accommodate one trillion HS in urban production over the two and a half centuries of the principate.

Notes

1. Finley's choice of comparisons is revealing of where he placed the Roman economy in the spectrum of development. Many of his comparisons were drawn from Shanin (1971) and cover a range including twentieth-century Russia and colonial Africa (1985a: ch. 4, nn. 29–30); Europe of the 1930s (ch. 4, n. 33); and postcolonial Brazil (ch. 4, n. 49)—none of which are "primitive societies."

2. Similarly, Rostovtzeff (1957: 145) noted that one of the main duties of the emperor in Rome and town magistrates elsewhere was to secure the basic food supply. "The conditions under which a plentiful supply of food had to be secured were not very favourable." In an integrated market, this sort of

supervision would have been superfluous because pricing would have drawn grain to areas in need.

3. Finley (1985a: 182) made a similar programmatic statement but did not develop it in a constructive fashion.

4. I am especially grateful to Lucas for permission to cite this work prior to publication.

5. This broad understanding, from the point of view of an agricultural economist, is the point of D. G. Johnson 2000.

6. Comparative studies show that the more skewed the wealth between rich landowners and tenants, the lower the productivity. See Rosenzweig and Binswanger 1993.

7. Duncan-Jones (1982) argues convincingly from the indirect evidence of returns to investment that Columella's one thousand HS per *iugum* is likely to be on the high side for land prices in Italy.

Chapter 12

Comment on Hitchner and Saller

AVNER GREIF

Was there economic growth in the Roman Empire or was there not? Did specialization, capital accumulation, and innovations brought about by investment in human capital and appropriate institutions improve the lives of those living in the Roman Empire? These two interesting chapters provide somewhat different, yet compatible, answers to these questions. Hitchner points out that the institutional structure provided by the empire was conducive to growth. Peace, the security of property rights, and a benevolent government enabled the Romans to benefit from growth, based—among other things—on the empire's rich natural endowment, technological changes, industrial development, and long-distance trade.

Saller, on the other hand, argues against casting the debate over the nature of the Roman economy in the above terms. Growth was fast and the Roman economy was market-oriented—an advanced economy from the perspective of that time and place. Compared to modern economies, however, growth was meager and unsustainable. As a matter of fact, Saller argues, this unsustainable growth is predicted by recent theories of economic development. The ultimate source for sustainable economic growth is technological inventions brought about by human capital. Since investment in productive human capital was small within the empire, we could not expect anything but unsustained economic growth.

There is no contradiction between these two positions. In a sense, Hitchner is elaborating on the sources and manifestations of growth that

239

Saller does not deny. Clearly, there is much to learn about and gain from elaborating on the extent and nature of economic changes that took place during the Roman period. Our knowledge of this historical period will not be complete until we sort out the facts to the best of our ability.

Saller and Hitchner are also in concurrence about the issue central to the study of the economy of this historical episode. They propose studying economic growth measured as average income per capita, and each highlights the importance of the three direct factors for economic growth that have been identified in economics: specialization, capital investment, and technological advance. Saller, however, argues that compared to the level of economic growth based on the latter factor achieved in the modern period, the Roman economy was clearly a failure. It was a failure because it was not marching like modern economies from one invention to another, thereby increasing the economy's production possibilities. This failure, in turn, reflects a lack of investment in human capital that, in turn, may reflect low life expectancy. People did not expect to live long enough to justify as large an investment in human capital as they do today.

I discuss the limitations of this view as a prologue to my more substantive point. Consider the contrafactual under which the Roman world is altered only in one respect: human life expectancy in this contrafactual world is the same as in modern economies. Let's say that life expectancy is the same as it was in England in 1820, just after the first wave of the technological and organizational changes that made it the first industrialized nation. As in any contrafactual, we will allow the residents of the Roman Empire, after the change, to pursue their economic and other objectives as they see fit. A literal interpretation of the scenario that Saller provides implies that the choices they would have made would have brought about industrialization and modern economic growth. But clearly Saller would not subscribe to such a view. Modern economic growth could not have happened in the first century AD. As a matter of fact, modern economic growth did not transpire in many of the contemporary economies in which modern medicine and technology have prolonged life expectancy. Longevity may be necessary for modern economic growth, but it is clearly not sufficient by itself.

Extended life expectancy would not have led to modern economic growth in the Roman Empire because—and this is my main point—it is misleading to view such growth as reflecting exogenous shifts in factors such as life expectancy or institutions. It is even misleading to consider modern economic growth as a phenomenon whose roots one will find in modern times. Modern economic growth reflects an economic, political, and social *process* through which European economies became the first modern economies. It is the climax of a gradual and long process of accumulation and construction of scientific knowledge, techniques, productive and organizational capacity, and of the institutional foundations of markets. It reflects the gradual emergence of the role of law and political freedom, as well as the social transformation of personal and economic relationships.

Thus, evaluating the economic implications of various historical events using the yardstick of the living standard of only those who were alive at the time is too limited. It ignores the implications of these events for future generations and on the process that gave birth to the modern economy.

To illustrate the point, consider one of the most practical things ever invented—the wheel. The economic importance of wheels, even in the information age, is rather clear. We are, after all, surrounded by wheels. Wheels, gear wheels, cranks, and the like are in our watches, cars, airplanes, tractors, trains, and, of course, computers and printers. When wheels were invented sometime prior to 3500 BC, they clearly increased the standard of living. By how much? Probably very little. After all, it very likely took a long time for this invention to spread: It was costly to manufacture wheels from tree trunks without an iron ax, and there were no roads to speak of. But the overall contribution of wheels to economic outcomes since they were invented is indisputable. The wheel is a "general purpose" technology upon which many other inventions have been built.

Returning to the Roman period, the above argument suggests expanding the study of the Roman economic system beyond its direct implication for the average income per capita of the empire's residents. It suggests considering the economic and other events that transpired during this time, while attending to the broader question of economic history: What were the contributions of this time and place to the process that made modern economic growth possible? It is clearly beyond my abilities to contribute an answer to this question. To show that there is merit in studying the contributions of the Roman period to the process bringing about modern economic growth, I will, nevertheless, give three examples of what such contributions might have been. As is well known, the waterwheel was invented in the Roman period. The contribution of this invention to the standard of living during the Roman period is considered to have been relatively small. While this may have been true, the question still remains: What was the contribution of this invention to the process of growth? The importance of the waterwheel in the medieval economy is well known (particularly after the transition away from the undershot Roman waterwheel to the overshot waterwheel). But what has (to the best of my knowledge) been ignored regarding the importance of the Roman waterwheel is that it constitutes a conceptual breakthrough. It was the first machine to capture nonanimated energy for on-land productive use, namely turning grinding stones. Use of the waterwheel represents the first time in human history that an "engine" was built—that the force of nature was used to turn wheels. Prior to this invention, grinding stones were rotated using animated power, and animated power was used to raise water to irrigate higher ground, but never before was the power of water used to replace the power of animals.

Similarly, the Roman period left the Europeans a less tangible heritage that, nevertheless, has been valuable in the production of knowledge. Specifically, Rome provided Europe with a unifying language, Latin, that enabled the European scientific community to interact across political borders. In the age we live in, language is not much of a barrier to intellectual exchange, but this was not always the case. As a matter of fact, much of the knowledge of the ancient world was not known in the West until it was translated into Latin from (mainly) Arabic and Greek in the high Middle Ages. The European intellectual community had a common language, and the contributions to modern economic growth of the interactions among members of this community across political borders are well known.

Finally, the Roman heritage in the West includes the Roman legal tradition. Many economists would agree that in order to bring about and support modern economic growth it is necessary to have a particular legal tradition—a legal tradition in which rules can be changed to fit the evolving needs of the economy and that ensures that individuals have property rights and freedom. Such a tradition exists in the Western world, and it is a legacy of the Roman period. It was then that the European legal tradition was formulated, and despite various challenges, it has survived the test of time. One can only wonder if modern economic growth could have occurred in Europe if it had possessed one of the alternative legal traditions that emerged elsewhere, such as the divine law that dominates the Muslim world.

Economic growth and stagnation in the Roman Empire is an important subject in and of itself, and both Saller's and Hitchner's chapters bring fresh insights to this issue. This investigation can be further enriched by considering a question central to Economic History: How did the events that transpired in the Roman Empire shape the process through which modern economic growth has developed?

Abbott, A. 2001. *Chaos of Disciplines*. Chicago.

Abell, P. 1996. "Sociological theory and rational choice theory." In *The Blackwell Companion to Social Theory*, ed. B. S. Turner, 252–73. Oxford.

Adams, R. McC. 1966. *The Evolution of Urban Societies*. New York.

———. 1974. "Anthropological reflections on ancient trade." *Current Anthropology* 15: 239–58.

———. 1981. *Heartland of Cities*. Chicago.

Agache, R. 1978. *La Somme pre-romaine et romaine*. Paris.

Alcock, Susan E. 1997. *The Early Roman Empire in the East*. Oxford Monograph 95. Oxford.

Allen, P. M. 1988. "Dynamic models of evolving systems." *System Dynamics Review* 4: 109–30.

———. 1997. "Models of creativity: Towards a new science of history." In *Time, Process and Structured Transformation in Archaeology*, ed. S. Van der Leeuw and J. McGlade, 39–56. London.

Allen, R. C. 1999. "Tracking the agricultural revolution." *Economic History Review* 52: 209–35.

———. 2001. "The great divergence in European wages and prices from the Middle Ages to the First World War." *Explorations in Economic History* 38: 411–47.

Allison, P. 1997. "Roman households: An archaeological perspective." In Parkins 1997a: 112–46.

Alston, L., T. Eggerston, and D. C. North, eds. 1996. *Empirical Studies in Institutional Change*. Cambridge.

Alston, R. 1998. "Trade and the city in Roman Egypt." In *Trade, Traders and the Ancient City*, ed. H. Parkins and C. Smith, 168–202. London.

Amouretti, M.-Cl., and J. P. Brun, eds. 1993. *La production du vin et de l'huile en Mediterranee*. Paris.

Amphores romaines et histoire économique. Dix ans de recherches. 1989. Rome: Collection de l'École française de Rome 114.

Anderson, P. 1974. *Passages from Antiquity to Feudalism*. London.

———. 1992. *A Zone of Engagement*. London.

Ando, C. 2000. *Imperial Ideology and Provincial Loyalty in the Roman Empire*. Berkeley.

Andreau, J. 1974. *Les affaires de Monsieur Jucundus.* Rome.

———. 1977. "Finley, la banque antique et l'économie moderne." *Annali della Scuola Normale Superiore di Pisa* 7: 1129–52. Classe di Lettere e Filosofia.

———. 1987. *La vie financière dans le monde romain. Les metiers de manieurs d'argent (IVe siècle av. J.-C.–III siècle ap. J-C).* Paris.

———. 1995. "Vingt ans après *L'Economie antique* de Moses I. Finley." *Annales. Histoire Sciences Sociales* 50: 947–60.

Andreau, J., and R. Étienne. 1984. "Vingt ans de recherché sur l'archaisme et la modernité des sociétés antiques." *Revue des etudes anciennes* 86: 55–83.

———. 1986. "Fernand Braudel, l'antiquité et l'histoire ancienne." *Quaderni di storia* 24: 5–21.

Andreau, J., and F. Hartog, eds. 1987–89. "La cité antique? A partir de l'oeuvre de Moses I. Finley." *Opus* 6–8.

Andreau, J., J-P. Vernant, and R. Descat, eds. 1994. *Économie antique: Les échanges dans l'antiquité: Le rôle de l'état.* Saint-Bertrand-de-Comminges.

Appadurai, A. 1996. *Modernity at Large: Cultural Dimensions of Globalization.* Minneapolis.

———. ed., 2001. *Globalization.* Durham, N.C.

Arafat, K., and C. Morgan. 1989. "Pots and potters in Athens and Corinth: A review." *Oxford Journal of Archaeology* 8: 311–46.

Archi, A., ed. 1984. *Circulation of Goods in Non-Palatial Contexts in the Ancient Near East.* Rome.

Archibald, Z. H., J. K. Davies, V. Gabrielsen, and G. J. Oliver, eds. 2001. *Hellenistic Economies.* London.

Ault, B. 1999. "*Koprones* and oil presses at Halieis: Interactions of town and country and the integration of domestic and regional economies." *Hesperia* 68: 549–73.

———. Forthcoming a. "Housing the poor and the homeless in ancient Greece." In *Households at the Margins of Greek Society,* ed. B. Ault and L. Nevett. Philadelphia.

———. Forthcoming b. *Excavations at Ancient Halieis.* Vol. 2, *Domestic Architecture and Household Assemblages in the Lower Town.* Bloomington, Ind.

Austin, M. 1986. "Hellenistic kings, war and the economy." *Classical Quarterly* 36: 450–66.

Austin, M., and P. Vidal-Naquet. 1973. *Économies et sociétés en Grèce ancienne.* Paris. English translation 1977.

Aymard, M. 2001. "De la Méditerranée à l'Asie: Une comparaison nécessaire." *Annales. Histoire Sciences Sociales* 56: 43–50.

Badan, O., J.-P. Brun, and G. Conges. 1996. "Les Bergeries romaines de la Crau d'Arles." *Gallia* 52: 263–310.

Bagnall, R. S. 1982/83. "Papyrology and Ptolemaic history: 1956–1980." *Classical World* 76: 13–21.

————. 1985a. "The camel, the wagon, and the donkey in later Roman Egypt." *Bulletin of the American Society of Papyrologists* 22: 1–6.

————. 1985b. *Currency and Inflation in Fourth-Century Egypt.* Atlanta: *Bulletin of the American Society of Papyrologists* supp. vol. 5.

————. 1992. "Landholding in late Roman Egypt: The distribution of wealth." *Journal of Roman Studies* 82: 128–49.

————. 1993a. *Egypt in Late Antiquity.* Princeton.

————. 1993b. "Slavery and society in late Roman Egypt." In *Law, Politics and Society in the Ancient Mediterranean World,* ed. B. Halpern and D. Hobson, 220–40. Sheffield.

————. 1995. *Reading Papyri, Writing Ancient History.* London.

————. 1997a. "Decolonizing Ptolemaic Egypt." In *Hellenistic Constructs: Essays in Culture, History, and Historiography,* ed. P. Cartledge, P. Garnsey, and E. Gruen, 225–41. Berkeley.

————. 1997b. *The Kellis Agricultural Account Book.* Oxford.

————. 1997c. "Missing females in Roman Egypt." *Scripta Classica Israelica* 16: 121–38.

Bagnall, R. S., and P. Derow. 1981. *Greek Historical Documents: The Hellenistic Period.* Atlanta: *Sources for Biblical Study* 16.

Bagnall, R. S., and B. W. Frier. 1994. *The Demography of Roman Egypt.* Cambridge.

Bailey, D. M., ed. 1996. *Archaeological Research in Roman Egypt.* Ann Arbor, Mich.: *Journal of Roman Archaeology* supp. vol. 19.

Bailyn, B. 1951. "Braudel's geohistory—a reconsideration." *Journal of Economic History* 11: 277–82.

Baker, P. 1999. "What is social science history, anyway?" *Social Science History* 23: 475–80.

Bang, P. F. 1998. "Antiquity between 'primitivism' and 'modernism.'" Center for Cultural Research, University of Aarhus, http://www.hum.au.dk//ckulturf/pages/publications/pfb/antiquity.htm.

Barker, G. W. W., D. D. Gilbertson, G. D. B. Jones, and D. J. Mattingly, 1996. *Farming the Desert: The UNESCO Libyan Valleys Survey.* 2 vols. Paris and London.

Barker, G. W., and J. A. Lloyd, eds. 1991. *Roman Landscapes. Archaeological Survey in the Mediterranean Region.* London.

Bartholomew, John. 1938. *Newnes' Modern World Atlas.* London.

Bates, R., A. Greif, M. Levi, J.-L. Rosenthal, and B. Weingast. 1998. *Analytic Narratives.* Princeton.

Baudrillard, J. 1981 [1972]. *For a Critique of the Political Economy of the Sign.* St. Louis, Mo.

Becker, G., K. Murphy, and R. Tamura. 1990. "Human capital, fertility, and economic growth." *Journal of Political Economy* 98 supp.: S12–S37.

Bellamy, P., and R. B. Hitchner. 1996. "The villas of the Vallée des Baux and the Barbegal mill: Excavations at La Merindole villa and cemetery." *Journal of Roman Archaeology* 9: 154–76.

Ben Lazreg, N., M. Bonifay, A. Drine, and P. Trousset. 1995. "Production et commercialisation des Salsamenta de l'Afrique ancienne." *Productions et exportations Africaines. Actualités archéologique en Afrique du nord antique et médiévale*. Aix-en-Provence.

Bentz, M. 1998. *Panathenäische Preisamphoren. Eine athenische Vasengattung und ihre Funktion vom 6.-4. Jh. v. Chr.* Basel: *Antike Kunst* Beiheft 18.

Berkhofer, R. F. 1995. *Beyond the Great Story: History as Text and Discourse.* Cambridge, Mass.

Berlev, O. 1997. "Bureaucrats." In *The Egyptians.*, ed. S. Donadoni, 87–119. Trans. R. Bianchi, A. L. Crone, C. Lambert, and T. Ritter. Chicago.

Berlinerblau, J., ed. 2001. *Heresy in the University: The Black Athena Controversy and the Responsibilities of American Intellectuals.* New Brunswick, N.J.

Bernal, M. 1987. *Black Athena.* Vol. 1. *The Fabrication of Ancient Greece, 1785–1985.* New Brunswick, N.J.

———. 2001. *Black Athena Writes Back.* Ed. D. C. Moore. Durham, N.C.

Bieżuńska-Małowist, I. 1977. *L'esclavage dans l'Égypte gréco-romaine.* Vol. 2. Wroclaw.

Bilde, P., et al., eds. 1993. *Centre and Periphery in the Hellenistic World.* Aarhus.

Binford, L. R. 1981a. "Behavioral archaeology and the 'Pompeii premise.'" *Journal of Anthropological Research* 37: 195–208.

———. 1981b. *Bones: Ancient Men and Modern Myths.* New York.

———. 1983. *In Pursuit of the Past.* Ed. John Cherry and Robin Torrence. New York.

Bingen, J. 1952. *Papyrus Revenue Laws.* Göttingen: *Sammelbuch griechischer Urkunden aus Ägypten* Beiheft 1.

———. 1978. *La papyrus revenue laws. Tradition grecque et adaptation hellénistique.* Opladen.

———. 1984. "Les tensions structurelles de la société ptolémaïque." In *Atti del XVII Congresso internazionale di papirologia*, 921–37. Naples.

Bintliff, J., P. Howard, and A. Snodgrass. 1999. "The hidden landscape of prehistoric Greece." *Journal of Mediterranean Archaeology* 12: 139–68.

Bintliff, J., and A. M. Snodgrass. 1988. "Off-site pottery distributions: A regional and interregional perspective." *Current Anthropology* 29: 506–13.

Blanton, R. 1994. *Houses and Households: A Comparative Study.* New York.

Blaug, M. 1992. *The Methodology of Economics.* 2d ed. Cambridge.

Blaut, J. M. 2000. *Eight Eurocentric Historians.* Westport, Conn.

Blier, S. 1987. *The Anatomy of Architecture: Ontology and Metaphor in Batammaliba Architectural Expression.* Cambridge.

Boak, A. E. R. 1943. *A History of Rome to 565 AD*. 3d ed. New York.

———. 1955. *Manpower Shortage and the Fall of the Roman Empire in the West*. Ann Arbor.

Boak, A. E. R., and H. C. Youtie. 1957. "Flight and oppression in fourth-century Egypt." In *Studi in onore di Aristide Calderini e Roberto Paribeni*, vol. 2: 325–37. Milan.

Bodel, J., ed. 2001. *Epigraphic Evidence: Ancient History from Inscriptions*. London.

Bongenaar, A. C. V. M., ed. 2000. *Interdependency of Institutions and Private Entrepeneurs*. Istanbul.

Bottéro, J. 1992. *Mesopotamia: Writing, Reasoning, and the Gods*. Trans. Z. Bahrani and M. van de Mieroop. Chicago.

Boulding, K. E. 1981. *Evolutionary Economics*. Beverly Hills.

———. 1987. "The economics of pride and shame." *Atlantic Economic Journal* 15: 10–19. Repr. in *Towards a New Economics. Critical Essays on Ecology, Distribution and Other Themes*, ed. K. E. Boulding. Aldershot.

———. 1992. *Towards a New Economics. Critical Essays on Ecology, Distribution and Other Themes*. Aldershot.

Bourdieu, P. 1977 [1972]. *Outline of a Theory of Practice*. Cambridge.

———. 1984 [1979]. *Distinction*. Cambridge, Mass.

———. 1990 [1970]. *The Logic of Practice*. Oxford.

Bowersock, G. W. 1986. "Rostovtzeff in Madison." *The American Scholar* 20: 391–400.

———. 1990. *Hellenism in Late Antiquity*. Ann Arbor.

Bowman, A. K. 1985. "Landholding in the Hermopolite nome in the fourth century AD." *Journal of Roman Studies* 75: 137–62.

———. 1994. "The Roman imperial army: Letters and literacy on the northern frontier." In *Literacy and Power in the Ancient World*, ed. A. K. Bowman and G. Woolf, 109–25. Cambridge.

Bowman, A. K., and D. Rathbone. 1992. "Cities and administration in Roman Egypt." *Journal of Roman Studies* 82: 107–27.

Bowman, A. K., and E. Rogan, eds. 1999. *Agriculture in Egypt from Pharaonic to Modern Times*. London: *Proceedings of the British Acacdemy* 96.

Bowman, A. K., and J. D. Thomas. 1994. *The Vindolanda Writing-Tablets (Tabulae Vindolandenses II)*. London.

Bradley, R. 1997. *Rock Art and the Prehistory of Atlantic Europe*. London.

———. 1998. *The Significance of Monuments*. London.

Brady, H. 1995. "Doing good and doing better. Symposium on *Designing Social Research* (II)." *Political Methodologist* 6.2: 11–19.

Brann, E. 1962. *The Athenian Agora VIII. Late Geometric and Protoattic Pottery*. Princeton.

Braudel, F. 1972a [1949]. *The Mediterranean and the Mediterranean World in the Age of Philip II*. Trans. S. Reynolds. London.

———. 1972b. "Personal testimony." *Journal of Modern History* 44: 448–67.

————. 2001 [1998]. *Memory and the Mediterranean.* Trans. S. Reynolds. London

Braunert, H. 1964. *Die Binnenwanderung. Studien zur Sozialgeschichte Ägyptens in der Ptolemäer- und Kaiserzeit.* Bonn: Bonner Historische Forschungen 26.

Bresson, A. 2000. *La cité marchande.* Paris.

Bresson, A., and P. Rouillard, eds. 1993. *L'emporion.* Paris.

Briant, P. 1982a. "Produktivkräfte, Staat und tributäre Produktionsweise im Achämenidenreich." In *Produktivkräfte und Gesellschaftsformationen in vorkapitalistischer Zeit,* ed. J. Hermann and I. Sellnow, 351–72. Berlin.

————. 1982b. *Rois, tributs et paysans.* Paris.

Brien-Poitevin, F. 1996. "Consommation des coquillages marins en Provence à l'époque romaine." *Revue archeologique de Narbonnaise* 29: 313–20.

Bringmann, K., and H. von Steuben. 1995. *Schenkungen hellenistischer Herrscher an Griechische Städte und Heiligtümer.* Vol. 1, *Zeugnisse und Kommentare.* Berlin.

Brown, A., and A. Deaton. 1972. "Models of consumer behavior: A survey." *Economic Journal* 82: 1145–1236.

Brun, J.-P. 1986. *L'oléoculture antique en Provence.* Paris.

————. 2003. "Les pressoirs à vin d'Afrique et de Maurétanie a l'époque romaine." *Africa* n.s. 1: 7–30.

Brun, J.-P., and G. Conges. 1994. "La villa viticole romaine des Toulons (Rians, Var)." *Annales de la société des sciences naturelles et d'archeologie de Toulon et du Var:* 219–41.

Bücher, K. 1893. *Die Enstehung der Volkswirtschaft.* Tübingen.

Burke, P. 1990. *The French Historical Revolution: The Annales School 1929–1989.* Stanford.

————. ed. 1991. *New Perspectives on Historical Writing.* Cambridge.

Burkert, W. 1992 [1984]. *The Orientalizing Revolution.* Trans. M. Pinder and W. Burkert. Cambridge, Mass.

Burnett, J. 1986. *A Social History of Housing, 1815–1970.* 2d ed. London.

Butzer, K. 1976. *Early Hydraulic Civilization in Egypt. A Study in Cultural Ecology.* Chicago.

————. 1980. "Long-term Nile flood variation and political discontinuities in pharaonic Egypt." In *From Hunters to Farmers: The Causes and Consequences of Food Production in Africa,* ed. J. D. Clark and S. A. Brandt. Berkeley.

Cameron, C. M., and S. Tomka, eds. 1993. *Abandonment of Settlements and Regions.* Cambridge.

Campbell, B. 1996. "Shaping the rural environment: Surveyors in ancient Rome." *Journal of Roman Studies* 86: 74–99.

Campbell, J. B. 1984. *The Emperor and the Roman Army, 31 BC–AD 235.* Oxford.

Cannadine, D. 1984. "The present and the past in the English Industrial Revolution." *Past and Present* 103: 131–72.

Carandini, A. 1985. *Settefinestre: Una villa schiavistica nell'Etruria romana.* Modena.

Carr, E. H. 1961. *What is History?* Harmondsworth, U.K.

Carrié, J.-M. 1982. "Le 'colonat du bas-empire': Un mythe historiographique?" *Opus* 1: 351–70.

———. 1983. "Un roman des origines: Les généalogies du 'colonat du bas-empire.'" *Opus* 2: 205–51.

Carson, A. 1999. *Economy of the Unlost.* Princeton.

Carsten, J., and S. Hugh-Jones, eds. 1995. *About the House: Lévi-Strauss and Beyond.* Cambridge.

Cartledge, P. 1997. Introduction to *Hellenistic Constructs: Essays in Culture, History, and Historiography,* ed. P. Cartledge, P. Garnsey, and E. Gruen, 1–19. Berkeley.

Cartledge, P., E. Cohen, and L. Foxhall, eds. 2001. *Money, Labour and Land: Approaches to the Economics of Ancient Greece.* London.

Cartledge, P., P. Garnsey, and E. Gruen, eds. 1997. *Hellenistic Constructs: Essays in Culture, History, and Historiography.* Berkeley.

Castells, M. 1996–98. *The Information Age: Economy, Society, and Culture.* 3 vols. Oxford.

Chaudhuri, K. N. 1985. *Trade and Civilisation in the Indian Ocean: An Economic History from the Rise of Islam to 1750.* Cambridge.

———. 1990. *Asia Before Europe: Economy and Civilisation of the Indian Ocean from the Rise of Islam to 1750.* Cambridge.

Cherry, J., J. Davis, and E. Mantzourani, eds. 1991. *Landscape Archaeology as Long-Term History.* Los Angeles.

Childe, V. G. 1950. "The urban revolution." *Town Planning Review* 21: 3–17.

Choquer, G., and F. Favory. 1991. *Les paysages de l'antiquité. Terres et cadastres de l'Occident romain.* Paris.

Clarke, G. W., ed. 1989. *Hellenism Rediscovered.* Cambridge.

Clarysse, W. 1979. "Large estate-holders in the Ptolemaic period." In *State and Temple Economy in the Ancient Near East,* ed. E. Lipinski, vol. 2: 731–43. Leuven.

Clarysse, W., and D. J. Thompson. Forthcoming. *Counting the People in Hellenistic Egypt.* 2 vols. Cambridge.

Clarysse, W., and K. Vandorpe. 1995. *Zenon, un homme d'affairs grec a l'ombre des pyramides.* Leuven.

———. 1997. "Viticulture and wine consumption in the Arsinoite nome (*P. Köln.* V 221)." *Ancient Society* 28: 67–73.

Coase, R. 1937. "The nature of the firm." *Econometrica* 4: 386–405.

Cohen, E. 1992. *Athenian Economy and Society: A Banking Perspective.* Princeton.

―――. 2001. Introduction to *Money, Labour and Land: Approaches to the Economics of Ancient Greece*, P. Cartledge, E. Cohen, and L. Foxhall, eds., 1–7. London.

Cole, S. 1996. *Nippur in Late Assyrian Times c. 755–612 BC.* Helsinki.

Cook, R. M. 1959. "Die Bedeutung der bemalten Keramik für den griechischen Handel." *Jahrbuch des deutschen archäologischen Instituts* 74: 114–23.

Cornell, T. 1983. "The End of Roman imperial expansion." In *War and Society in the Roman World*, eds. J. Rich and G. Shipley. London.

Cornell, T., and K. Lomas, eds. 1995. *Urban Society in Roman Italy*. London.

Cotton, H. M., W. E. H. Cockle, and F. Millar. 1995. "The papyrology of the Roman Near East: A survey." *Journal of Roman Studies* 85: 214–35.

Coucouzeli, A. 1999. "Architecture, power, and ideology in Dark Age Greece: A new interpretation of the Lefkandi Toumba building." In *Proceedings of the XVth International Congress of Classical Archaeology, Amsterdam, July 12–17, 1998*, ed. P. Docter and E. Moorman, 126–29. Amsterdam.

Courty, M.-A., P. Goldberg, and R. MacPhail. 1989. *Soils and Micromorphology in Archaeology*. Cambridge.

Cox, C. 1998. *Household Interests: Property, Marriage Strategies, and Family Dynamics in Ancient Athens*. Princeton.

Crafts, N. F. R. 1985. "English workers' real wages during the Industrial Revolution: some remaining problems." *Journal of Economic History* 45: 139–44.

Crane, R. 1967. *The Idea of the Humanities and Other Essays*. Vol. 1. Chicago.

Crawford, D. J. 1971. *Kerkeosiris: An Egyptian village in the Ptolemaic Period*. Cambridge.

―――. 1973. "The opium poppy. A study in Ptolemaic agriculture." In *Problèmes de la terre en Grèce ancienne*, ed. Moses I. Finley, 223–51. Paris.

Crielaard, J. P., and J. Driessen. 1994. "The hero's home." *Topoi* 4: 251–70.

Curtis, R. I. 1991. *Garum and Salsamenta: Production and Commerce in Materia Medica*. Leiden: *Studies in Ancient Medicine* 3.

D'Altroy, T., and T. Earle. 1985. "Staple finance, wealth finance and storage in the Inka political economy." *Current Anthropology* 26: 187–206.

Dandamaev, M. 1979. "State and temple in Babylonia in the first millennium BC." In *State and Temple Economy in the Ancient Near East*, ed. E. Lipinski, vol. 2: 589–96. Leuven.

―――. 1982. "The Neo-Babylonian Elders." In *Sources and Languages of the Ancient Near East*, ed. J. N. Postgate et al., 37–41. Warminster.

―――. 1983. "Aliens and the community in Babylonia in the 6th–5th centuries BC." *Recuils de la Societé Jean Bodin pour l'histoire comparative des insitutions* 41: 133–45.

———. 1988. "The Neo-Babylonian popular assembly." In *Sulmu*, ed.
P. Vavrousek and V. Soucek, 63–71. Prague.

———. 1996. "An age of privatization in ancient Mesopotamia." In *Privatization in the Ancient Near East and Classical World.*, M. Hudson and
B. A. Levine, 197–210. Cambridge, Mass.

David, P. 1985. "Clio and the economics of QWERTY." *American Economic Review* 75: 332–37.

Davies, J. K. 1984. "Cultural, social, and economic features of the Hellenistic world." In *Cambridge Ancient History* VII, part 1, ed. F. W. Walbank,
A. E. Astin, M. W. Frederiksen, and R. M. Ogilvie, 257–320. 2d ed.
Cambridge.

———. 1998. "Ancient economies: Models and muddles." In *Trade, Traders and the Ancient City*. ed. H. Parkins and C. Smith, 225–56.
London.

———. 2001. "Hellenistic economies in the post-Finley era." In *Hellenistic Economies*, ed. Z. H. Archibald, J. K. Davies, V. Gabrielsen, and
G. J. Oliver, 11–62. London.

De Ligt, L. 1993. *Fairs and Markets in the Roman Empire: Economic and Social Aspects of Periodic Trade in a Pre-Industrial Society*. Amsterdam.

De Long, J. B., and A. Shleifer. 1993. "Princes and merchants: City growth before the Industrial Revolution." *Journal of Law and Economics* 36:
671–702.

De Robertis, F. 1971. *Storia delle corporazioni e del regime associativo nel mondo romano*. Vols. 1–2. Bari.

De Soto, H. 2000. *The Mystery of Capital*. New York.

Deimel, A. 1931. *Sumerische Tempelwirtschaft zur Zeit Urukaginas und seiner Vorgänger*. Rome.

Deininger, J. 1985. "Die politischen Strukturen des mittlemeerisch-vorderorientalischen Altertums in Max Webers Sicht." In *Max Webers Sicht des antiken Christentums*, ed. W. Schluchter, 72–110. Frankfurt.

Depauw, M. 1997. *A Companion to Demotic Studies*. Brussels: *Papyrologica Bruxellensia* 28.

———. 2000. *The Archive of Teos and Thabis from Early Ptolemaic Thebes*.
Brussels.

Descat, R. 1995. "*L'économie antique* et la cité grecque." *Annales Histoire Sciences Sociales* 50: 961–89.

Diakonoff, I. M. 1954. "Sale of lands in pre-Sargonic Sumer." *Papers of the 23rd International Congress of Orientalists*. Moscow.

———. ed. 1969. *Ancient Mesopotamia*. Moscow.

———. 1974. "Slaves, helots and serfs in early antiquity." *Acta Antiqua* 22:
45–78.

———. 1982. "The structure of Near Eastern society before the middle of the 2nd millennium BC." In *Oikumene*, ed. I. Hahn, vol. 3: 7–100. Budapest.

———. 1991. "General outline of the first period of the history of the ancient world and the problem of the ways of development." In *Early Antiquity*, ed. I. M. Diakonoff, 27–66. Trans. A. Kirjanov. Chicago.

Dietler, Michael. 1995. "The cup of Gyptis: Rethinking the colonial encounter in Early Iron Age Western Europe and the relevance of world-systems models." *Journal of European Archaeology* 3: 89–111.

———. 1997. "The Iron Age in Mediterranean France: Colonial encounters, entanglements, and transformations." *Journal of World Prehistory* 11: 269–357.

Dietz, S., L. L. Sebaï, and H. Ben Hassen. 1996. *Africa Proconsularis. Regional Studies in the Segermes Valley of Northern Tunisia*. Copenhagen.

Dixit, A., and B. J. Nalebuff. 1991. *Thinking Strategically*. New York.

Docter, R., and E. Moorman, eds. 1999. *Proceedings of the XVth International Congress of Classical Archaeology, Amsterdam, July 12–17, 1998*. Amsterdam.

Donadoni, S., ed. 1997. *The Egyptians*. Trans. R. Bianchi, A. L. Crone, C. Lambert, and T. Ritter. Chicago.

Drecoll, C. 1997. *Die Liturgien im römischen Kaiserreich des 3. und 4. Jh. n. Chr.* Stuttgart: *Historia* Einzelschriften 116.

Drinkwater, J. F. 1997. Review of *Die regionale Mobilität in Gallien nach den Inschriften des 1. bis 3. Jahrhunderts nach Chr.*, by L. Wierschowski (Stuttgart 1995: *Historia* Einzelschrift 91). *Britannia* 28: 511–12.

Drobak, J., and J. Nye, eds. 1997. *Frontiers of the New Institutional Economics*. New York.

Drougou, S., and I. Vokotopoulou. 1989. "Olynthos—i oikia BVII₁." To *Archaiologiko Ergo sti Makedonia kai Thraki* 3: 339–50.

Droysen, J. G. 1836. *Geschichte der Diodochen*. Berlin.

duBois, P. 2001. *Trojan Horses: Saving the Classics from Conservatives*. New York.

Dunbabin, K. 1978. *The Mosaics of Roman North Africa*. Oxford.

Duncan-Jones, R. P. 1982. *The Economy of the Roman Empire: Quantitative Studies*. 2d ed. Cambridge.

———. 1990. *Structure and Scale in the Roman Economy*. Cambridge.

———. 1994. *Money and Government in the Roman Empire*. Cambridge.

Duttenhöfer, R. 1994. *Ptolemäische Urkunden aus der Heidelberger Papyrus-Sammlung (P. Heid. VI)*. Heidelberg.

Dyson, S. 1998. *Ancient Marbles to American Shores*. Philadelphia.

Eagleton, T. 1983. *Literary Theory: An Introduction*. Minneapolis.

Edwards, C., ed. 1999. *Roman Presences: Receptions of Rome in European Culture, 1789–1945*. Cambridge.

Ehrlich, I. 1990. "The problem of development: Introduction." *Journal of Political Economy* 98 supp.: S1–S11.

Eisenstadt, S. N. 1963. *The Political Systems of Empires: The Rise and Fall of the Historical Bureaucratic Societies.* New York.

Eisman, M. 1974. "Nikosthenic amphorai: The J. Paul Getty Museum amphora." *Getty Museum Journal* 1: 43–51.

Elat, M. 1987. "Der *tamkaru* im neuassyrischen Reich." *Journal of the Social and Economic History of the Orient* 30: 233–54.

Ellickson, R. C., and C. Thorland 1995. "Ancient land law: Mesopotamia, Egypt, Israel." *Chicago-Kent Law Review* 71: 321–411.

Elton, G. 1967. *The Practice of History.* Glasgow.

Engels, D. 1990. *Roman Corinth.* Chicago.

Engels, F. 1972 [1884]. *Origins of the Family, Private Property, and the State.* Ed. E. Leacock. London.

Eph'al, I. 1978. "The western minorities in Babylonia in the 6th–5th centuries BC.: Maintenance and cohesion." *Orientalia* n.s. 47: 74–90.

Ermarth, E. D. 1992. *Sequel to History: Postmodernism and the Crisis of Historical Time.* Princeton.

Etienne, R. 1991. "Architecture et démocratie." *Topoi* 1: 39–47.

Eyre, C. J. 1999. "Village economy in Pharaonic Egypt." In *Agriculture in Egypt from Pharaonic to Modern Times,* ed. A. K. Bowman and E. Rogan, 33–60. London: *Proceedings of the British Acacdemy* 96.

Fales, F. M. 1984a. "The Neo-Assyrian Period." In *Circulation of Goods in Non-Palatial Context in the Ancient Near East,* ed. A. Archi, 207–20. Rome.

———. 1984b. "A survey of Neo-Assyrian land sales." In *Land Tenure and Social Transformation in the Middle East.* ed. T. Khalidi, 1–13. Beirut.

Falkenstein, A. 1954. "La cité-temple sumérienne." *Cahiers d'histoire mondiale* 1: 784–814.

Fantham, E. 1994. *Roman Literary Culture.* Baltimore.

Favory, F., A. Parodi, P. Poupet, and C. Raynaud. 1994. "Lunel-Viel et son territoire." In *Les campagnes de la France mediterranéenne micro-régionales,* ed. P. Favory and J.-L. Fiches, 163–235. Paris.

Feinstein, C. 1998. "Pessimism perpetuated: Real wages and the standard of living in Britain during and after the Industrial Revolution." *Journal of Economic History* 58: 625–58.

Figueira, T. 1998. *The Power of Money.* Philadelphia.

Fikhman, I. F. 1997. Review of *Reading Papyri, Writing Ancient History,* by Roger Bagnall (London). *Scripta Classica Israelica* 16: 279–85.

Filow, B. 1934. *Die Grabhügelnekropole bei Duvanlij in Südbulgarien.* Sofia.

Finley, M. I. 1952. "Multiple charges on real property in Athenian law: New evidence from an Agora inscription." In *Studi in onore di Vincenzo Arangio-Ruiz*, vol. 3: 473–91. Naples.

———. 1964. "Between slavery and freedom." *Comparative Studies in Society and History* 6: 233–49. Repr. in *Economy and Society in Ancient Greece*, ed. B. D. Shaw and R. P. Saller, 116–32. London.

———. 1965. "Classical Greece." In *Second International Conference of Economic History*. Vol. 1, *Trade and Politics in the Ancient World:*, ed. M. I. Finley, 11–35. Paris.

———. 1970. "Aristotle and economic analysis." *Past and Present* 47: 3–25.

———. 1975. *The Use and Abuse of History*. New York.

———. 1977. "The ancient city: From Fustel de Coulanges to Max Weber and beyond." *Comparative Studies in Society and Ancient History* 19: 305–27. Repr. in *Economy and Society in Ancient Greece*, ed. B. D. Shaw and R. P. Saller, 3–23. London.

———. 1980. *Ancient Slavery and Modern Ideology*. London.

———. 1981. *Economy and Society in Ancient Greece*. Ed. B. D. Shaw and R. P. Saller. London.

———. 1985a [1973]. *The Ancient Economy*. Rev. ed. London.

———. 1985b. *Ancient History: Evidence and Models*. London.

———. 1999. *The Ancient Economy*. Revised ed. Berkeley.

Floud, R. 1994. "The heights of Europeans since 1750: A new source for European economic history." In *Stature, Living Standards, and Economic Development*, ed. J. Komlos, 9–24. Chicago.

Floud, R., and D. McCloskey, eds. 1994. *The Economic History of Britain Since 1700*. 2d ed. 2 vols. Cambridge.

Floud, R., K. Wachter, and A. Gregory. 1990. *Height, Health and History: Nutritional Status in the United Kingdom, 1750–1980*. Cambridge.

Fogel, R. W., and G. R. Elton. 1983. *Which Road to the Past?* New Haven.

Forbes, H. A. 1982. "Strategies and soils: Technology, production, and environment in the peninsula of Methana, Greece." Ph.D. diss., University of Pennsylvania. Repr. in University Microfilms International, Ann Arbor, Mich., no. 822 7269.

Foster, B. 1981. "A new look at the Sumerian temple state." *Journal of the Economic and Social History of the Orient* 24: 225–41.

Fotiadis, M. 1995. "Modernity and the past-still-present: Politics of time in the birth of regional archaeological projects in Greece." *American Journal of Archaeology* 99: 59–78.

Frame, G. 1984. "The 'first families' of Borsippa during the Early Neo-Babylonian Period." *Journal of Cuneiform Studies* 36: 67–80.

Francovich, R., and H. Patterson, eds. 2000. *Extracting Meaning from Ploughsoil Assemblages*. Oxford.

Frank, A. G. 1998. *ReOrient: Global Economy in the Asian Age.* Berkeley.

Frank, A. G., and B. K. Gills, eds. 1993. *The World System: Five Hundred Years or Five Thousand?* London.

Frankenstein, S. 1979. "The Phoenicians in the far west: A function of Neo-Assyrian imperialism." In *Power and Propaganda: A Symposium on Ancient Empires.*, ed. M. T. Larsen, 263–94. Copenhagen.

Franko, G. F. 1988. "*Sitometria* in the Zenon archive: Identifying Zenon's personal documents." *Bulletin of the American Society of Papyrologists* 25: 13–98.

Fraser, P. M. 1972. *Ptolemaic Alexandria.* 3 vols. Oxford.

Frayn, J. M. 1993. *Markets and Fairs in Roman Italy. Their Social and Economic Importance from the Second Century BC to the Third Century AD.* Oxford.

French, A. 1964. *The Growth of the Athenian Economy.* London.

Friedman, T. 2000. *The Lexus and the Olive Tree: Understanding Globalization.* Rev. ed. New York.

Frier, B. W. 1989. "A new papyrology?" *Bulletin of the American Society of Papyrologists* 26: 217–26.

———. 1999. "Roman demography." In *Life, Death, and Entertainment in the Roman Empire:*, ed. D. S. Potter and D. J. Mattingly, 85–112. Ann Arbor, Mich.

Fulle, G. 1997. "The international organization of the Arretine *terra sigillata* industry: Problems of evidence and interpretation." *Journal of Roman Studies* 87: 111–55.

Furubotn, E. G., and R. Richter. 1997. *Institutions and Economic Theory: The Contribution of the New Institutional Economics.* Ann Arbor, Mich.

Gallant, T. W. 1991. *Risk and Survival in Ancient Greece. Reconstructing the Rural Domestic Economy.* Stanford.

Garlan, Y. 1988 [1982]. *Slavery in Ancient Greece.* Trans. J. Lloyd. Ithaca, N.Y.

Garnsey, P. 1988. *Famine and Food Supply in the Graeco-Roman World.* Cambridge.

Garnsey, P., and R. P. Saller. 1987. *The Roman Empire: Economy, Society and Culture.* London.

Gascou, J. 1985. "Les grands domaines, la cité et l'état en Égypte byzantine (Recherches d'histoire agraire, fiscale et administrative)." *Travaux et Mémoires* 9: 1–90.

Gates, S., and B. Humes. 1997. *Games, Information, and Politics.* Ann Arbor, Mich.

Geertz, C. 1973. *The Interpretation of Cultures.* New York.

Gelb, I. J. 1969. "On the alleged temple and state economies in ancient Mesopotamia." In *Studi in onore di E. Volterra*, vol. 6: 137–54. Milan.

———. 1972. "The Arua institution." *Révue d'Assyriologie* 66: 1–32.

Gerring, J. 2001. *Social Science Methodology: A Criterial Framework.* Cambridge.

Giardina, A., ed. 1986. *Società romana e impero tardoantica*. 3 vols. Rome and Bari.

Giardina, A., and A. Schiavone, eds. 1981. *Società romana e produzione schiavisticà*. 3 vols. Rome and Bari.

Giddens, A. 1999. *Runaway World*. London.

Gilbertson, D. D. 1996. "Explanations: Environment as agency." In G. Barker, ed., *Farming the Desert. The UNESCO Libyan Valleys Survey*. Vol. 1, *Synthesis*: 291–317. Tripoli.

Gledhill, J., and M. T. Larsen. 1982. "The Polanyi paradigm and a dynamic analysis of archaic states." In *Theory and Explanation in Archaeology*, ed. C. Renfrew, M. J. Rowlands, and B. A. Segraves, 197–229. New York.

Goldsmith, R. W. 1984. "An estimate of the size and structure of the National Product of the early Roman Empire." *Review of Income and Wealth* 30: 263–88.

———. 1987. *Premodern Financial Systems: A Historical Comparative Study*. Cambridge.

Goldstone, J. 1991. *Revolution and Rebellion in the Early Modern World*. Berkeley.

———. 1998. "The problem of the 'Early Modern' world." *Journal of the Economic and Social History of the Orient* 41: 249–84.

———. 2000. "The rise of the West—or not? A revision to socio-economic history." *Sociological Theory* 18: 175–92.

———. 2002. "Efflorescences and economic growth in world history: Rethinking the 'rise of the West' and the Industrial Revolution." *Journal of World History* 13: 323–89.

Gould, P., and R. White. 1986 [1974]. *Mental Maps*. London.

Grafton, A. 1991. *Defenders of the Text: The Traditions of Scholarship in an Age of Science, 1450–1800*. Cambridge, Mass.

Grandjean, Y. 1988. *Études thasiennes*. Vol. 12, *Recherches sur l'habitat thasien à l'époque grecque*. Athens.

Granovetter, M. 1985. "Economic action and social structure: The problem of embeddedness." *American Journal of Sociology* 91: 481–510.

———. 1990. "The old and the new in economic sociology." In *Beyond the Marketplace*, ed. R. Friedland and A. F. Robertson, 89–112. New York.

Gras, M. 1995. *La Méditerrannée archaïque*. Paris.

Green, P. 1990. *Alexander to Actium: The Historical Evolution of the Hellenistic Age*. Berkeley.

Greene, J. A. 1993. *Ager et "Arosot": Rural Settlement and Agrarian History of the Carthaginian Countryside*. Redditch.

Greene, K. 1986. *The Archaeology of the Roman Economy*. London.

———. 1994. "Technology and innovation in context: The Roman background to mediaeval and later developments." *Journal of Roman Archaeology* 7: 22–33.

———. 1997. *Roman Pottery*. Berkeley.

————. 2000. "Technological innovation and economic progress in the ancient world: M. I. Finley reconsidered." *Economic History Review* 52: 29–59.

Grenfell, B. P., and J. P. Mahaffy. 1896. *Revenue Laws of Ptolemy Philadelphus.* Oxford.

Gress, D. 1998. *From Plato to NATO: The Idea of the West and Its Opponents.* New York.

Grunert, S. 1980. "Ägyptische Erscheinungsformen des Privateigentums zur Zeit der Ptolemäer: Grundeigentum." *Altorientalische Forschungen* 7: 51–76.

Gunter, A., ed. 1992. *The Construction of the Ancient Near East.* Copenhagen: *Culture & History* 11.

Gutman, H. 1975. *Slavery and the Numbers Game.* Champaign, Ill.

Haas, C. 1997. *Alexandria in Late Antiquity.* Baltimore.

Haber, S. 1999. "Anything goes: Mexico's 'new' cultural history." *Hispanic American Historical Review* 79: 299–319.

————. 2001. "Mission statement." http://www.stanford.edu/group/sshi/mission_statement.html.

Hamilton, G. 1994. "Civilizations and the organization of economies." In *The Handbook of Economic Sociology,* ed. N. Smelser and R. Swedberg, 183–205. Princeton.

Haines, M., and R. Steckel. 2000. *Childhood Mortality and Nutritional Status as Indicators of Standard of Living.* Cambridge, Mass.: National Bureau of Economic Research Historical Paper 121.

Hamilakis, Y. 1999. "La trahison des archéologues: Archaeological practice as intellectual activity in postmodernism." *Journal of Mediterranean Archaeology* 12: 60–79.

Hansen, M. H. 1999. *The Athenian Democracy in the Age of Demosthenes.* 2d ed. London.

Hanson, V. D., and J. Heath. 1998. *Who Killed Homer?* New York.

Hardt, M., and A. Negri. 2000. *Empire.* Cambridge, Mass.

Hardy, E. R. 1931. *The Large Estates of Byzantine Egypt.* New York.

Harris, E. C. 1993. *Principles of Archaeological Stratification.* 2d ed. London.

Harris, W. V. 1979. *War and Imperialism in Republican Rome, 320–70 BC.* Oxford.

————. 1989. "Child-exposure in the Roman Empire." *Journal of Roman Studies* 84: 1–22.

————. ed., 1993. *The Inscribed Economy: Production and Distribution in the Roman Empire in the Light of the Instrumentum Domesticum.* Ann Arbor, Mich.: *Journal of Roman Archaeology* supp. vol. 6.

————. 1999. "Demography, geography and the sources of Roman slaves." *Journal of Roman Studies* 89: 62–75.

Harrison, A. R. W. 1968. *The Law of Athens*. Vol. 1, *The Family and Property*. Oxford.

Harvey, D. 1989. *The Condition of Postmodernity*. Oxford.

Haselgrove, C. 1987. "Culture process on the periphery: Belgic Gaul and Rome during the late Republic and early Empire." In *Centre and Periphery in the Ancient World*, ed. M. Rowlands, M. T. Larsen, and K. Kristiansen, 104–24. Cambridge.

Hausman, D. and M. McPherson. 1996. *Economic Analysis and Moral Philosophy*. Cambridge.

Heichelheim, F. 1970. *An Ancient Economic History*. 2d ed. Leiden.

Hexter, J. H. 1972. "Fernand Braudel and the *monde braudelien*." *Journal of Modern History* 44: 480–539.

Hingley, R. 2000. *Roman Officers and English Gentlemen: Imperialism and the Origin of Archaeology*. London.

Hitchner, R. B. 1988. "The Kasserine Archaeological Survey, 1982–86." *Antiquités africaines* 24: 7–41.

———. 1990. "The Kasserine Archaeological Survey—1987." *Antiquités africaines* 30: 231–60.

———. 1994. "Image and reality: The changing face of pastoralism in the Tunisian high steppe." In *Landuse in the Roman Empire*. Rome.

———. 1995a. "Prospection archéologique à Entressen." *Les Amis du Vieil Istres* 17: 15–26.

———. 1995b. "Irrigation, terraces, dams and aqueducts in the region of Cillium (mod. Kasserine)." In *Productions et exportations Africaines. Actualités archéologique en Afrique du nord antique et médiévale*, 143–57. Aix-en-Provence.

———. 1999. "More Italy than Provence? Archaeology, texts, and culture change in Roman Provence." *Transactions of the American Philological Association* 129: 375–79.

Hodder, I. 1982a. *Symbols in Action: Ethnoarchaeological Studies of Material Culture*. Cambridge.

———. 1982b. *The Present Past*. London.

———. 1986. *Reading the Past*. Cambridge.

———. 1990. *The Domestication of Europe*. Oxford.

———. 1991. *Archaeological Theory in Europe: The Last Fifty Years*. London.

———. ed., 2001. *Archaeological Theory Today*. Cambridge.

Hodder, I., and C. Orton. 1976. *Spatial Analysis in Archaeology*. Cambridge.

Hodder, I., M. Shanks, et al. 1995. *Interpreting Archaeology*. Oxford.

Hoepfner, W., and G. Brands, eds. 1996. *Basileia: Die Paläste der hellenistischen Könige*. Mainz.

Hoepfner, W., and E.-L. Schwandner, eds. 1994 [1986]. *Haus und Stadt im klassischen Griechenland*. 2d ed. Munich.

Hoepfner, W., E.-L. Schwandner, and W. Schuller, eds. 1989. *Demokratie und Architektur*. Munich.

Hopkins, D. 1997. "Agriculture." In *The Oxford Encyclopedia of Archaeology in the Ancient Near East*, ed. E. Meyers, vol. 1: 22–30. Oxford.

Hopkins, K. 1980. "Taxes and trade in the Roman empire." *Journal of Roman Studies* 70: 101–25.

———. 1983. Introduction to *Trade in the Ancient Economy*, ed. P. Garnsey, K. Hopkins, and C. R. Whittaker, ix–xxv. Cambridge.

———. 1995/96. "Rome, taxes, rents and trade." *Kodai: Journal of Ancient History* 6/7: 41–75. Repr. in *The Ancient Economy*., eds. W. Scheidel and S. von Reden, 190–230. Edinburgh (2002).

———. 2000. "Rents, taxes, trade and the city of Rome." In *Mercati permanenti e mercati periodici nel mondo romano*, ed. E. Lo Cascio, 253–67. Bari.

Hopkins, N. S. 1987. *Agrarian Transformation in Egypt*. Boulder, Colo.

Horden, P., and N. Purcell. 2000. *The Corrupting Sea: A Study of Mediterranean History*. Oxford.

Horrell, S. 1996. "Home demand and British industrialization." *Journal of Economic History* 56: 561–604.

Howgego, C. 1995. *Ancient History from Coins*. London.

Hudson, M., and B. A. Levine, eds. 1996. *Privatization in the Ancient Near East and Classical World*. Cambridge, Mass.

Hunt, L., ed. 1989. *The New Cultural History*. Berkeley.

Jameson, M. H. 1977/78. "Agriculture and slavery in classical Athens." *Classical Journal* 73: 122–41.

Jameson, M. H., C. Runnels, and T. van Andel. 1994. *A Greek Countryside*. Stanford.

Janssen, J. J. 1975. "Prolegomena to the study of Egypt's economic history during the New Kingdom." *Studien zur Altägyptischen Kultur* 3: 127–85.

———. 1981. "Die Struktur der pharäonischen Wirtschaft." *Göttinger Miszellen* 48: 59–77.

Jew, D. 1999. "Food, silver, trade and liturgies: Modelling the Athenian economy." M.Phil. thesis, Cambridge University.

Joannès, F. 1989. *Archives de Borsippa: La famille Ea-ilûta-bâni*. Geneva.

Johnson, A. C. 1936. *Roman Egypt to the Reign of Diocletian*. Baltimore.

———. 1951. *Egypt and the Roman Empire*. Ann Arbor, Mich.

Johnson, A. C., and L. C. West. 1949. *Byzantine Egypt: Economic Studies*. Princeton: *Princeton University Studies in Papyrology* 6.

Johnson, D. G. 2000. "Population, food, and knowledge." *American Economic Review* 90: 1–14.

Jones, A. H. M. 1964. *The Later Roman Empire, 284–602; A Social, Economic and Administrative Survey*. Oxford.

Jones, E. L. 1987 [1981]. *The European Miracle*. 2d ed. Oxford.

————. 2000 [1988]. *Growth Recurring: Economic Change in World History.* 2d ed. Oxford.

Jones, J. E., A. J. Graham, and L. H. Sackett. 1973. "An Attic country house below the Cave of Pan at Vari." *Annual of the British School at Athens* 68: 355–452.

Jones, J. E., L. H. Sackett, and A. J. Graham. 1962. "The Dema House in Attica." *Annual of the British School at Athens* 57: 75–114.

Jongman, W. 1988. *Economy and Society at Pompeii.* Amsterdam.

Jördens, A. 1995. "Sozialstrukturen im Arbeitstierhandel des kaisezeitlichen Ägypten." *Tyche* 10: 37–100.

Kaplony-Heckel, U. 1963. *Die demotischen Tempeleide.* Wiesbaden.

Kardulias, P. N., ed. 1999. *World-Systems Theory in Practice.* Lanham, Md.

Keay, S. J. 1988. *Roman Spain.* Berkeley.

Keenan, J. G. 1980. "Aurelius Phoibammon, son of Triadelphus: A Byzantine Egyptian land entrepreneur." *Bulletin of the American Society of Papyrologists* 17: 145–54.

————. 1981. "On village and polis in Byzantine Egypt." *Proceedings of the XVIth International Congress of Papyrology,* 479–485. Chico, Calif.

————. 1982. "Papyrology and Roman history: 1956–1980." *Classical World* 76: 23–31.

————. 1993. "Papyrology and Byzantine historiography." *Bulletin of the American Society of Papyrologists* 30: 137–44.

Kehoe, D. P. 1990. "Pastoralism and agriculture." *Journal of Roman Archaeology* 3: 386–98.

————. 1992. *Management and Investment on Estates in Roman Egypt During the Early Empire.* Bonn.

————. 1997. *Investment, Profit, and Tenancy: The Jurists and the Roman Agrarian Economy.* Ann Arbor, Mich.

Kellner, H. 1979. "Disorderly conduct: Braudel's Mediterranean satire." *History and Theory* 18: 197–222.

Kelly, M. 1997. "The Dynamics of Smithian Growth." *The Quarterly Journal of Economics* 112: 939–64.

Kemp, B. 1989. *Ancient Egypt.* London.

Khalidi, T., ed. 1984. *Land Tenure and Social Transformation in the Middle East.* Beirut.

Kiderlen, M. 1995. *Megale Oikia. Untersuchungen zur Entwicklung aufwendiger griechischer Stadthausarchitektur.* Hürth.

King, G., R. Keohane, and S. Verba. 1994. *Designing Social Inquiry: Scientific Inference in Qualitative Research.* Princeton.

Kinser, S. 1981. "*Annaliste* paradigm? The geohistorical structuralism of Fernand Braudel." *American Historical Review* 86: 63–105.

Klamer, A., D. N. McCloskey, and R. Solow, eds. 1988. *The Consequences of Economic Rhetoric.* Cambridge.

Knapp, A. B. 1993. "Thalassocracies in Bronze Age eastern Mediterranean trade: Making and breaking a myth." *World Archaeology* 24: 332–47.

Koenen, L. 1996. "The carbonized archive from Petra." *Journal of Roman Archaeology* 9: 177–88.

Kohl, P. 1987. "The ancient economy, transferable technologies and the Bronze Age world-system: A view from the northeastern frontier of the Ancient Near East." In *Centre and Periphery in the Ancient World*, ed. M. Rowlands, M. T. Larsen, and K. Kristiansen, 13–24. Cambridge.

Kolendo, J. 1991. *Le colonat en Afrique sous le haut-empire.* Paris.

Komlos, J. 1996. *The Biological Standard of Living in Europe and America, 1700–1900: Studies in Anthropometric History.* Chicago.

Kopcke, G., and I. Tokumaru, eds. 1992. *Greece Between East and West, 10th–8th Centuries BC.* Mainz.

Kreps, S. 1990. *A Course in Microeconomic Theory.* Princeton.

Kristiansen, K., ed. 1985. *Archaeological Formation Processes.* Copenhagen.

———. 1998. *Europe Before History.* Cambridge.

Kugler, R. L., and E. L. Frost, eds. 2001. *The Global Century: Globalization and National Security.* 2 vols. Washington, D.C.

Kuhn, T. 1970 [1962]. *The Structure of Scientific Revolutions.* 2d ed. Chicago.

Kuhrt, A. 1995. *The Ancient Near East c. 3000–330 BC.* 2 vols. London.

———. 1998. "The Old Assyrian merchants." In *Trade, Traders and the Ancient City.* ed. H. Parkins and C. Smith, 16–30. London.

Kuklick, S. 1996. *Puritans in Babylon.* Princeton.

Kula, W. 1976 [1962]. *An Economic Theory of Feudalism.* London.

Kümmel, H. M. 1979. *Familie, Beruf und Amt im spätbabylonischen Uruk.* Berlin.

Kurke, L. 1991. *The Traffic in Praise: Pindar and the Poetics of Social Economy.* Ithaca, N.Y.

———. 1999. *Coins, Bodies, Games, and Gold: The Politics of Meaning in Archaic Greece.* Princeton.

Lang, F. 1996. *Archaische Siedlungen in Griechenland: Struktur und Entwicklung.* Berlin.

Larsen, M. T. 1967. *Old Assyrian Caravan Procedures.* Istanbul.

———. ed., 1979. *Power and Propaganda: A Symposium on Ancient Empires.* Copenhagen.

———. 1996. *The Conquest of Assyria.* New York.

Lassère, J-M. 1977. *Ubique Populus. Peuplement et mouvements de population dans l'Afrique romaine de la chute de Carthage a la fin de la dynastie des Sevères (146 a. C.–235 p. C.).* Paris.

Laubenheimer, F. 1989. "Le vin Gaulois." *Revue des etudes anciennes* 91: 5–22.

———. 1990. *Les amphores en Gaule.* Paris.

———. ed. 1992. *Les amphores en Gaule. Production et circulation*. Paris (*Annales littéraires de l'Université de Besançon* 474).

Lawson, T. 1997. *Economics and Reality*. London.

Lee, J. Z., and F. Wang. 1999. *One Quarter of Humanity: Malthusian Mythology and Chinese Realities*. Cambridge, Mass.

Leemans, W. F. 1983. "Trouve-t-on des 'communautés royales' dans l'ancienne Mésopotamie?" In *Les communautés rurales*, 43–106. Paris.

Lefkowitz, M. 1996. *Not Out of Africa*. New York.

Lefkowitz, M., and G. Rogers, eds. 1996. *Black Athena Revisited*. Durham, N.C.

Leveau, P. 1993. "Mentalité économique et grand travaux: Le drainage du lac Fucin." *Annales ESC* 48: 3–16.

———. 1995. "De la céréalculture et de l'élévage à la production de blé et de viande (l'apport de l'archéologie)." In *Du latifundium au latifundio, Bordeaux III, 17–19 decembre 1992*, 357–81. Paris.

———. 1996. "The Barbegal water mill in its environment: Archaeology and the economic and social history of antiquity." *Journal of Roman Archaeology* 9: 137–53.

Leveau, P., P. Sillières, and J.-P. Vallat. 1993. *Campagnes de la Méditerranée romaine Occident*. Paris.

Lévi-Strauss, C. 1949. *Elementary Structures of Kinship*. Boston.

Lewis, D. M. 1966. "After the profanation of the Mysteries." In *Ancient Society and Institutions*, ed. Ernst Badian, 177–91. Oxford.

Lewis, M. 1997. *Millstone and Hammer: The Origins of Water-Power*. Hull, UK.

Lewis, N. 1970. "Greco-Roman Egypt: Fact or fiction?" *Proceedings XII Congress of Papyrology*: 3–14. Toronto: *American Studies in Papyrology* 7. Repr. in *On Government and Law in Roman Egypt*, N. Lewis, 138–49. Atlanta: *American Studies in Papyrology* 33.

———. 1983. *Life in Egypt Under Roman Rule*. Oxford.

———. 1984. "The Romanity of Roman Egypt: A growing consensus." *Atti XVII Congresso di Papirologia*, 1077–84. Naples. Repr. in *On Government and Law in Roman Egypt*, N. Lewis, 298–305. Atlanta: *American Studies in Papyrology* 33.

———. 1995. *On Government and Law in Roman Egypt*. Atlanta: *American Studies in Papyrology* 33.

Lind, M. 2000. "The second fall of Rome." *The Wilson Quarterly* (Winter). http://wwics.si.edu/OUTREACH/WQ/WQSELECT/ROME/HTM.

Lindert, P. 1994. "Unequal living standards." In *The Economic History of Britain Since 1700*, ed. R. Floud and D. McCloskey, vol. 1: 357–86. 2d. ed. Cambridge.

Lindert, P., and J. Williamson. 1983. "English workers' living standards during the Industrial Revolution: A new look." *Economic History Review* 36: 1–25.

———. 1985. "English workers' real wages: A reply to Crafts." *Journal of Economic History* 45: 145–53.

Lipinski, E., ed. 1979. *State and Temple Economy in the Ancient Near East.* 2 vols. Leuven.

Liverani, M. 1975. "Communautés de village et palais royal dans la Syrie du IIème millénaire." *Journal of the Economic and Social History of the Orient* 18: 146–64.

———. 1979. "Economie della fattorie palatine ugaritiche." *Dialoghi d'archeologia* 2: 57–72.

———. 1984. "Land tenure and inheritance in the ancient Near East: The interaction between 'palace' and 'family' sectors." In *Land Tenure and Social Transformation in the Middle East.*, ed. T. Khalidi, 33–44. Beirut.

———. 1987. "The collapse of the Near Eastern regional system at the end of the Bronze Age: the case of Syria." In *Centre and Periphery in the Ancient World,* ed. M. Rowlands, M. Larsen, and K. Kristiansen, 66–73. Cambridge.

———. 1997. "Lower Mesopotamian fields: South vs. north." In *Ana sadi Labnani lu allik. Festschrift für W. Rölling,* ed. B. Pongratz-Leisen, H. Kühne, and P. Xella, 219–27. Neukirchen.

———. 1998. *Uruk, la prima città.* Rome.

———. 1999. "The role of the village in shaping the ancient Near Eastern landscape." In *Landscapes (XLIV rencontre assyriologique internationale),* 37–47. Padua.

Lo Cascio, E. 1994. "The Roman Principate: The impact of the organization of the Empire on production." In *Production and Public Powers in Classical Antiquity,* eds. E. Lo Cascio and D. W. Rathbone. Cambridge.

———., ed. 2000. *Mercati permanenti e mercati periodici nel mondo romano.* Bari.

Lucas, G. 2001. *Critical Approaches to Fieldwork: Contemporary and Historical Archaeological Practice.* London.

Lucas, R. E., Jr. 1998. "The Industrial Revolution: Past and future." University of Chicago working paper. Originally presented as the 1996 Kuznets Lectures, Yale University.

———. 2002. *Lectures on Economic Growth.* Cambridge, Mass.

Lyotard, J-F. 1984. *The Postmodern Condition: A Report on Knowledge.* Minneapolis.

Maekawa, K. 1980. "Female weavers and their children." *Acta Sumerologica* 2: 81–125.

Mann, M. 1986. *The Sources of Social Power.* Vol. 1. Cambridge.

Manning, J. G. 2003. *Land and Power in Ptolemaic Egypt: The Structure of Land Tenure.* Cambridge.

———. Forthcoming. "A Ptolemaic agreement concerning a donkey with

an unusual warranty clause. The strange case of P. dem. Princ. I."
Enchoria 28.

Marchand, S. 1996. *Down from Olympus: Archaeology and Philhellenism in Germany, 1750–1970.* Princeton.

Marchand, S., and A. Grafton. 1997. "Martin Bernal and his critics." *Arion* 3d ser. 5: 1–35.

Marfoe, L. 1987. "Cedar forest to silver mountain: Social change and the development of long-distance trade in early Near Eastern societies." In *Centre and Periphery in the Ancient World*, ed. M. Rowlands, M. T. Larsen, and K. Kristiansen, 25–35. Cambridge.

Marx, K. 1964 [1857/58]. *Precapitalist Economic Formations.* Ed. E. Hobsbawm. London.

Marx, K., and F. Engels. 1848. *The Communist Manifesto.* New York.

Mathisen, R., and H. Sivan, eds. 1996. *Shifting Frontiers in Late Antiquity.* Aldershot.

Mattern, S. P. 1999. *Rome and the Enemy. Imperial Strategy in the Principate.* Berkeley.

Mattingly, D. J. 1994. *Tripolitania.* Ann Arbor, Mich.

———. 1997a. "Beyond belief? Drawing a line beneath the consumer city." In *Roman Urbanism*, ed. H. Parkins, 210–18. London.

———. 1997b. "Africa, a landscape of opportunity?" In *Dialogues in Roman Imperialism*, ed. D. J. Mattingly, 117–39. Portsmouth, R.I.

Mattingly, D. J., and R. B. Hitchner. 1993. "Technical specifications of some North African olive presses of Roman date," In *La production du vin et de l'huile en Méditerranée,* ed. Marie-Claire Amouretti and Jean-Pierre Brun, 439–62.

———. 1995. "Roman Africa: An archaeological survey." *Journal of Roman Studies* 85: 165–213.

Mattingly, D. J., and J. Salmon, eds. 2001. *Economies Beyond Agriculture in the Classical World.* London.

Maxfield, V. A. 1996. "The eastern desert forts and the army in Egypt during the Principate." In *Archaeological Research in Roman Egypt*, ed. D. M. Bailey, 9–19. Ann Arbor, Mich.: *Journal of Roman Archaeology* supp. vol. 19.

Mazarakis Ainian, A. 1997. *From Rulers' Dwellings to Temples: Architecture, Religion and Society in Early Iron Age Greece (1100–700 BC.).* Jonsered.

———. Forthcoming. "Architecture and social structure in Early Iron Age Greece." In *Building Communities: House, Settlement and Society.*, ed. R. Westgate and J. Whitley. London.

McClellan, M. C. 1997. "The economy of Hellenistic Egypt and Syria. An archeological perspective." In *Ancient Economic Thought*, ed. B. B. Price, 172–87. London.

McCloskey, D. N. 1998 [1985]. *The Rhetoric of Economics*. 2d ed. Madison, Wis.

McCorristen, J. 1997. "The fiber revolution. Textile extensification, alienation, and social stratification in ancient Mesopotamia." *Current Anthropology* 38: 517–49.

McDonald, W. A., W. Coulson, and J. J., Rosser, eds. 1983. *Excavations at Nichoria in Southwest Greece*. Vol. 3, *Dark Age and Byzantine Occupation*. Minneapolis.

McKinnon, M. 1994. "Living standards, 1870–1914." In *The Economic History of Britain Since 1700*, eds. R. Floud and D. McCloskey, vol. 2: 265–90. 2d ed. Cambridge.

McNeill, W. 1949. *A History of Western Civilization*. Chicago.

Meiggs, R. 1973. *Roman Ostia*. 2d ed. Oxford.

Menzel, B. 1981. *Assyrische Tempel*. 2 vols. Rome.

Millar, F. 1977. *The Emperor in the Roman World, 31 BC–AD 337*. London.

Miller, M. 1997. *Athens and Persia in the Fifth Century BC*. Cambridge.

Millet, M. 1990. *The Romanization of Britain*. Cambridge.

Millett, P. 1991. *Lending and Borrowing in Ancient Athens*. Cambridge.

———. 2001. "Productive to some purpose? The problem of ancient economic growth." In *Economies Beyond Agriculture in the Classical World*, ed. D. J. Mattingly and J. Salmon, 17–48. London.

Mokyr, J. 1987. "Has the Industrial Revolution been crowded out? Some reflections on Crafts and Williamson." *Explorations in Economic History* 24: 293–319.

———. 1990. *The Lever of Riches: Technological Creativity and Economic Progress*. New York.

Möller, A. 2000. *Naukratis*. Oxford.

Monkkonen, E. 1994. "Lessons of social science history." *Social Science History* 18: 161–68.

Moorey, P. R. S. 1987. "On tracking cultural transfers in prehistory: The case of Egypt and lower Mesopotamia in the fourth millennium BC." In *Centre and Periphery in the Ancient World*, ed. M. Rowlands, M. T. Larsen, and K. Kristiansen, 36–46. Cambridge.

Morris, I. 1987. *Burial and Ancient Society: The Rise of the Greek City-State*. Cambridge.

———. 1991. "The early polis as city and state." In *City and Country in the Ancient World*, ed. J. Rich and A. Wallace-Hadrill, 24–51. London.

———. 1992. *Death-Ritual and Social Structure in Classical Antiquity*. Cambridge.

———. 1994. "The Athenian economy twenty years after *The Ancient Economy*." *Classical Philology* 89: 351–66.

———. 1998. "Beyond democracy and empire: Athenian art in context." In *Democracy, Empire, and the Arts in Fifth-Century Athens*, ed. D. Boedeker and K. Raaflaub, 59–86. Cambridge, Mass.

———. 1999a. Foreword to *The Ancient Economy*, by M. I. Finley, ix–xxxvi. Rev. ed. Berkeley.

———. 1999b. "The social and economic archaeology of Greece: An overview." In *Proceedings of the XVth International Congress of Classical Archaeology, Amsterdam, July 12–17, 1998*, ed. P. Docter and E. Moorman, 27–33. Amsterdam.

———. 2000. *Archaeology as Cultural History: Words and Things in Iron Age Greece.* Oxford.

———. 2001. "Hard surfaces." In *Money, Labour and Land: Approaches to the Economics of Ancient Greece*, ed. P. Cartledge, E. Cohen, and L. Foxhall, 8–43. London.

———. 2003. "Mediterraneanization." *Mediterranean Historical Review* 18: 30–55.

———. 2004. "Classical archaeology." In *Blackwell Companion to Archaeology.*, ed. J. Bintliff, 253–71. Oxford.

Morris, S. P. 1992. *Daidalos and the Origins of Greek Art.* Princeton.

Morrow, J. 1994. *Game Theory for Political Scientists.* Princeton.

Nash, D. T., and M. D. Petraglia, eds. 1987. *Natural Formation Processes and the Archaeological Record.* Oxford: British Archaeological Reports 352.

Nelson, R. R., and S. G. Winter. 1982. *An Evolutionary Theory of Economic Change.* Cambridge, Mass.

Neumann, J. 1987a. "Zum Problem des privaten Bodeneigentums in Mesopotamien." In *Das Grundeigentum in Mesopotamien*: 29–48. Berlin.

———. 1987b. *Handwerk in Mesopotamien.* Berlin.

Neumann, J., and S. Parpola. 1987. "Climatic change in the eleventh-tenth century eclipse of Assyria and Babylonia." *Journal of Near Eastern Studies* 46: 161–82.

Nevett, L. 1999. *House and Society in the Ancient Greek World.* Cambridge.

———. 2000. "A real estate 'market' in classical Greece? The evidence of town housing." *Annual of the British School at Athens* 95: 329–44.

North, D. C. 1981. *Structure and Change in Economic History.* New York.

———. 1985. "Transaction costs in history." *Journal of European Economic History* 14: 557–76.

———. 1990. *Institutions, Institutional Change and Economic Performance.* Cambridge.

North, D., and R. Thomas. 1973. *The Rise of the Western World: A New Economic History.* Cambridge.

Oakley, J., and S. Rotroff. 1992. *Debris from a Public Dining Place in the Athenian Agora.* Princeton: *Hesperia* supp. vol. 25.

Oates, J., ed. 1993. *Ancient Trade: New Perspectives.* London: *World Archaeology* 24.3.

Ober, J. 1998. *Political Dissent in Democratic Athens.* Princeton.

Oelsner, J. 1976. "Erwägungen zum Gesellschaftsaufbau Babyloniens von der neubabylonischen bis zur achämenidischen Zeit (7.-4. Jh. v. u. Z.)." *Altorientalische Forschungen* 4: 131–49.

———. 1984. "Die neu- und spätbabylonische Zeit." In *Circulation of Goods in Non-Palatial Context in the Ancient Near East*, ed. A. Archi, 221–40. Rome.

———. 1987. "Grundbesitz/Grundeigentum im achämenidischen und seleukidischen Babylonien." *Jahrbuch für Wirtschaftsgeschichte: sonderband:* 117–34.

Offer, A. 1997. "Between the gift and the market: The economy of regard." *Economic History Review* 50: 450–76.

Oppenheim, A. L. 1957. "A bird's-eye view of Mesopotamian economic history." In *Trade and Market in the Early Empires.*, ed. K. Polanyi, C. M. Arensberg, and H. W. Pearson, 27–37. Glencoe, Ill.

———. 1967. "Essay on overland trade in the first millennium BC." *Journal of Cuneiform Studies* 21: 236–54.

———. 1977 [1964]. *Ancient Mesopotamia: Portrait of a Dead Civilization.* Rev. ed. Chicago.

Ormerod, P. 1994. *The Death of Economics.* London.

———. 1998. *Butterfly Economics.* London.

Orrieux, C. 1981. "Les comptes privés de Zénon à Philadelphie." *Chronique d'Égypte* 56: 314–40.

———. 1983. *Les papyrus de Zenon. L'horizon d'un grec en Égypte au IIIe Siècle avant J. C.* Paris.

———. 1985. *Zénon de Caunos, parépidèmos et le destin grec.* Paris.

Orsted, P. et al. 1992. "Town and countryside in Roman Tunisia." *Journal of Roman Archaeology* 5: 69–96.

Orton, C. 2000. *Sampling in Archaeology.* Cambridge.

Parker, A. J. 1990. "The wines of Roman Italy." *Journal of Roman Archaeology* 3: 325–31.

Parker, G. 1974. "Braudel's 'Mediterranean': The making and marketing of a masterpiece." *History* 59: 238–43.

Parker, R. 1983. *Miasma.* Oxford.

Parkins, H., ed. 1997a. *Roman Urbanism.* London.

———. 1997b. "The 'consumer city' domesticated?" In *Roman Urbanism*, ed. H. Parkins, 83–111. London.

———. 1998. "Time for change? Shaping the future of the ancient economy." In *Trade, Traders and the Ancient City*, ed. H. Parkins and C. Smith, 1–15. London.

Parkins, H., and C. Smith, eds. 1998. *Trade, Traders and the Ancient City.* London.

Parpola, S. 1995. "The construction of Dur-Sarrukin in the Assyrian royal correspondence." In *Khorsabad le palais de Sargon II, roi d'Assyrie*, ed. A. Caubert, 47–77. Paris.

Pasquinucci, M., and F. Trément, eds. 2000. *Non-Destructive Techniques Applied to Landscape Archaeology*. Oxford.

Paterson, J. 1998. "Trade and traders in the Roman world: Scale, structure, and organisation." In *Trade, Traders and the Ancient City*, ed. H. Parkins and C. Smith, 149–67. London.

Patterson, C. 1998. *The Family in Greek History*. Cambridge, Mass.

Payne, A., A. Kuttner, and R. Smick, eds. 2000. *Antiquity and its Interpreters*. Cambridge.

Payne, S. 1972. "Partial recovery and sample bias: The results of some sieving experiments." In *Papers in Economic Prehistory*, ed. E. Higgs, 49–64. Cambridge.

Peacock, D. 1982. *Pottery in the Roman World*. London.

Peacock, D., F. Bejaoui, and N. Ben Lazreg. 1990. "Roman pottery production in central Tunisia." *Journal of Roman Archaeology* 3: 59–84.

Pearson, M., and M. Shanks. 2001. *Theatre/Archaeology*. London.

Pestman, P. W. 1990. *The New Papyrological Primer*. Leiden.

———. 1995. "A family archive which changes history. The archive of an anonym." In *Hundred-Gated Thebes*, ed. S. P. Vleeming, 91–100. Leiden.

Pestman, P. W., et al. 1981. *A Guide to the Zenon Archive*. Leiden: *Papyrologica Lugduno-Batava* 21.

Pettegrew, D. 2001. "Chasing the classical farmstead: assessing the formation and signature of rural settlement in the Greek landscape." *Journal of Mediterranean Archaeology* 14: 189–209.

Plaumann, G. 1910. *Ptolemais in Oberägypten. Ein Beitrag zur Geschichte des Hellenismus in Ägypten*. Leipzig: Leipzig historische Abhandlungen 18.

Polanyi, K. 1944. *The Great Transformation*. Boston.

———. 1947. "Our obsolete market mentality: Civilization must find a new thought pattern." *Commentary* 3: 109–17.

———. 1957. "The economy as an instituted process." In *Trade and Market in the Early Empires.*, ed. K. Polanyi, C. M. Arensberg, and H. W. Pearson, 243–70. Glencoe, Ill.

———. 1960. "On the comparative treatment of economic institutions in antiquity." In *City Invincible*, ed. C. Kraeling and R. McC. Adams, 329–50. Chicago.

———. 1977. *The Livelihood of Man*. Ed. H. W. Pearson. New York.

Polanyi, K., C. M. Arensberg, and H. W. Pearson, eds. 1957. *Trade and Market in the Early Empires*. Glencoe, Ill.

Pomeranz, K. 2000. *The Great Divergence: China, Europe, and the Making of the Modern World Economy*. Princeton.

Pomeroy, S. 1997. *Families in Classical and Hellenistic Greece: Representations and Realities*. Oxford.

Popham, M., P. Calligas, and L. H. Sackett, eds. 1993. *Lefkandi*. Vol. 2, *The Protogeometric Building at Toumba*. Part 2, *The Excavation, Architecture and Finds*. Athens: British School at Athens supp. vol. 23.

Postgate, J. N. 1972. "The role of the temple in the Mesopotamian secular economy." In *Man, Settlement and Urbanism*, ed. P. J. Ucko, R. Tringham, and G. W. Dimbleby, 811–25. London.

———. 1974. *Taxation and Conscription in the Assyrian Empire*. Rome.

———. 1979. "The economic structure of the Assyrian Empire." In *Power and Propaganda: A Symposium on Ancient Empires*, ed. M. T. Larsen, 193–221. Copenhagen.

———. 1989. "The ownership and exploitation of land in Assyria in the 1st millennium BC." In *Reflets des deux fleuves: volume de mélanges offerts à André Finet*, ed. M. Lebeau and Ph. Talon, 141–52. Leuven.

———. 1992. *Early Mesopotamia: Society and Economy at the Dawn of History*. London.

Potter, T. W. 1981. "The Roman occupation of the central Fenland." *Britannia* 12: 79–133.

———. 1989. "Recent work on the Roman Fens of eastern England and the question of imperial estates." *Journal of Roman Archaeology* 2: 267–74.

Powell, M. A. 1978. "Götter, Könige und 'Kapitalisten' in Mesopotamien des 3. Jahrtausends v. u. Z." *Oikumene* 2: 127–43.

Préaux, C. 1939. *L'Économie royale des Lagides*. Brussels.

———. 1947. *Les Grecs en Égypte d'après les archives de Zénon*. Brussels.

———. 1978. *Le monde hellénistique. La Grèce et l'Orient de la mort d'Alexandre à la conquête romaine de la Grèce (323–146 av. J.-C.)*. 2 vols. Paris.

Pritchett, W. K. 1956. "The Attic stelai, part II." *Hesperia* 25: 175–328.

Raaflaub, K., and E. Müller-Luckner, eds. 1993. *Anfänge politischen Denkens in der Antike*. Munich.

Randsborg, K. 1991. *The First Millennium AD in Europe and the Mediterranean*. Cambridge.

Rathbone, D. 1989. "The ancient economy and Graeco-Roman Egypt." In *Egitto e storia antica dall'ellenismo all'età romana: Bilancio di un confronto. Atti del Colloquio internazionale Bologna, 31 agosto—2 settembre 1987*, ed. L. Criscuolo and G. Geraci, 159–76. Bologna.

———. 1990. "More (or less?) economic rationalism in Roman agriculture." *Journal of Roman Archaeology* 3: 432–36.

———. 1991. *Economic Rationalism and Rural Society in Third-Century AD Egypt: The Heroninos Archive and the Appianus Estate*. Cambridge.

———. 1994. "Ptolemaic to Roman Egypt: The death of the *dirigiste* state?" In *Production and Public Powers in Antiquity*, E. Lo Cascio and D. Rathbone, 29–40. Milan: *Proceedings of the Eleventh International Economy History Congress* B1.

———. 1996. "Monetisation, not price-inflation, in third-century Egypt." In *Coin Finds and Coin Use in the Roman World:*, ed. C. E. King and D. G. Wigg, 321–39. Berlin: *Studien zur Fundmünzen der Antike* 10.

Rauh, N. K. 1993. *The Sacred Bonds of Commerce. Religion, Economy and Trade Society at Hellenistic and Roman Delos, 166–87 BC.* Amsterdam.

Rawski, T. G. 1996. "Issues in the study of economic trends." In *Economics and the Historian*, ed. T. G. Rawski, 15–59. Berkeley.

Ray, D. 1998. *Development Economics.* Princeton.

Reder, M. 1999. *Economics.* Chicago.

Reddy, W. 1992. "Postmodernism and the public sphere." *Cultural Anthropology* 7: 135–68.

Reger, G. 1994. *Regionalism and Change in the Economy of Independent Delos, 314–167 BC.* Berkeley.

———. 1997. "The price histories of some imported goods on independent Delos." In *Économie antique: prix et formation des prix dans les economies antiques*, ed. J. Andreau, P. Briant, and R. Descat, 53–72. Saint-Bertrand-de-Comminges.

Reese, D. S. 1979–80. "The exploitation of Murex shells: Purple-dye and lime production at Side Khrebish, Benghazi (Berenice)." *Libyan Studies* 11: 79–93.

Renfrew, C. 1975. "Trade as action at a distance." In *Ancient Civilization and Trade*, ed. J. Sabloff and C. C. Lamberg-Karlovsky, 3–59. Albuquerque, N.M.

Renfrew, C., and P. Bahn. 2001. *Archaeology.* 3d ed. London.

Renger, J. 1971. "Notes on the goldsmiths, jewelers, and carpenters of Neo-Babylonian Eanna." *Journal of the American Oriental Society* 91: 494–503.

———. 1984. "Patterns of non-institutional trade and non-commercial exchange in ancient Mesopotamia at the beginning of the second millennium BC." In *Circulation of Goods in Non-Palatial Context in the Ancient Near East*, ed. A. Archi, 31–123. Rome.

———. 1994. "On economic structures in ancient Mesopotamia." *Orientalia* n.s. 63: 157–208.

———. 1995. "Institutional, communal, and individual ownership or possession of arable land in ancient Mesopotamia from the end of the fourth to the end of the first millennium BC." *Chicago-Kent Law Review* 71: 269–319.

———. 1996. "Handwerk und Handwerker im alten Mesopotamien." *Archiv für Orientalforschung* 23: 211–31.

Reynolds, L. G. 1986. *Economic Growth in the Third World. An Introduction.* New Haven.

Rich, J., and A. Wallace-Hadrill, eds. 1991. *City and Country in the Ancient World*. London.

Rihll, T. E., and A. E. Wilson. 1991. "Modelling settlement structures in ancient Greece: New approaches to the polis." In *City and Country in the Ancient World*, ed. J. Rich and A. Wallace-Hadrill, 59–95. London.

Robinson, D. M. 1931–52. *Excavations at Olynthus*. Vols. 2–7, 10, 12–14. Baltimore.

Robinson, D. M., and P. A. Clement. 1938. *Excavations at Olynthus*. Vol. 9, *The Chalcidic Mint and the Coins Found in 1928–1934*. Baltimore.

Robinson, D. M., and A. J. Graham. 1938. *Excavations at Olynthus*. Vol. 8, *The Hellenic House*. Baltimore.

Roccati, A. 1997. "Scribes." In *The Egyptians.*, ed. S. Donadoni, 61–85. Trans. R. Bianchi, A. L. Crone, C. Lambert, and T. Ritter. Chicago.

Röllig, W. 1976. "Der altmesopotamische Markt." *Welt des Orients* 8: 286–95.

Rosenzweig, M. R., and H. P. Binswanger. 1993. "Wealth, weather risk, and the composition of profitability of agricultural investments." *Economic Journal* 103: 56–78.

Rostovtzeff, M. I. 1922. *A Large Estate in Egypt in the Third Century BC*. Madison.

——. 1935/36. "The Hellenistic world and its economic development." *American Historical Review* 41: 231–52.

——. 1941. The *Social and Economic History of the Hellenistic World*. 3 vols. Oxford.

——. 1957. *The Social and Economic History of the Roman Empire*. 2d ed. Revised by P. M. Fraser. Oxford.

Roth, M. T. 1989. "A case of contested status." In *DUMU-E2–DUB-BA-A: Studies in Honor of Åke W. Sjöberg*, ed. H. Behrens, D. Loding, and M. T. Roth, 481–89. Philadelphia.

Rowlands, M., M. T. Larsen, and K. Kristiansen, eds. 1987. *Centre and Periphery in the Ancient World*. Cambridge.

Rowlandson, J. 1985. "Freedom and subordination in ancient agriculture: The case of the *basilikoi georgoi* of Ptolemaic Egypt." *History of Political Thought* 6: 327–47.

——. 1996. *Landowners and Tenants in Roman Egypt. The Social Relations of Agriculture in the Oxyrhynchite Nome*. Oxford.

Rowntree, Seebohm. 1901. *Poverty: A Study of Town Life*. London.

Ruby, P., ed. 1999. *Les princes de la protohistoire*. Naples and Paris.

Rueschemeyer, D., P. Evans, and T. Skocpol, eds. 1985. *Bringing the State Back In*. Cambridge.

Runciman, W. G. 1983. *A Treatise on Social Theory* I. Cambridge.

Rupprecht, H.-A. 1994. *Kleine Einführung in die Papyruskunde*. Darmstadt.

Said, E. 1978. *Orientalism*. New York.

Ste. Croix, G. E. M. de. 1983 [1981]. *The Class Struggle in the Ancient Greek World*. Corrected ed. London.

Salviat, F. 1986. "Cadastre et amenagement: Quinte Curce, les *insulae furianae*, le *fossa augusta* et la localisation du cadastre C d'Orange." *Revue archeologique du Narbonaisse* 19: 101–16.

Samuel, A. E. 1971. "P. Tebt. 703 and the Oikonomos." In *Studi in onore di E. Volterra*, vol. 2: 451–60. Milan.

————. 1983. *From Athens to Alexandria: Hellenism and Social Goals in Ptolemaic Egypt*. Leuven: Studia Hellenistica 26.

————. 1984. "The money economy and the Ptolemaic peasantry." *Bulletin of the American Society of Papyrologists* 21: 187–206.

————. 1989. *The Shifting Sands of History: Interpretations of Ptolemaic Egypt*. Lanham, Md.

————. 1997. "Assumptions, economics, and the origins of Europe." In *Ancient Economic Thought*, ed. B. B. Price, 211–37. London.

Samuelson, P., and W. Nordhaus. 1998. *Economics*. 16th ed. New York.

Sandy, B. D. 1989. *The Production and Sale of Vegetable Oils in Ptolemaic Egypt*. Bulletin of the American Society of Papyrologists supp. vol. 6. Atlanta.

Sbonias, K. 1999. "Introduction to issues in demography and survey." In *Reconstructing Past Population Trends in Mediterranean Europe*, ed. J. Bintliff and K. Sbonias, 1–20. Oxford.

Scheibler, I. 1983. *Griechische Töpferkunst. Herstellung, Handel und Gebrauch der antiken Tongefässe*. Munich.

Scheidel, W. 1996. *Measuring Sex, Age and Death in the Roman Empire: Explorations in Ancient Demography*. Ann Arbor, Mich.: Journal of Roman Archaeology supp. vol. 21.

————. 1997. "Quantifying the sources of slaves in the early Roman Empire." *Journal of Roman Studies* 77: 156–69.

————. 1999. "Emperors, aristocrats, and the grim reaper: Towards a demographic profile of the Roman élite." *Classical Quarterly* 49: 254–81.

————. 2001a. "Progress and problems in Roman demography." In *Debating Roman Demography*, ed. W. Scheidel, 1–91. Brill.

————. 2001b. *Death on the Nile: Disease and the Demography of Roman Egypt*. Leiden.

————. 2001c. "Roman age structure: Evidence and models." *Journal of Roman Studies* 91: 1–26.

Scheidel, W., and S. von Reden, eds. 2002. *The Ancient Economy*. Edinburgh.

Schiffer, M. B. 1976. *Behavioral Archeology*. New York.

————. 1985. "Is there a Pompeii premise?" *Journal of Anthropological Research* 41: 18–41.

————. 1987. *Formation Processes of the Archaeological Record*. Albuquerque, N.M.

Schnapp, A. 1996. *The Discovery of the Past.* London.

Schneider, A. 1920. *Die sumerische Tempelstadt. Die Anfänge der Kulturwirtschaft.* Essen.

Schumpeter, J. 1934. *The Theory of Economic Development: An Inquiry into Profits, Capital, Credit, Interest, and the Business Cycle.* Cambridge, Mass.

Scott, J. W. 1991. "The evidence of experience." *Critical Inquiry* 17: 773–97.

Seidl, E. 1970. *Bodennutzung und Bodenpacht nach den demotischen Texten der Ptolemäerzeit.* Vienna.

Sen, A. 1999. *Development as Freedom.* Oxford.

Shanin, T., ed. 1971. *Peasants and Peasant Societies: Selected Readings.* Harmondsworth.

Shanks, M. 1992. *Experiencing the Past: On the Character of Archaeology.* London.

———. 1996. *Classical Archaeology of Greece: Experiences of the Discipline.* London.

Shanks, M., and C. Tilley. 1987a. *ReConstructing Archaeology.* Cambridge.

———. 1987b. *Social Theory and Archaeology.* Albuquerque, N.M.

Shaw, B. D. 1981. "Rural markets in North Africa and the political economy of the Roman empire." *Antiquités africaines* 17: 37–83.

———. 1982. "Lamasba: An ancient irrigation community." *Antiquités africaines* 18: 37–83.

———. 1984. "Water and society in the ancient Maghreb: Technology, property, and development." *Antiquités africaines* 20: 121–73.

———. 1991. "The noblest monuments and the smallest things: Wells, walls and aqueducts in the making of Roman Africa." In *Future currents in aqueduct studies,* ed. T. Hodge, 63–91. Leeds.

———. 1992. "Under Russian eyes." *Journal of Roman Studies* 82: 216–28.

———. 1993. "The early development of M. I. Finley's thought: The Heichelheim dossier." *Athenaeum* 81: 177–99.

———. 1996. "Seasons of death: Aspects of mortality in imperial Rome." *Journal of Roman Studies* 86: 100–38.

———. 2001. "Challenging Braudel: A new vision of the Mediterranean." *Journal of Roman Archaeology* 14: 419–53.

Shaw, B. D., and R. Saller. 1981. "Editors' introduction." In M. I. Finley, *Economy and Society in Ancient Greece,* ix–xxvi. London.

Shelton, J. 1976. "Land register: Crown tenants at Kerkeosiris." In *Collectanea Papyrologica: Texts Published in Honor of H. C. Youtie,* ed. A. E. Hanson, 111–52. Bonn.

Sherratt, S., and A. Sherratt. 1993. "The growth of the Mediterranean economy in the early first millennium BC." *World Archaeology* 24: 361–78.

Shipley, G. J. 1993. "Distance, development, decline? World-systems analysis and the 'Hellenistic' world." In *Centre and Periphery in the Hellenistic World,* ed. P. Bilde et al., 271–84. Aarhus.

Sidebotham, S. E., and W. Z. Wendrich. 1996. *Berenike 1995.* Leiden.

Silberman, N. 1982. *Digging for God and Country: Exploration, Archaeology, and the Secret Struggles for the Holy Land, 1799–1918.* New York.

Silver, M. 1983. *Prophets and Markets: The Political Economy of Ancient Israel.* Boston.

———. 1985. *Economic Structures of the Ancient Near East.* London.

———. 1994. *Economic Structures of Antiquity.* Westport, Conn.

Smelser, N., and R. Swedberg. 1994. "The sociological perspective on the economy." In *The Handbook of Economic Sociology,* ed. N. Smelser and R. Swedberg, 3–26. Princeton.

Smith, A. 1970 [1789]. *The Wealth of Nations Books I–III.* Ed. A. Skinner. Harmondsworth, U.K.

Snell, D. C. 1977. "The activities of some merchants of Umma." *Iraq* 39: 45–50.

———. 1982. *Ledgers and Prices. Early Mesopotamian Merchant Accounts.* New Haven, Conn.

Snodgrass, A. M. 1980. *Archaic Greece: The Age of Experiment.* London.

———. 1987. *An Archaeology of Greece.* Berkeley.

———. 1994. "Response: The archaeological aspect." In *Classical Greece: Ancient Histories and Modern Archaeologies,* ed. I. Morris, 197–200. Cambridge.

Soja, E. 2000. *Postmetropolis: Critical Studies of Cities and Regions.* Oxford.

Solow, R. 1956. "A contribution to the theory of economic growth." *Quarterly Journal of Economics* 70: 65–94.

Soros, G. 2002. *George Soros on Globalization.* New York.

Springborg, P. 1992. *Republicanism and the Oriental Prince.* Chapel Hill, N.C.

Sparkes, B., and L. Talcott. 1970. *The Athenian Agora.* Vol. 12, *Black and Plain Pottery of the Sixth, Fifth, and Fourth Centuries BC.* Princeton.

Stavropoullos, Ph. 1938. "Ieratiki oikia en Zostiri tis Attikis." *Archaiologiki Ephemeris:* 1–31.

Steckel, R. 1995. "Stature and the standard of living." *Journal of Economic Literature* 33: 1903–40.

———. 1997. *Industrialization and Health in Historical Perspective.* Cambridge, Mass.: National Bureau of Economic Research Historical Paper 118.

Steckel, R., and R. Floud, eds. 1997. *Health and Welfare During Industrialization.* Chicago.

Steckel, R. H., and J. C. Rose. 2002. *The Backbone of History.* Cambridge.

Steinkeller, P. 1996. "The organization of crafts in third millennium Babylonia. The case of potters." *Altorientalische Forschungen* 23: 232–53.

Stern, E. M. 1999. "Roman glassblowing in its cultural context." *American Journal of Archaeology* 103: 441–84.

Stissi, V. 1999. "Why do numbers count? A plea for a wider approach to excavation pottery." In *Proceedings of the XVth International Congress of Classical Archaeology, Amsterdam, July 12–17, 1998*, ed. P. Docter and E. Moorman, 404–7. Amsterdam.

Stokes, G. 2001. "The fates of human societies." *American Historical Review* 106: 508–25.

Stolper. M. W. 1985. *Entrepeneurs and Empire: The Murasû Archive, the Murasû Firm, and Persian Rule in Babylonia*. Leiden.

———. 1994. "Mesopotamia, 482–330 B.C." In *Cambridge Ancient History*, ed. D. M. Lewis et al., vol. 6: 234–60. 2d ed. Cambridge.

Stone, D. L. 1997. "The development of an imperial territory: Romans, Africans, and the transformation of the rural landscape of Tunisia." Ph.D. diss., University of Michigan.

Stone, E. 1987. *Nippur Neighborhoods*. Chicago.

Stray, C. 1998. *Classics Transformed: Schools, Universities, and Society in England, 1830–1960*. Oxford.

Swedberg, R. 1991. "Major traditions of economic sociology." *Annual Review of Sociology* 17: 251–76.

———. 1998. *Max Weber and the Idea of Economic Sociology*. Princeton.

Szelenyi, I., and E. Kostello. 1998. "Outline of an institutionalist theory of inequality: The case of socialist and postcommunist eastern Europe." In *The New Institutionalism in Sociology*, ed. M. Brinton and V. Nee, 305–26. New York.

Tandy, D. W. 1997. *Warriors into Traders. The Power of the Market in Early Greece*. Berkeley.

Tarn, W. W., and G. T. Griffith. 1952. *Hellenistic Civilization*. 3d ed. London.

Taylor, A., ed. 1975. *The Standard of Living in Britain in the Industrial Revolution*. London.

Tchernia, A. 1986. *Le vin de l'Italie romaine*. Rome.

Temin, P. 2001. "A market economy in the early Roman Empire." *Journal of Roman Studies* 91: 169–81.

———. 2002. "Price behavior in ancient Babylon." *Explorations in Economic History* 39: 46–60.

Tetlock, P., and A. Belkin. 1996. "Counterfactual thought experiments in world politics." In *Counterfactual Thought Experiments in World Politics*, eds. P. Tetlock and A. Belkin, 1–38. Princeton.

Thomas, J. 1996. *Time, Culture and Identity: An Interpretive Archaeology*. London.

———. 1999. *Understanding the Neolithic*. London.

Thompson, D. J. 1988. *Memphis Under the Ptolemies*. Princeton.

———. 1997. "Policing the Ptolemaic countryside." In *Akten des 21. Internationalen Papyrologenkongresses Berlin, 13.-19.8.1995*, ed. B. Kramer et al., 961–66. Berlin.

————. 1999. "New and old in the Ptolemaic Fayyum." In *Agriculture in Egypt from Pharaonic to Modern Times*, ed. A. K. Bowman and E. Rogan, 123–38. London: *Proceedings of the British Academy 96.*

Thompson, D. J., and G. Hawthorn. 1995. "The demography of Roman Egypt." *Journal of Roman Archaeology* 8: 483–88.

Tilley, C. ed. 1990. *Reading Material Culture*. Oxford.

————. 1991. *Material Culture and Text: The Art of Ambiguity*. London.

————. ed., 1993. *Interpretative Archaeology*. Oxford.

————. 1994. *A Phenomenology of Landscape*. Oxford.

————. 1996. *An Ethnography of the Neolithic*. Cambridge.

————. 1999. *Metaphor and Material Culture*. Oxford.

Tilley, C. 1984. *Big Structures, Large Processes, Huge Comparisons*. New York.

————. 1992. *Capital, Coercion, and European States, AD 990–1992*. Oxford.

Tomber, R. S. 1996. "Provisioning the desert: Pottery supply to Mons Claudianus." In *Archaeological Research in Roman Egypt*, ed. D. M. Bailey, 39–49. Ann Arbor, Mich.: *Journal of Roman Archaeology* supp. vol. 19.

Tosi, M. 1984. "The notion of craft specialization and its representation in the archaeological record of early states." In *Marxist Perspectives in Archaeology*, ed. M. Spriggs, 22–52. Cambridge.

Trigger, B., B. Kemp, D. O'Connor, and A. Lloyd. 1983. *Ancient Egypt: A Social History*. Cambridge.

Trousset, P. 1992. "La vie littorale et les ports dans la Petite Syrte á l'époque romain." In *Afrique du Nord antique et médiévale. Spectacles, vie portuaire, religions. Actes du Ve colloque international sur l'histoire et l'archéologie de l'Afrique du Nord (Avignon, 9–13, avril 1990)*, 317–32. Paris.

————. 1996. "Les oases presahariennes dans l'antiquite: partage de l'eau et division du temps." *Antiquités africaines* 22: 161–91.

Turner, E. G. 1980. *Greek Papyri. An Introduction*. Oxford.

————. 1984. "Ptolemaic Egypt." In *Cambridge Ancient History* VII, part 1, ed. F. W. Walbank, A. E. Astin, M. W. Frederiksen, and R. M. Ogilvie, 118–74. 2d ed. Cambridge.

Turner, F. M. 1981. *The Greek Heritage in Victorian Britain*. New Haven.

Usher, D. 1980. *The Measurement of Economic Growth*. Oxford.

van de Mieroop, M. 1987. *Crafts in the Early Isin Period*. Louvain.

————. 1997. *The Ancient Mesopotamian City*. Oxford.

————. 1999. *Cuneiform Texts and the Writing of History*. London.

Van der Leeuw, S., and J. McGlade, eds. 1997. *Time, Process and Structured Transformation in Archaeology*. London.

van der Spek, R. J. 1987. "The Babylonian city." In *Hellenism in the East*, A. Kuhrt and S. Sherwin-White, 57–74. London.

van Driel, G. 1989. "The Murasûs in context." *Journal of the Social and Economic History of the Orient* 32: 203–29.

Van Minnen, P. 1986. "The volume of the Oxyrhynchite textile trade."
    Münstersche Beiträge zur antiken Handelsgeschichte 5.2: 88–95.
———. 1987. "Urban craftsmen in Roman Egypt." *Münstersche Beiträge zur
    antiken Handelsgeschichte* 6.1: 31–88.
Van Ossel, P. 1992. *Établissements ruraux de l'Antiquité tardive dans le nord de la
    Gaule.* Paris.
Van Ossel, P., and P. Ouzoulias. 2000. "Rural settlement economy in northern
    Gaul in the late empire: An overview." *Journal of Roman Archaeology* 13:
    133–60.
Van Wees, H. 1992. *Status Warriors: War, Violence, and Society in Homer and
    History.* Amsterdam.
Vandorpe, K. 1994. "Museum archaeology, or how to reconstruct Pathyris
    archives." In *Acta Demotica. Acts of the Fifth International Conference for
    Demotists. Pisa, 4th–8th September 1993*, 289–300. Pisa: *Egitto e Vicino
    Oriente* 17.
Veenhof, K. R. 1972. *Aspects of Old Assyrian Trade and its Terminology.* Leiden.
Vera, D. 1987. "Enfiteusi, colonato et transformazioni agrarie nell'Africa
    Proconsulaire del tardo impero." *Africa Romana* 4: 267–93.
———. 1988. "Terra e lavoro nell'Africa romana." *Studia Storica* 29: 967–92.
Verhoogt, A. 1997. *Menches, Komogrammateus of Kerkeosiris. The Doings and
    Dealings of a Village Scribe in the Late Ptolemaic Period (120–110 BC).*
    Leiden.
Veyne, P. 1976. *Le pain et le cirque. Sociologie historique d'un pluralisme politique.*
    Paris.
Vickers, M., and D. Gill. 1994. *Artful Crafts.* Oxford.
Vidal-Naquet, P. 1965. "Économie et société dans la Grèce ancienne: L'oeu-
    vre de Moses I. Finley." *Archives européenes de sociologie* 6: 111–48.
———. 1967. Le bordereau d'ensemencement dans l'Égypte ptolémaique. *Pa-
    pyrologica Bruxellensia.* 5.
von Freyberg, H. U. 1989. *Kapitalverkehr und Handel im römischen Kaiserreich
    (27 BC–235 AD).* Freiburg.
von Reden, S. 1995. *Exchange in Ancient Greece.* London.
———. 1997a. "Money, law and exchange: Coinage in the Greek polis."
    Journal of Hellenic Studies 117: 154–76.
———. 1997b. "Money and coinage in Ptolemaic Egypt: Some preliminary
    remarks." In *Akten des 21. Internationalen Papyrologenkongresses Berlin,
    13.-19.8.1995*, ed. B. Kramer et al., 1003–8. Stuttgart.
Voth, H-J. 2001. "The longest years: New estimates of labor input in England,
    1760–1830." *Journal of Economic History* 61: 1065–82.
Waetzoldt, H. 1972. *Untersuchungen zur neusumerischen Textilindustrie.* Rome.
Walbank, F. W., A. E. Astin, M. W. Frederiksen, and R. M. Ogilvie, eds.
    1984. *Cambridge Ancient History* VII, part 1. 2d ed. Cambridge.

Wallace, S. L. 1938. *Taxation in Egypt from Augustus to Diocletian*. Princeton.

Wallerstein, I. 1976. *The Modern World System: Capitalist Agriculture and the Origins of the European World-Economy in the Sixteenth Century*. Vol. 1. New York.

Walter, U. 1993. *An der Polis teilhaben. Bürgerstaat und Zugehörigkeit im archaischen Griechenland*. Stuttgart: *Historia* Einzelschrift 82.

Walter-Karydi, E. 1994. *Die Nobilitierung des Wohnhauses. Lebensform und Architektur im spätklassischen Griechenland*. Konstanz.

Warburton, D. 1997. *State and Economy in Ancient Egypt*. Freiburg.

Weber, M. 1950 [1919/20]. *General Economic History*. Trans F. Knight. New York.

———. 1958 [1921]. *The City*. Glencoe, Ill.

———. 1968. *Economy and Society*. Ed. Guenther Roth and Claus Wittich. Berkeley.

———. 1976a [1904/5]. *The Protestant Ethic and the Spirit of Capitalism*. Ed. A. Giddens. New York.

———. 1976b [1909]. *The Agrarian Sociology of Ancient Civilizations*. Trans. R. I. Frank. London.

Webster, T. B. L. 1972. *Athenian Culture and Society*. London.

Weinberg, J. P. 1976. "Bemerkungen zum Problem 'der Vorhellenismus' in Vorderer Orient." *Klio* 58: 5–20.

Wes, M. A. 1990. *Michael Rostovtzeff, Historian in Exile: Russian Roots in an American Context*. Stuttgart.

West, L. C., and A. C. Johnson. 1944. *Currency in Roman and Byzantine Egypt*: Princeton: *Princeton University Studies in Papyrology* 5.

West, M. L. 1966. *Hesiod: Theogony*. Oxford.

———. 1997. *The East Face of Helicon*. Oxford.

White, H. 1973. *Metahistory: The Historical Imagination in Nineteenth-Century Europe*. Baltimore.

White, K. D. 1970. *Roman Farming*. London.

Whitelaw, T. 1983. "The settlement at Fournou Korifi Myrtos and aspects of Early Minoan social organization." In *Minoan Society*, ed. Olga Krzyszkowska and Lucia Nixon, 323–45. Bristol.

Whittaker, C. R. 1995. "Do theories of the ancient city matter?" In *Urban Society in Roman Italy*, ed. T. Cornell and K. Lomas, 9–26. London.

———. 1996. "Moses Finley." *Proceedings of the British Acacdemy* 94: 459–72.

———. 1997. "Markets and fairs." *Journal of Roman Archaeology* 10: 420–22.

Wikander, Ö. 1984. *Exploitation of Water-Power or Technological Stagnation? A Reappraisal of the Productive Forces in the Roman Empire*. Lund.

Williamson, J. 1984. "British mortality and the value of life, 1781–1831." *Population Studies* 38: 157–72.

Wilson, A. 1995. "Water-power in North Africa and the development of the horizontal water-wheel." *Journal of Roman Archaeology* 8: 499–510.
———. 1999. "Commerce and industry in Roman Sabratha." *Libyan Studies* 30: 29–52.
———. 2000. "The water-mills on the Janiculum." *Memoirs of the American Academy in Rome* 45: 219–46.
———. 2002. "Machines, power and the ancient economy." *Journal of Roman Studies* 92: 1–32.
Winckelmann, J. J. 1880 [1764]. *History of Ancient Art.* New York.
Winterer, C. 2002. *The Culture of Classicism: Ancient Greece and Rome in American Intellectual Life, 1780–1910.* Baltimore.
Wittfogel, K. 1957. *Oriental Despotism.* New Haven, Conn.
Wong, R. B. 1998. *China Transformed: Historical Change and the Limits of European Experience.* Ithaca, N.Y.
———. 2001. "Entre monde et nation: Les régions braudéliennes en Asie." *Annales Histoire Sciences Sociales* 56: 5–41.
Woodmansee, M., and M. Osteen, eds. 1999. *The New Economic Criticism: Studies at the Intersection of Literature and Economics.* London.
Woolf, G. 1990. "World-systems analysis and the Roman empire." *Journal of Roman Archaeology* 3: 44–58.
———. 1996. "Monumental writing and the expansion of Roman society in the early empire." *Journal of Roman Studies* 86: 22–39.
———. 1998. *Becoming Roman. The Origins of Provincial Civilization in Gaul.* Cambridge.
Wrigley, E. A. 1988. *Continuity, Chance and Change.* Cambridge.
Zaccagnini, C. 1981. "Modo di produzione asiatico e Vicino Oriente antico." *Dialoghi di Archaeologia* 3: 3–65.
———. 1989. "Asiatic Mode of Production and ancient Near East: Notes towards a discussion." In *Production and Consumption in the Ancient Near East,* ed. C. Zaccagnini, 1–126. Budapest. Repr. and trans. from *Dialoghi di archeologia* n.s. 3 (1981).
Zamora, J. A. 1997. *Sobre el modo de produccion asiatico en Ugarit.* Madrid-Zaragossa.

INDEX

Abandonment processes, 118
Adams, R. McC., 49
Aegean, Bronze Age in, 6
Agency, 99
Agora, Athenian, 119
Agricultural productivity, 197
Ainian, M., 111, 115
Alcibiades, 100, 122
Alexander, 6
Alexandria, 178, 195, 199
Allen, R., 22
(An)durāru, 77
Ammianus, 135
Ammotopos, 111
Amphoras, 104; Panathenaic prize, 118
Andocides, 118
Androtion, 151
Ankyronpolis (el-Hibeh), 170
Annona, 227
Ano Voula, 113
Antaiopolis (Egypt), 197
Apion papers, 200
Apollonios, 172
Appianus, estate of, 194
Archives, 74, 167, 184n; from Dead Sea,
    188, 204n
Argolid Exploration Project, 123
Aristophanes, 118
Arles, grain mill at, 225
Arretine pottery, 217
Arsinoe, 179
Arsinoite nome, 168
Ashur, 53
Asiatic Mode of Production, 49, 64
Athenian orators, 92
Athens, 100, 142; population of, 159
Attic stelai, 118, 122
Ault, B., 113
Avaritia, 213

Bagnall, R., 169
Bagradas River, 216
Bang, P. F., 228
Barbegal, 214, 216
Belgic Gaul, pre-Roman, 139
Bentz, M., 96
Berenike (Egypt), 196
Bernal. M., 9, 17
Binford, L., 99
Bit ritti, 80
Blanton, R., 113
Blaug, M., 160
Boak, A., 192
Boeckh, A., 27
Boniface IV, 97
Borsippa, 80
Bourdieu, P., 113
Bowman, A., 189
Brady, H., 34
Braudel, F., 9, 15
Brown, P., 190
Bu Njem (Libya), 189
Bücher, K., 49
Bücher-Meyer debate, 174
Bullion, 151
Bureaucracy, 176, 178
Burial, 95
Burkert, W., 17–18

Cabotage, 20
Canal building, 80
Capital investment, 234
Capitalism, 208
Carr, E., 21
Census, Ptolemaic, 168
Centralization, 55
Centuriation, 213
Chayanov, A. V., 128
Chemtou (Tunisia), 214

281